PIONEERS
AND
HOMEMAKERS

SUNY Series in Israeli Studies
Russell Stone, Editor

PIONEERS
AND
HOMEMAKERS

Jewish Women in Pre-State Israel

Edited by
Deborah S. Bernstein

State University of New York Press

Published by
State University of New York Press, Albany

© 1992 State University of New York

Printed in the United States of America

For information, address State University of New York
Press, State University Plaza, Albany, N.Y., 12246

Production by Diane Ganeles
Marketing by Fran Keneston

Library of Congress Cataloging-in-Publication Data

Pioneers and homemakers : Jewish women in pre-state Israel / edited by
  Deborah S. Bernstein.
      p.   cm. — (SUNY series in Israeli studies)
    Includes bibliographical references and index.
    ISBN 0-7914-0905-8 (alk. paper). — ISBN 0-7914-0906-6 (alk. paper
  : pbk.)
    1. Women, Jewish—Palestine—History—20th century. 2. Feminism-
  -Palestine—History—20th century. 3. Palestine-
  -History—1917-1948. I. Bernstein, Deborah. II. Series.
  HQ1728.5.P56 1992   91-21247
  305.48'696—dc20   CIP

10 9 8 7 6 5 4 3 2 1

In memory of my mother,
Sylvia Levinthal Bernstein

Contents

Part III. Women's Rights, Women's Spheres

Illustrations

Preface

An anthology is a collective project. The combined work of many people gives it its special character. This anthology is a collective enterprise in more respects than one. It is, above all, the result of the interest and effort of the eleven contributors. Most of the chapters, while based on previous work, were written especially for this collection. It also presents, to a major extent, the "state of the art." It gives the reader an overall view of much of the work which has been done so far, in a range of disciplines, concerning women's experience, action and status in the *Yishuv*, the formative, pre-state period of Israeli society. I am hopeful that it can thus show the extent to which the vacuum in our knowledge is slowly beginning to fill, the new insight which has been obtained, as well as the many intriguing questions waiting for documentation and research.

The idea of assembling a collection of articles on women in the *Yishuv* began to emerge as I was working on an earlier project on Jewish women workers in Palestine of the 1920s and 1930s. As I met with other researchers from a number of disciplines, I realized that there was potential for much more writing concerning women than had already been done and published. There were unpublished Masters and Doctoral theses, there were studies that contained information on women which had not been written up, there were beginnings that needed encouragement and a supportive framework. Not all this potential resulted in articles included in this anthology, but much of it did.

The idea of an anthology met with much enthusiasm. The contributors, besides writing their individual articles, were available for comments and advice, and often encouraged me to continue with the project when it seemed that there was still a long way to go. In addition, many colleagues helped me as the work proceeded, and I would especially like to thank Nira Reiss for her generous help and advice and Dafna Erdinest-Vulcan for her editorial assistance. I also received much essential help from the University of Haifa, and would especially like to thank Yael Metzer, Director of Public Relations, Aliza Brown of the Research Authroity, and Arlet Adler, director of KIDMAH—A Project for the Advancement and Involvement of Women. Special thanks also to Dalia Talmon and to Danielle Friedlander for the attentive typing of the manuscript. It is our hope that the readers will share our enthusiasm and continue to advance our knowledge and understanding far beyond their present state.

Introduction

A new chapter of Jewish history began in Palestine in the late nineteenth century.* A new wave of Jewish settlement was underway, initiated by the Zionist Movement, a political and social movement for the establishment of a national home for the Jews in Palestine—*Eretz Israel*. Modern political Zionism developed during this time in Europe. The World Zionist Movement, and its leading organization, the World Zionist Organization, established in 1897, served as umbrella structures incorporating a variety of social and political ideologies of which the rebuilding of Zion as a Jewish homeland was the binding element. Immigration continued through the turn of the century and the first half of the twentieth century, primarily from Eastern Europe and to a much lesser extent from Moslem countries. It led to the establishment of numerous new settlements, urban and rural, new social movements and organizations and eventually to the consolidation of a semi-autonomous Jewish entity known as the New *Yishuv*, or simply the *Yishuv* (meaning in Hebrew—the Settlement).

Women were there from the very start. They were part of every wave of immigration. They settled, singly and in families, in all types of settlement: the early rural settlements—the *moshavot*, the communal kibbutzim and *kvutzot*, the cooperative *moshavim* and, of course, the towns and cities. The story of their immigration and settlement is thus part of the story of the period. And yet, it has not been told. Their experiences, actions and struggles, their daily lives and their special moments have been passed over with hardly a mention. At times their very existence has been erased. This is true for much of the documentation of the period and at least as true, probably even more so, for the recent study of the *Yishuv*. Women have either been ignored, or put on a "pioneering

---

*Special thanks to Dafna Izraeli for her insightful and helpful comments on an earlier draft of this Introduction.

1

pedestal", where they became the subject of a myth, according to which the *Halutza*, the pioneering woman, worked and struggled hand in hand, shoulder to shoulder, with her male comrade. In neither case were women's own voices heard. Women's demands and needs were conceived, at best, as their own problem, rather than a challenge to the whole community, men as well as women, in their attempt to build a new society.

But the women were not merely fighting for their own rights. Their aspiration was to change the essence of gender relations in the new Jewish society. They attempted, in different ways and at different levels of coherence and articulation, to break down the barriers between the male and the female spheres. In some cases, they attempted to enter the male sphere, in others to add value and social significance to the female sphere. They aspired to be part of the building of a new society, and to be acknowledged as such; to establish a new society in which men and women would work together to create something of value. These aspirations were not realized. However hard they tried, both as individuals and in organized struggle, as all the articles in this collection will show, however significant their achievements were, they did not change gender relations, they did not break down men's monopoly on all that was important, powerful and valued. They did not gain control over their lives.

The young women immigrants came from a highly patriarchal, gender segregated, traditional Jewish society. The men controlled all positions of power and prestige and were uncontested heads of community and family. The orthodox Jewish world was clearly divided into gender spheres, as Rhonda Berger-Sofer writes, "Internally, there is a strict division between the sexes with almost no social interaction occurring between males and females who are not nuclear family members. While the ideal roles for the women are as wives and mothers, the ideal roles for the men are as religious ritual observers and Torah scholars" (Berger-Sofer, 1982:9). The home was woman's domain. While it was by no means her only sphere, it was by far the most important. Her prescribed role within the home was seen as an essential obligation to the maintenance of the Jewish community. The norms and traditions that determined the centrality of the domestic sphere for women were validated by the religious law which established three commandments for women alone, all three relating to the proper conduct within home and family (Weissler, 1986). Within home and family the women enjoyed a strong position (Zborowski and Herzog, 1952:124;

Weinberg, 1988:xix), but many women were also the providers for their families, as earning a livelihood was frequently considered a woman's job and an extension of her work in the home. This was true of most pre-industrial Europe, but in the Jewish community of Eastern Europe women were, at times, the sole providers for their families while the men studied the holy scriptures (Baum et al., 1975:67).

Women worked in a wide range of occupations typical of women in a pre-industrial and industrializing society, and of the economic role of the Jewish community as mediator and supplier of services for the host society. These included marketing of goods, making and selling of food and drink (including liquor), tavern-keeping, sewing and embroidery, gardening in rural areas and domestic work, as well as industrial work in textile, clothing and food workshops and factories (Weinberg, 1988:1–21; Baum et al. 1975: 55–71; Lestschinsky, 1961:28–30). Although the contribution of women was essential to the home and to the economy, the most important spheres in the life of the Jewish community—public leadership and religious scholarship—remained beyond their boundaries.

By the end of the nineteenth century the traditional, relatively static Jewish society of Eastern Europe was undergoing far-reaching changes. Severe political restrictions were imposed on Jews, including their removal from the countryside into the towns and cities of the Pale of Settlement, and their exclusion from a wide range of occupations which had been essential to the Jewish economy. These changes were accompanied by rapid proletarianization on the one hand and a dramatic spread of poverty on the other (Lestschinsky, 1961:127–47). At the same time, cultural and ideological change was taking place. The movement of Enlightenment, the *Haskala*, which had begun in the mid-nineteenth century in central and western Europe, eroding the total predominance of the orthodox leadership, was gaining support in the more traditional Jewish world of the Pale of Settlement as well. Secular education was expanding and many parents, especially of the middle-class, began to provide education for their daughters, as well as for their sons. Women had previously often learned to read and write but by the end of the nineteenth century many had begun to attend secular schools—elementary schools, gymnasia and, in a much smaller number of cases, even university courses (Baum et al., 1975:72–74).

The combination of impoverishment and political persecution

on the one hand and education on the other, led to the development of radical movements within the Jewish community, in close conjunction with the growth of radical and revolutionary movements in the host society, in Russia. Women played an important role in these developments. They were part of the emerging Jewish proletariat of the newly educated (primarily middle-class) young generation, and of the various radical movements in which the young Jews enlisted, including the revolutionary socialist Russian movements, the Bund—the Jewish Socialist workers' movement, and the socialist-Zionist movement. Jewish society was on the move. People were moving from villages to towns, from towns to cities, from Eastern to Western Europe and above all to America. Some of the Jews, affected by and affiliated with the Zionist movement, headed to Palestine. Much of what happened to the women who immigrated to Palestine can be understood in the context of the society from which they came. The opposition with which women met from some sectors of the Jewish community in Palestine stemmed from the desire of the latter to lead a traditional, even ultra-orthodox, way of life. Many women, on the other hand, desired to break away from the traditional society that excluded them from full participation in the most valued spheres of life.

Zionist immigration to Palestine began, according to the accepted chronology, in 1882.[1] Palestine at the time was part of the Ottoman Empire, a poor underdeveloped territory, drawing unto itself the increasing interest of the European powers due to its strategic and religious significance. Jewish immigration continued in a cyclical form, portrayed in the historiography of the Yishuv, as consecutive waves of immigration (*Aliyah*), each identified according to its place in the series, and to its distinct social and ideological characteristics. As the historiography of the Yishuv has developed, to a large extent, in relation to these waves of immigration, a brief description of each will be useful (Eisenstadt, 1967; Bein, 1954).

The First Aliyah began in 1882 and continued, intermittently, until 1903. Most of the immigrants came from Russia and were affiliated with the *Hibbat Zion* movement, a section of the Zionist movement that called for immediate immigration to Palestine. They were lower middle-class families, with some means of their own. As the men, rather than the women, were politically active in Russia, the decision to immigrate was largely taken by them, with the women, in most cases, following—more or less willingly—in their footsteps. They established moshavot, agricultural villages based on privately-owned farms, most of which were eventually supported financially by the charities of the Baron de Rothschild. They led a traditional Jewish life and, as private enterprise farmers, became an important component of the new middle-class. The women, many of whom were deeply committed to their life in the moshavot, faced a difficult struggle to achieve public recognition and participation (see Aaronsohn; Berlovitz).

The Second Aliyah, 1904–1918, was composed largely of Labor Zionist immigrants: young, single immigrants, known as *halutzim* (men pioneers) and *halutzot* (women pioneers) (singular: *halutz* and *halutza*). The constitution of the second wave of immigration was predominantly male, with a small minority of 17–18 percent young women (Blum, 1980:5). They had no financial means of their own, and were thus dependent for their livelihood on both the farmers of the moshavot and on the public funds of the World Zionist Organization (WZO). The young men, and to a much greater extent the young women, faced extreme hardship in their attempts to become agricultural workers, "to conquer labor" as the (highly masculine) expression was, at the time. They created the labor movement, later to become the dominant and hegemonic force in the Yishuv, and also set the foundations of the women workers' movement. This Aliyah is therefore considered the one which formed the future pattern for the Yishuv. It established the rudiments of future organizations and formulated dominant values, among them the concept of the new Hebrew woman—a worker, pioneer and comrade. In consequence the Second Aliyah has won most attention both in the popular myths of the period and in sociological and historical studies. A relatively large number of articles in this collection are related to the women of the Second Aliyah, primarily those of Margalit Shilo; Dafna Izraeli; Shulamit Reinharz; Musia Lipman and Deborah Bernstein and Nurit Govrin.

The Third Aliyah began in 1919, with the end of the First World War, and lasted until 1923. Ottoman rule had ended and the British military and then civil rule of Palestine began, with the commitment of His Majesty's Government—expressed by the Balfour Declaration (1917)—to the establishment of a Jewish National Home in Palestine. Zionist expectations ran high, as did socialist fervor in the aftermath of the Russian Revolution. Most immigrants, of whom 36 percent were women (Gertz, 1947:98),[2] belonged to the labor movement. They were young men and women, in their late teens and early twenties, who often were organized in collectives, prior to immigration. Collectives eased the initial transition for many of the young women. Nevertheless, they soon faced acute difficulties of finding employment, when many of the immigrants left their collectives or when the latter disbanded. In these years many of the goals of the Second Aliyah were implemented and major institutions took shape, the most important being the Histadrut—the General Federation of Hebrew Labor (1920). The Women Workers' Movement was formally established that year as well (see Izraeli).

The Fourth Aliyah, from 1924 to 1931, was composed largely of petit-bourgeois families from Poland, who arrived with small amounts of private capital. The gender composition of this immigration was far more balanced than in previous immigrations, both because of the larger proportion of families, and because of the increase in the proportion of women among the single, labor-oriented immigrants (Gertz, ibid). The immigrants of the Fourth Aliyah settled in the urban centers and ushered in a period of economic prosperity and full employment, at least for the male workers. The women of the petit-bourgeois immigrant families were largely housewives. The women workers still had difficulty finding employment in the urban economy which focused largely on construction work. In 1927, an economic depression set in as the result of the sudden halt of immigration from Poland and of the capital inflow which had accompanied it.

Slow economic recovery, together with the rise of Hitler in Europe, led to the last large wave of immigration, the Fifth Aliyah from 1932 to 1939 (or through World War Two, as well). This was the largest immigration, composed of approximately 50 percent middle-class families from Germany, and 50 percent labor immigrants (Gertz, 1947:103). Women were slightly over half of all immigrants arriving in Palestine between 1932–1939 and continued to comprise half of all immigrants in the following years (Gertz, 1947:98). This immigration was accompanied by the largest inflow of private capital, brought by the middle-class German immigrants, which once again led to economic prosperity. The urban centers and economy expanded, and the occupational opportunities for women became more professionally specialized and diversified. This short lived prosperity was soon followed by a slump when the threat of war became imminent and immigration from Europe all but stopped. It was followed, once again, by economic expansion during the war years geaered to the needs of the British army in the region.

Between 1882 and 1948 the Jewish population of Palestine increased dramatically, changing the composition of the Palestine population in general. Reliable statistics are available only from 1919, the beginning of the British rule. From 1919 to 1945, Jewish immigration amounted to approximately 335,000 immigrants, approximately 172,000 men and 158,000 women (Gertz, ibid.) The Jewish population of Palestine, according to the first census carried out by the British in 1922, grew from approximately 83,800 in 1922 to 174,600 in 1931, the year of the second census, and to 554,000 in 1945 (Gertz, 1947:46). This increase in absolute numbers changed the percentage of the Jews in the total population from 11.1 percent in 1922 to 30.6 percent in 1945, according to the figures of the mandate government, and to 32.0 percent, according to the figures of the Jewish Agency (Gertz, 1947:47). This rapid growth took place under the relatively supportive rule of the British Mandate which, notwithstanding its occasional disagreement with the Jewish leadership and despite the opposition of the Palestinian Arab leadership and majority, allowed large scale Jewish immigration, capital inflow and the purchase of land, at least until 1939, and recognized the political institutions of the Yishuv. These policies enabled the Jewish Yishuv to become a semi-autonomous entity, a state-in-the-making, according to an expression current at the time. This formative period in the building of the nation—the composition of the Jewish population, the institutional structure, the allocation of power, and the ideological priorities—was also formative in the structuring of gender relations.

The Yishuv was a politicized community, highly divided, with groups in conflict on a number of crucial issues. What type of society would the new Jewish society strive to be? An egalitarian society? A socialist one? A society of free enterprise? A religious society? A pluralistic society where immigrants from Moslem countries would share power and cultural influence with the dominant European immigration? These issues became the foci of controversy and conflict between the Labor Movement and its various opponents, just as they divided the Labor Movement internally. Political segmentation within the Yishuv was exacerbated by the impact of factors surrounding it—the dependence of the Yishuv on the public funding of the World Zionist Organization, its dependence on the British Mandate government in determining immigration, land and labor policies, and its struggle against the opposition of the Arab majority. Thus, the experience of the pre-state years was one of creative social experimentation in the formation of a new society on the one hand, and struggle and conflict on numerous fronts on the other hand.

These special and complex features of the period shaped women's experience and consciousness. Internal division created opportunities for new groups to emerge and to stake their claims. Among them were various groups of women who, in a variety of ways, voiced their demands for full participation in the making of the new society. Women of almost all sectors, except for the women of the veteran Jewish orthodoxy, demanded the vote (see Sylvie Fogiel-Bijaoui). Women workers demanded their share of the labor market, as well as of traditional male occupations, and created support systems and services to help them achieve their goals (Dafna Izraeli). Middle-class women organized to create new welfare services (Hanna Herzog). At the same time internal divisions in the Yishuv created a split among women, which was highly detrimental to achieving many of their goals. Women, especially the more active and militant ones, belonged to the different social camps and political parties. The high level of politicization of the community, as well as its internal segmentation, placed a high premium on the loyalty of women to their respective political and social groups. It also led to a highly centralized political system which exercised, as Dafna Izraeli argues in her study of the women workers' movement, strong social control on women by the leadership of the various sectors.

Against this background of political commitment and intersecting struggles, women had to gain priority for "their" issues., the redefinition of the division between male and female, the breakdown of barriers, and the end to the marginalization of women and women's spheres. While some men actually opposed equality for women, in principle, most did not care enough to devote much attention or thought to the subject. At times, when women's needs were compatible with, or even reinforced, goals identified with national revival, they won support and sympathy (see Shilo on the attitude of Arthur Ruppin, senior Zionist official in Palestine). Indifference or oversight, however, were far more common. The general milieu served as an encouraging context, in some respects, for women to advance their goals, as it was accepting of social innovation and change. The concept of a new society, anad especially an egalitarian one, seemed to open the way for women to change their traditional position. At the same time, it was also a difficult time to wage a battle for new relations between women and men, as other struggles were to gain unquestioned primacy, even in the eyes of most women. This is still very much the case.

Historiography

The study of women in the Yishuv has developed at the intersection of two trends in the study of Israeli society. The first, beginning around the mid-1970s, was the re-examination of the Yishuv. The second, the study of women in contemporary Israeli society, which began at approximately the same time, or slightly later.

The Re-examination of the Yishuv

Until the mid-1970s, the study of the Yishuv bore the imprint of the hegemony of the Labor Movement. This was evident in the topics studied and ignored, in the implicit and explicit interpretations, and in the myths and images accepted by the historiography of the period. During the 1970s, the Labor Movement, i.e., the Labor Alignment party and the Histadrut, suffered a rapid decline in power and status. By 1977 the Labor party had lost its political control for the first time in fifty years. The decline and downfall of the Labor Movement had a profound impact on the study of the Yishuv, the period in which the Labor Movement had gained its power, and which it eventually glorified by myths conveyed through the system of education, literary works, the mass media and not least, academic scholarship.

New perspectives began to emerge. These can be characterized by two main trends. The first, the study of social groups previously ignored; such as Druyan's (1981) work on the Yemenite immigration during the years 1882–1914; Herzog's (1986) study of the Sephardi and Yemenite political organizations; Shavit's (1983) work on the Revisionist movement and Drori's (1981) writing on bourgeois groups such as the manufacturers and the household owners. Thus the Yishuv society began to emerge as far more diverse socially, politically, and ideologically than the treatment by the Labor Movement tended to reveal.

The second trend, probably even more influential in bringing about a new understanding of the period, has been the re-examination of long-held images and myths, and their subjection to systematic and skeptical scrutiny. Three studies that challenged dominant myths concerning the Labor Movement were those of

Yonathan Shapiro (1976) who argued for the primacy of power over ideology in the development of the Histadrut; Zvi Sussman (1973) who demonstrated the striking inequality of wages between skilled and unskilled labor in contrast to the prevailing ideology of equality; and Anita Shapira (1977) who convincingly showed that "Hebrew labor" was never actually fully realized despite the well-known image of the pioneer tilling the land and drying the swamps. In the milieu of the 1970s, with growing criticism being levelled at the Labor party and the Histadrut for the gap between their ideology and their actual structure and practice, such a revision of the past was accepted by many as a welcome new approach.

The Study of Women in Contemporary Israeli Society

Until the mid-1970s the status of women was a "non-issue" in Israel. The general notion that women had been and still were equal prevailed in public opinion and was reflected in the absence of almost any academic study related to women.[3] After all, sociological study was oriented primarily to "social problems" and women's status was not defined as one. Even as late as 1986, Izraeli and Tabory argue that "Israeli social scientists writing about social problems, social conflicts, and social stratification have generally omitted any discussion of the status of women as problematic . . . or have subsumed the discussion within the general topic of family . . . "(1986:664–5). However, while students of "social problems" continued to ignore the issue of women's status, it became a subject of study for those scholars, primarily women, who increasingly challenged the assumption of women's equality (for early works, see Aloni, 1976; Padan-Eisenstark, 1973; Hazelton, 1977; Brandow, 1980). This development was influenced by events both outside and within the academic world. A small, but articulate, Feminist movement appeared in Israel in the early 1970s. Marcia Friedman, one of the leading Feminist activists, was elected to the Knesset in 1973 on a civil rights list and raised the issue of violence against women for the first time. In 1975, Israel's Prime Minister established a Commission on the Status of Women to advise the government on the "means to advance equality and partnership between men and women". This action was taken within the framework of the United Nations' Decade on Women, and in response to pressure exerted by the women's caucus in the Labor Alignment party (Izraeli and Tabori, 1987:463–82). A wide range of women were involved in the work of the commission: politicians, academic scholars, trade union activists, social workers, army officers and others. The commission delivered its report in 1978. The work of the commission sensitized many of its members to the issue of women's inequality, gave the issue at least momentary public hearing and created the need for research which would provide greater knowledge and understanding of the many issues raised (Izraeli, 1987:37–53). At the same time, the development of women's studies abroad influenced women within academia, giving legitimacy to this new field of study.

The study of women in contemporary Israeli society began with the argument that women's status differed strikingly from the commonly accepted image of equality and liberation (e.g., Padan-Eisenstark, 1973; Brandow, 1980:403). As can be seen, the element of re-examination emerged rather early on in the study of women. Initially the critique of contemporary inequality still assumed that equality had been achieved in the past and had somehow been lost (e.g., Padan-Eisenstark, 1973; Clapsaddle, 1976). Before long this assumption concerning women's status in the Yishuv, was questioned. Thus the two trends converged, and the re-examination of women in the Yishuv joined the "myth breaking" trend already in full swing.

Many of the articles in this collection are, at least in part, an outcome of this process. The reader will see that many of the articles refer to the prevailing images of the past as a frame of reference for presenting new questions and new evidence. And yet, the dispelling of myths, as a research agenda, has its own risks and drawbacks. If the researcher remains tied to the recent myth, either by accepting or by rejecting it, the myth still dictates the questions asked. Were women equal to men in the Yishuv? The answer quite soon appears as a clearly negative one, reiterated by all students of the subject regardless of specific period, sphere of life, social group and so forth. It then becomes essential to move on from the "negative" though necessary stage of rejecting a misleading image, to the phrasing of new questions—what *was* the position of women, what did they aim for, *what did they do*, what were the attitudes, actions and reactions of the men, their comrades and husbands on the one hand and the male leadership on the other. What did women actually achieve—how and why . . . It is to these questions that the anthology is aimed: beginning with the rejection of the myth of the pioneering woman, the halutza, as being the typical woman of the Yishuv, it moves on to chart new images, tell new stories, and present the women's own voices, dilemmas and action.

New Themes

The studies in this anthology are varied. They stem from different disciplines (sociology, history, geography and literature), deal with different sub-periods (First Aliyah, Second Aliyah), various spheres of life (politics, family, culture) and social groups (the women of the Labor Movement; women of the middle-class; Yemenite women). Three themes, however, recur in almost all of the articles: filling the vacuum or telling the untold tale, social change, and the dynamics of the private and the public.

Filling the Vacuum—Telling the Untold Tale

Until recently, very little had been written on women in the Yishuv. Large anthologies, such as the *Second Aliyah Book*, edited by Bracha Habas (Habas, 1947) and the *Third Aliyah Book*, edited by Yehuda Erez (Erez, 1964), devoted a special chapter to women, rich with impressive tales, and then all but ignored them in the other hundreds of pages.[4] Other publications did even less. The myth of women's equality was taken for granted and the silence only reinforced it. The new study of the Yishuv, the application of systematic research from the perspective of a variety of disciplines, left the issue of gender untouched. A number of examples will suffice.

The scholarly interest in the Yishuv led to the appearance of a number of new journals. A quick survey of two of these is surprising even to the skeptic. The earlier of the two, *Me'asef* (meaning in Hebrew, "Collection"), is subtitled "Writings in the Study of the Jewish Workers Movement", and is published by Givat Haviva, the study center of the Kibbutz *Ha'artzi*, the left wing of the Kibbutz Movement. The journal began to appear in 1971, one volume a year, containing approximately fifteen items including articles, documents, memoirs, and reviews. In the eighteen volumes to appear so far, there have been only two items on women, both dealing with the same woman, written by the same author: an article and a document on Manya Shohat, written (or annotated) by Yaacov Goldstein in 1972 and 1979 respectively (Goldstein, 1972; 1979). The only other article of relevance to women is a long and illuminating article by M. Levin, "The Family in a Revolutionary Society: Norms and manners among the members of the Bund" (1982–3). Thus, even a journal published by those relatively more committed to gender equality, and dealing with social movements with a similar commitment, hardly acknowledge the existence of women.

A second journal, called *Kivunim* (meaning in Hebrew, "Directions"), which appeared between 1978 and 1987, is a quarterly, subtitled "A Journal for the Study of Judaism and Zionism". In slightly over forty issues, each containing nine to ten articles, only three deal with women. Furthermore, while well over half of all the articles deal with the Jewish settlement in Palestine and somewhat less than half with world Jewish events, in the case of women, all three articles concern women outside of Palestine and of the Zionist movement: Rosa Luxemburg (Weistreich, 1978), Grace Agilar (Schonfeld, 1986) and women in the Jewish society of Persia (Levi, 1987). If Jewish women existed in Palestine, or anywhere in the Jewish national awakening, the study of the Zionist movement and the Yishuv has certainly not "seen" them there.

Additional insight into the absence of women from recent study can be gained from an article by Ruth Fierer (1984) entitled "The Rise and Fall of the Pioneering Myth". It is an important article as it deals with the formation and evolution of a central social myth, described as follows:

> A group of pioneers of heroic character, rebel against the historic oppressive circumstances and go out to conquer the ancient Land of Israel. The pioneers struggle in the motherland against grave difficulties: the virgin soil, deathly swamps, Arabs and hostile authorities. By the force of their will power and self sacrifice they overcome the difficulties, with the pure gun in the one hand and the plow in the other, while at their feet spread the bountiful and green fields and orchards. Before their eyes the nation is reborn and reunited with its land, as in the days of the First and Second Temple (1984:15).

This is very clearly the myth of the *male* pioneer, *Halutz*. The women do not belong to the material or the language from which this myth is woven: they did not hold the gun in one hand and the plough in the other . . . they did not "conquer" the land, nor did they penetrate the "virgin" soil . . . And yet Fierer makes no mention either of the male essence of the pioneering myth, nor of the existence of another, closely related, "female" myth, that of the Halutza. Most articles in this volume take this latter myth as a reference point. We seem to have forgotten that this myth of the Halutza, which has had an important impact on the consciousness of Israeli women, has also been relegated to the margins and beyond.

A number of factors help explain this total lack of interest:

• The marginality of the issue. Although the Zionist movement supported women's equality, in principle, and Labor Zionism was committed, ideologically, to women's equality, the issue was driven to the margins by the struggle for national existence, for the "building of the land" (*Binyan Ha'aretz*), for the "conquest of labor" (*Kibush Ha'avoda*), for the right to immigration and so forth. Even the women themselves often gave priority to other struggles, as argued, for example, by Berlovitz and by Fogiel-Bijaoui.

• Few women held positions of power and of leadership. It is these positions which are the most documented and studied, leaving all other segments, women among them, on the sidelines.

• Few women, even among the activist and influential ones, left collected volumes of speeches and public writings, as did many of the men. Their impact on the library shelves is even smaller than it was in actual public life. The documentation left by women is often of a very different nature, that of private writing, mainly letters and diaries, which have begun to play an important role in the reclaiming of the past lives of women.

• The private spheres. Just as women were relatively absent from the political and public spheres, the spheres where their voice was heard remained largely undocumented. Public activity which dealt with the more personal dimensions of life—welfare, health, child-care, etc.—was given far less attention than political power struggles. The private spheres, which occupied much of women's time and energy, and shaped much of their life chances, were hardly referred to in public debate, let alone systematically documented.

• Male bias in the writing of history. The feminist critique that historical writing has ignored women and made them invisible (Bridenthal et al., 1987; Gordon et al., 1976), is blatantly evident in the new, as well as the old, historiography of the Yishuv, as demonstrated above,[5] and as argued in many of the studies included in this volume.

Each article in this anthology contributes, in its way, to filling the large vacuum of knowledge on women's experience. This has been done, in most cases, within the accepted categories for the study of the Yishuv. The distinctions between chronological waves of immigration,[6] between types of settlements, between the Labor Movement and the middle-classes, etc., has been retained, as has the new attention to previously neglected social groups. Thus many of the articles are clearly located in specific *Aliyot*—the First Aliyah (Yaffa Belovitz; Ran Aaronsohn) or the Second Aliyah

(Margalit Shilo; Musia Lipman and Deborah Bernstein; Nurit Govrin; Shulamit Reinharz); many of the articles deal with the women of the Labor Movement who, due to their affiliation with the dominant movement of the Yishuv, were more prominent and therefore more closely studied than other groups of women (Dafna Izraeli; Margalit Shilo; Deborah Bernstein; Sylvie Fogiel-Bijaoui; Shulamit Reinharz; Musia Lipman and Deborah Bernstein), while additional articles deal with women belonging to other social groups, such as the middle-classes (Hanna Herzog) and the Yemenite women (Nitza Druyan).

These articles add a new dimension to the existing parameters of time and social group. They not only refer to the women within these contexts, they put them at center stage, they deal with them as social actors, having their own voice, their own creation. They enter new spheres previously neglected (e.g., Bernstein on the family, Fogiel-Bijaoui on motherhood), and make use of new sources to illuminate women's experience (Aaronsohn's presentation of annotated letters; Lipman and Bernstein's discussion of pioneering women's diaries). Social experimentation by women becomes the focus of study in Izraeli's study of the Women Workers' Movement; in Shilo's study of the women's training farm, in Reinharz's study of Manya Shohat and the Collective in Sejera, in Fogiel-Bijaoui's analysis of the way women in kibbutzim coped with their inequality and in Herzog's study of middle-class women's organizations. These new subjects go way beyond the initial question of equality between men and women.

Women and Social Change

The Zionist enterprise was, in essence, an enterprise of social change, an attempt at transforming the Jewish people from a persecuted minority in the diaspora to a sovereign majority in the old-new Jewish homeland (and eventually, state). There are two additional dimensions of change, deeply embedded both in the experience and in the historiography of the Yishuv. First, a change in the nature of Jewish society, the transformation into a new type of society, egalitarian and labor-oriented, according to the basic tenets of the Labor Movement. Second, the transformation of the individual, of the diaspora Jew, into a productive, creative and proud Hebrew person. Women shared in all these facets of change. But they faced additional challenges, unique to them. They had to free themselves from the specific gender definition of traditional patriarchal Jewish society, where women were subordinated to men both in the family and in the community. From the first step, the process of change was far more difficult for them than for the men. The very act of immigration, of leaving family and community, was far more difficult for the young women who came on their own, and thus entailed a far deeper rejection of the past. In Palestine, they not only had to join in the struggles conducted by the men of the various social groups, they also had to struggle against the latter's conception of appropriate gender roles. The transformation of the diaspora Jew into the new "Hebrew" was not gender neutral. The very language describing the new Hebrew, as noted above in discussing the myth of the Halutz, was male language. The woman aspired to become a new "Hebrew woman". To do this she had to transform herself, and yet, how could self-transformation of her social role be achieved when the partners to this role, the men, were not engaged in the same process?[7] Could she become a different women if she was not treated differently? Could she establish new gender relations when men showed no inclination to give up any of their prerogatives, either in the public or in the private domain?

The process of change was an all encompassing one, it included individual identity, collective consciousness, formation of organization and the adoption of strategies of action. Most articles in this volume deal with some of these aspects. There were women who arrived in Palestine primarily because of their husband's decision to immigrate. They had no previous intention of transforming themselves. According to Ran Aaronsohn and Yaffa Berlovitz, who deal with the women of the First Aliyah, there were few new models these women could follow, as they developed a new sense of involvement in and commitment to their new society, and this often led, according to Berlovitz, to bewilderment and doubt. Even the Labor Movement women were often unclear as to the models they wanted to adopt. Margalit Shilo discusses the various models suggested in the women's training farm—some women aspired to emulate men, to try and be just like the pioneering man, the halutzim; others wanted to be their helpmates—working hand in hand at their separate and suitable tasks; still others offered to try and follow in the footsteps of the Russian revolutionary women or maybe to learn from the Arab peasant women who worked in the fields and milked the cows. The search for new models implies the development of consciousness of the need for, and possibility of, change. Both Sylvie Fogiel-Bijaoui and Dafna Izraeli discuss the importance of such consciousness for effective action, while Nitza Druyan discusses the implications of lack of consciousness in relation to the Yemenite women, who arrived in Palestine at the same time. Though unintended, their immigration to Palestine entailed a significant change, as it often happened that the women were the only ones able to obtain income for the family, and were thus brought into closer contact with the new world around them. Nevertheless, little change took place in their social and public status, nor were they able to organize to try and bring about such change.

Many of the writers are concerned with strategies of action for change. A variety of strategies emerge: the demand for equal duties, rather than equal rights, as argued by Sylvie Fogiel-Bijaoui for women in the kibbutz; the transformation of self through the acquisition of new skills, a route of self-emancipation, as shown by Margalit Shilo regarding the women's training farm; the formation of organizations to advance "women's spheres", as demonstrated by Hanna Herzog in relation to women of the middle-class; the formation of a women's movement, autonomous yet affiliated to the larger movement with which the women identified, as in the case of the women of the Labor Movement studied by Dafna Izraeli; and finally, the multiple strategies for obtaining the power to win the vote, as shown by Sylvie Fogiel-Bijaoui in her study of one of women's most important achievements.

The Private and the Public

Feminist critique of the study of society (e.g., Nicholson, 1976) has argued against the separation of the public from the private spheres as two independent, unrelated spheres of society. It is argued that such a separation is artificial and misleading, in that it implies that there are different principles of analysis to be brought to each of these overall spheres, and that what happens in one is of basically little analytic or practical concern to the other. On the contrary, the critique argues, the "private" sphere—the sphere of personal relations, the family, everyday experiences—is deeply embedded in the economic, political and social structure of society. At the same time, these "public" domains are often affected, changed or produced by processes within the "private" sphere, such as socialization and gender consciousness.

In the Yishuv, the public sphere of political, military and labor activity had unquestioned priority. Not only was it considered the more important sphere, it was seen as the *most* important, as it, and only it, was related to the "conquest of labor" and the "building of the land". While it is possible to see the relation between the "public" and the "private" spheres in the Yishuv as an integration of the two with collectivistic principles guiding both spheres, it can be argued that the "private" was expected to subordinate itself to the "public", with little recognition of its own social significance. The women were caught, possibly trapped, between their identification with the dominant ideology on the one hand, and the importance they themselves gave to their private experience and their personal world, on the other.

The articles in this volume show, in numerous cases, the depth of the relationship between the private and public spheres. The private sphere, the daily experience of family life and personal relations, was concretely shaped by the public sphere—by the political situation, by economic conditions, by social movements, etc., as argued by Bernstein in her study of the urban working-class family and women's daily experience. But, even more significant, the private was *experienced* by the individual women, as located in and related to a larger public reality. This is most striking in the annotated documents included in the anthology, the fragments of diaries presented by Deborah Bernstein and Musia Lipman and the letters annotated by Ran Aaronsohn. Almost every sentence reverberates with the intermeshing of spheres and experiences. The diary and letters are genres of writing which would seem to enable the most candid expression of intimate feelings of love, passion, and bitter despair. And yet, even in this private form of writing, the public sphere appears to be so basic to the women's feeling of self as to be always present, at times as a source of reassurance and satisfaction, at others as part of the sense of loss and bewilderment. The commitment to and involvement with the public is, in turn, invested, in many cases, with an urgency and passion which, once again, seem to link the "personal" and the "political".

The twelve articles in this collection are divided into three sections. The first, "Between Tradition and Change." deals with the early immigration and its impact on women who continued to live in a relatively traditional community, at least as far as gender relations were concerned. The second section "Women of the Labor Movement," contains studies of women who belonged to, or were affiliated with, the labor movement. The dominant position and innovative character of the labor movement and the women workers' movement attracted many of the students of the period, hence the relatively large number of articles in this section. The third section, "Women's Rights, Women's Spheres," contains two articles which deal mainly with women of the middle-class and their organized attempts to secure women's rights and advance those spheres which have always been identified as women's spheres.

Before letting the articles speak for themselves, a brief comment on language and terminology is called for. The articles speak in different voices, both of the writers and of the women portrayed. The women, one must remember, spoke and wrote between one hundred and fifty years ago. Even when they spoke Hebrew, their language was different from the living, spoken language we use today. It was not only newly acquired by the women immigrants; it was a language in "the making". Thus an element of verbal awkwardness, of stiffness, is often noted, even in translation. But the difference runs deeper. Their language was replete with expressions of public commitment and ideological fervor, which today sounds either artificial, pompous, or even insincere. At that time, for those women however, it was the most suitable form to express, albeit in a somewhat stilted manner, their thoughts and experiences. The style and the content were part and parcel of the people and their experience.

The contributors to this volume come from different disciplines, bringing different styles, forms of analysis and types of data. I have attempted, as the editor, to leave in the variability, introducing only that unity necessary for systematic reading, such as the form of notation and referencing. And yet one term calls for a special comment. The reader will note that two different terms have been used to refer to the place where the events occurred—Palestine and Eretz Israel (or Eretz Yisrael). Without going into the history of the name Palestine, suffice to note that before the establishment of the State of Israel, and especially during the British Mandate, Palestine was the name of the territory and political entity west of the Jordan river. The government appointed by the British was called the Government of Palestine, there was Palestinian citizenship (for both Jews and Arabs living in the territory) as well as Palestinian currency. Jews used the term Palestine (*Palestina*) both in everyday speech and in writing, as did the British and the Arabs. The Jews also used the Hebrew term Eretz Yisrael, meaning the Land of Israel. Today both terms have acquired additional connotations. "Palestine", refers to an Arab (Palestinian-Arab) country or state, while Eretz Israel brings to mind an exclusively Jewish entity. Neither of these connotations is fully satisfying for the period under study. As each term is rich, even rife, with connotations, I chose to allow the authors the prerogative of choosing the term they felt most appropriate for their writing.

Notes

1. It is difficult to set an exact date for the beginning of the new national immigrations, as compared to the previous religious immigration. The year 1882 marks the beginning of the immigration from Russia of the *Hibbat Zion* (Love of Zion) movement, a section of the World Zionist Movement which called for immediate immigration to Palestine. It became known as the First Aliyah. This, at least by implication, ignores the involvement of some of the earlier settlers in the building of the new national entity. It also ignores the Yemenite immigration which took place at the same time, which Druyan discusses in this volume. Thus, we have an additional example of bias introduced into the accepted historiography, reinforcing the centrality of the labor movement and its immediate predecessors.

2. Among the "bachelors" and "spinsters", to use the categories of the formal statistics, which mainly refer to the labor immigrants, women were only approximately twenty-five percent (Gertz, 1947:98).

3. The fact that Golda Meir was prime-minister also created the impression that there were no special problems for women. Quite the contrary. Israel could serve as an example of an egalitarian society.

4. The larger of the two collections is the *Third Aliyah Book*. It contains two volumes, and all of nine hundred pages. Of these, one whole section of approximately forty-five pages is devoted to the women pioneers. In all other sections, devoted to all spheres of work and types of settlements, women are hardly ever mentioned. Nevertheless, in both collections there is a lot of implicit material on women.

5. An additional publication, probably with the highest academic standing, is *Zionism: A collection for the study of the Zionist Movement and the Jewish Yishuv*. It is published by the Institute for the Study of Zionism of the Tel Aviv University and has appeared annually since 1970. Not one article in this publication deals with women. It is beyond our scope in this Introduction to deal with the ways in which the historiography excludes women, focusing on issues which did not involve women on the one hand, and ignoring them where they were, on the other.

6. Given far more knowledge concerning women in the Yishuv in the future, possibly a different periodization will prove more useful.

7. I would like to thank Dafna Izraeli for this important point.

References

Aloni, Shulamit. 1976. *Women as People*. Tel Aviv: Mabat (Hebrew).

Baum, Charlotte, Paula Hyman and Sonya Michel. 1975. *The Jewish Woman in America*. New York: Dial Press.

Bein, Alex. 1954. *The History of Jewish Agricultural Settlement in Palestine*. Tel Aviv: Massada (Hebrew).

Berger-Sofer, Rhonda. 1982. "Ideological Separation but Structural Interaction. The Relationship of Purity and Segregation to the Roles of Men & Women in a Jewish *Haredi* Community" (unpublished manuscript).

Bernstein, S. Deborah. 1987. *The Struggle for Equality, Urban Women Workers in Prestate Israeli Society*. New York: Praeger.

Blum, Shulamit. 1980. *The Woman in the Labor Movement During the Second Aliyah*. Ma. A. Dissertation. Tel Aviv University (Hebrew).

Brandow, K. Selma. 1980. "Ideology, Myth, and Reality: Sex Equality in Israel." *Sex Roles* 6, 3:403–419.

Bridenthal, Renate, Claudia Koonz and Susan Stuard (eds.). 1987. *Becoming Visible: Women in European history*. Houghton Mifflin: Boston. Second edition.

Clapsaddle, Carol. 1976. "Flight from Feminism: The Case of the Israeli Woman," pp. 202–217 in *The Jewish Woman*, edited by Elizabeth Koltun. New York: Schoken Books.

Drori, Yigal. 1981. *Hahugim Ha'ezrahi'im in the Jewish "Yishuv" in Eretz-Israel, 1920–1929*. Ph.D. Dissertation. Tel Aviv University (Hebrew).

Eisenstadt, S. N. 1967. *Israeli Society*. London: Weidenfeld and Nicolson.

Erez, Yehuda. 1964. *The Third Aliyah Book*. Tel Aviv: Am Oved (Hebrew).

Fierer, Ruth. 1984. "The Rise and Fall of the Pioneering Myth." *Kivunim*, 23:5–23 (Hebrew).

Gertz, A. 1947. *Statistical Handbook of Palestine*. Jerusalem: Department of Statistics of the Jewish Agency.

Goldstein, Yaacov. 1972. "Manya Shohat and Brit Shalom." *Me'asef*, 4:124–143 (Hebrew).

———. 1979. "The Medem-Shohat Debate." *Me'asef*, 11:130–142 (Hebrew).

Gordon, D. Ann, Mari Jo Buhl and Nancy Scorm Dye. 1976. "The Problem of Women's History," pp. 75–92 in *Liberating Women's History*, edited by Berenice A. Carroll. Urbana: University of Illinois Press.

Habas, Bracha. 1947. *The Second Aliyah Book*. Tel Aviv: Am Oved (Hebrew).

Hazelton, Leslie. 1977. *Israeli Women: The Reality Behind the Myths*. New York: Simon and Schuster.

Herzog, Hanna. 1986. *Political Ethnicity—The Image and Reality*. Tel Aviv: Hakibbutz Hameuchad (Hebrew).

Izraeli, N. Dafna and Ephraim Tabori. 1986. "The Perception of Women's Status in Israel as a Social Problem." *Sex Roles* 14, 11/12:663–679.

Izraeli, N. Dafna. 1987. "Status of Women in Israel," pp. 37–53 in *Encyclopedia Judaica Year Book 1986–7*. Jerusalem: Keter.

Izraeli, N. Dafna and Ephraim Tabori. 1987a. "The Political Context of Feminist Attitudes in Israel." *Gender and Society* 2, 4:463–482.

Lestschinsky, Jacob. 1961. *The Jewish Dispersion, Social and Economic Development of Jewish Communities in Europe and America in the Last Centuries*. Jerusalem: Bialik Institute.

Levi, Azaria. 1987. "The Woman in The Jewish Society of Persia." *Kivunim*, 34:117–127 (Hebrew).

Levin, M. 1982–3. "The Family in a Jewish Revolutionary Society—Norms and Practices among the Members of the Bund." *Me'asef*, 13:109–127; 14:157–173 (Hebrew).

Nicholson, Linda, J. 1976. "Feminist Theory: The Private and the Public," pp. 221–230 in *Women and Philosophy: Towards a Theory of Liberation*, edited by Carol C. Gould and Marx W. Wartofsky. New York: Putnam.

Padan-Eisenstark, Dorit. 1973. "Are Israeli Women Really Equal? Trends and Patterns in Israeli Women's Labor Force Participation: A Comparative Analysis." *Journal of Marriage and the Family* 35, 3:538–546.

Schonfeld, Amyra. 1986. "Grace Agilar—A Forgotten Author." *Kivunim*, 30:113–123 (Hebrew).

Shapira, Anita. 1977. *The Futile Struggle—The Jewish Labor Controversy 1929–1939*, Tel Aviv: Hakibbutz Hameuchad (Hebrew).

Shapiro, Yonathan. 1976. *The Formative Years of the Israeli Labor Party*. London: Sage.

Shavit, Yaacov. 1983. *The Revisionist Movement: The Plan for Colonizatory Regime and Social Ideas 1925–1935*. Tel Aviv: Hadar (Hebrew).

Sussman, Zvi. 1973. "The Determination of Wages of Unskilled Labor in the Advanced Section of the Dual Economy in Mandatory Palestine." *Economic Development and Cultural Change* 22, 1:95–113.

Weinberg, Sydney S. 1988. *The World of Our Mothers*. Chapel Hill: University of North Carolina Press.

Weissler, Chava. 1986. "The Traditional Piety of Ashkenazic Women," pp. 245–275 in *Jewish Spirituality*, edited by Arthur Green. London: Routledge and Kegan Paul.

Weistreich, Robert. 1978. "The Jewish Origins of Rosa Luxemburg." *Kivunim*, 1:71–87 (Hebrew).

Zborowski, Mark and Elizabeth Herzog. 1952. *Life is with People*. New York: Schoken Books.

Figure 1. Women Workers, 1924.

Part I

Between Tradition and Change

A wave of Jewish immigration to Palestine began in 1882. It became known in Zionist historiography as the First Aliyah, to distinguish it from all preceding Jewish immigration. Thus a demarcation line was drawn between the Jewish community which had developed in Palestine during the nineteenth century—the Old Yishuv—and the community which grew out of the later immigrations beginning at the end of the nineteenth century—the New Yishuv. The former was characterized as traditional, conservative and non-productive, while the latter was seen as its polar opposite, a community based on social experimentation, nationalistic spirit, European modernism and secularism. The immigration from Yemen, which took place during the same period as the First Aliyah from Eastern Europe, was largely ignored, as it clearly did not fit into this popular dichotomy.

However, a closer scrutiny of women's position in society indicates that the demarcation between Old and New Yishuv was not so clear and sharp as we have been led to believe (some of the other faults found in the above distinction have been discussed in the Introduction). The "New" had much of the "Old" contained within it, as far as women were concerned, especially in the early decades of Zionist immigration. This is evident in the life style of many of the immigrants, in their traditional conception of the Jewish community of family and of gender relations.

The East European First Aliyah and the immigration from Yemen were immigrations of families. In both cases the women played a very small role in the decision to immigrate. They followed their husbands' decision, and did not appear to attach any special significance to their immigration in terms of their own role as women in the community and in society. Women were seen, and continued to see themselves, as the traditional helpmates to their husbands and homemakers to their families. However, as the three articles in this section reveal, the actual experience of women was

25

far more complex. The transition to a new country and community, under changed circumstances, brought about a change in the lives of women, even as they continued to fulfill their traditional (and subordinate) role. The need to care for their families in a new environment, facing crisis, challenge, and hardship, created a new determination and a sense of communal involvement. But these transformations, unacknowledged by the men of the community, were riddled with ambivalence and insecurity. The sense of new involvement and strength was accompanied by unasked questions and often, as Yaffa Berlovitz and Nitza Druyan argue, by a sense of bewilderment and frustration.

The peripheral role of women in the *moshavot* and the Yemenite communities accounts for the scarcity of documentation referring to them and for the fact that their situation has not been examined in later studies. Ran Aaronsohn, Yaffa Berlovitz and Nitza Druyan have, therefore, had to discover and make use of a variety of less conventional sources—letters, oral poetry, women's tales of their life-story and literature written by women. These sources are used not only to document what has been excluded in historiography so far, but even more significantly, as Berlovitz emphasizes, to bring forth the woman's own voice—"her opinions, her thoughts, her emotional reactions and most important her interpretation of that soul-stirring historic event, the return to Zion."

Ran Aaronsohn presents a unique view of women's experience through two letters sent by a woman of whom we know only that she was a "settler's wife." The two letters portray not only her day to day life and work, but also her feelings and sense of what was happening to her and around her, from her vantage point within her own home. She appears to be a typical "settler's wife"—"the wife of K."—a woman who followed her husband, grieving her departure from all that was close, familiar and civilized to go to a far-off land, and live "among the stones of the field". And yet, less than half a year later, she writes that "the land is like a Garden of Eden laid out before us." She seems to be content both with the community she has found herself in, of which she has learned much in the meantime, and with her own work in the farm and at home. She is an enterprising and hard-working woman. "The wife of K.", concludes Aaronsohn, "accepted her role as a homemaker and a wife with modesty but not with servility, and fulfilled her role with a sense of her own worth, without a feeling of passivity."

The "settler's wife" did not question her position or express any awareness of her inferior status as a woman. In this respect she was probably similar to many of the other women in the moshavot. The women of whom Berlovitz writes, the women authors of the First Aliyah, were very different. They were well educated, versed in the Hebrew language and Zionist ideology. They were committed to the new national goals and were convinced that these entailed a renaissance for women as part of the national awakening. And yet, they were painfully aware of women's actual exclusion and subordination. The two leading authors Yaffa Berlovitz studies, Hemdah Ben-Yehuda and Nehamah Pukhachewsky, both call for change. Hemdah Ben-Yehuda sees the source of women's subordination in their inferior education. Pukhachewsky identifies a deeper level of subordination. All around her, women appeared to be victims of male exploitation. The Yemenite woman, whom she portrays with great compassion and admiration, a woman of strong character who maintained her proud bearing under extreme hardship, was totally subordinate to the man who clung to his old ways, thus limiting any potential for change in their community. But, as Berlovitz argues, Pukhachewsky saw as much exploitation, though more sophisticated in form, among the East European Ashkenazi immigrants. Even those women who were aware of the prejudices against them seemed to her to lack the daring to fight for their new convictions. Pukhachewsky's protest, according to Berlovitz, was directed to the man—the "new male"—"not only because he dominates women in their private lives but because he undermines her every attempt to free herself of the conventions of the past and assure her equal rights, for these, after all, were the declared principles of the national revival."

The Yemenite women Nitza Druyan studies were, as yet, far removed from feminist awareness. They came from an extremely conservative community whose members immigrated to Eretz Israel to continue rather than change their traditional-religious way of life. Nevertheless, the changed circumstances both in Jerusalem and in the moshavot, where the Yemenites served as a labor force for the independent farmers, made women in many cases the sole wage-earners, and created a major upheaval in the relations between men and women. "The employed women", claims Druyan "were gradually gaining self-confidence because of their income. They also became more socially sophisticated, acquiring knowledge in the ways of the world that the men lacked altogether." The community, still totally dominated by the men, reacted by applying force and coercion, both legally and physically. The fascinating story of Shoshanna Bassin, quoted at length by Druyan, tells of a

young girl who saw new options opening up around her and chose
to follow them, even at the cost of breaking with her family and
community. The Yemenite women at the turn of the century, argues Druyan, could not express their protest as did some Ashkenazi women of the First Aliyah, nor form protest movements as
did the women of the Second Aliyah (see Part II). "They lacked a
coherent awareness of their changing status . . . they were still in
their frustration stage which was manifest in more personal than
communal avenues."

1

Through the Eyes of a Settler's Wife: Letters From the *Moshava*

——— *Ran Aaronsohn* ———

Introduction*

Both men and women took part in the resumption of Jewish settlement in the Land of Israel during modern times. Most of the twenty-eight moshavot (private rural settlements) of the First Aliyah (Jewish immigration to Israel), (1882–1904), came into existence as family communities (Aaronsohn, 1983). Nevertheless, it is possible to assume from the source material of the period, as well as from memoirs committed to writing at a later date, that the role of women in the settlement effort was minor and marginal in comparison with the role of men. This is a mistaken assumption, in my opinion.

The sources, especially the primary sources, were written mostly by men, as may be expected in a society of immigrants with a traditional character. One of the first and only sources written by a woman living in one of the moshavot is presented below.*

The purpose of this chapter is to depict some features of the life of a woman and her surroundings (e.g., her house and her community) in the moshavot of the early period of modern Jewish settlement, by presenting original source material: two letters which were written during the years 1889 and 1890 by a woman who settled in Zikhron Yaakov, one of the first Jewish moshavot in the Land of Israel.

The chapter is divided into three sections. The opening section

---

*I would like to thank Dr. Debbie Bernstein, Dr. Ilan Solomon, and especially Professor Ruth Kark, for their comments and contributions to the writing of this article.

discusses the role of the woman in the early moshavot, in the source material of the period written by women, and the document presented below. The middle section includes the document itself, which consists of two letters, as well as a series of notes clarifying various references in the two letters. The final section consists of a discussion of the document as a means of examining the role of the woman and the family in the moshavot of the First Aliyah on the one hand, and as a reflection of general trends and settlement processes, on the other.

Our assumption, which we will try to back up with the help of the two letters, is that the highly personalized descriptions provided by the author in her letters enable us to draw conclusions on two levels: the "micro" level involving events in the daily life of the author and her immediate surroundings, and the "macro" level involving events in the life of the community. Needless to say, this paper makes no attempt at assessing the factual validity of all the details given in the source material; such an assessment requires, of course, corroboration from other sources.

As a result, the discussion which follows will go beyond the details described in the letters (which are quite interesting in their own right), and will emphasize the allusions to the broader framework of general developments which characterized the early moshavot. Thus, the reactions of the author to the problems which she encountered when settling in Zikhron Yaakov, will be used as a basis for depicting the characteristics of the society of the early moshavot as well as the position of women in this society.

A. Source Material of the Early Settlement Period Pertaining to Women

Even though most of the wives of the settlers were relatively educated, they did not participate in the life of the community by writing. Thus, there was a paucity of written documentation regarding their lives which created a historiographical bias against them. Nevertheless, it is possible to glean information regarding some of the early women settlers from the sources. In general, this information pertains to women who were unusual in terms of their independent activities, mostly single women, who were not overshadowed by men. Three such women who were active in the first decade of settlement are Golda Miloslawsky, a widow who immigrated to Israel (then Palestine) with her family and cultivated her small property in the young settlement of Nes Tziona; Batya Makov, who separated from her husband in order to immigrate to Israel and settled with her sons and daughters in the moshava of Rehovot, which had just been founded; and Ita Felman, who continued living with her large family in their orange grove ("Bayara") which had been established in an Arab village near Jaffa by her husband. (For information about the first two, see Smilansky, 1943, 1:234–51; for information about the third, see Aaronsohn, 1985:244–245,255).

Only a few of the married women settlers left a lasting impression. These were mostly educated women, who had studied abroad and were active in the Jewish settlement in the realms of culture and society. Several of these women became the first modern Hebrew women writers: Nehamah Pukhachewsky of Rishon le'Tzion, Hanna Trager-Barnett of Petah Tikva, and Yehudit Harari of Rehovot (Berlovitz, 1984). These women, of course, left us their own writing. However, this consisted, for the most part, of memoirs and literary compositions written at a later time, with the exception of some of the letters of Nehama Pukhachewsky (for more information about her, see Smilansky, 1943, 1:242–244).

In fact, even in the atypical and relatively more advanced groups of settlers, such as the *Bilu'im* of Gedera and some of the founders of Rishon le'Tzion, it seems that the role of the women was not significantly different than in the other moshavot: they were housewives and helpmates of the men (Smilansky, 1943, 1:214–221). Only a few women managed to break through the tight embrace of family life and make an imprint on the society which was being created, as a result of their professions and the strength of their personalities (Aaronsohn, 1989).

From among the few examples, I would like to mention two women who belonged to the same family: the doctor Fanya Belkind, and her sister, the midwife Olga, who was the wife of Yehoshua Hankin. The latter was the only woman who was the subject of an entry in *Personalities of the First Aliyah* which, included fifty–five bibliographic essays (Eliav, 1981, 2:414. For more information about Olga Hankin, see Smilansky, 1944, 2:132–142). There were others who were employed outside of their homes and worked in the communal services of the moshavot, mostly in the administration of the Baron de Rothschild, in the realms of education and medicine (Aaronsohn, 1985: 487–93). However, none of them left behind written source material documenting their lives.

Zikhron Yaakov was typical in this regard. The independence

of the wives of the settlers was extremely limited, as were their communal activities and even the amount of time devoted to work on their husbands' farms. A few descriptions do exist as to their activities. Mostly, these are descriptions of men regarding the activities of exemplary women, such as the members of the Aaronsohn family, Sara and her mother Malka, who did not leave us written records of their own. The amount of source material written by women is very limited; and nearly all of the source material consists of memoirs written at a later date (Bessa Leibman, in Samsonov, 1942; Buskala-Guttman, 1966).

However, the lack of sources pertaining to women does not indicate their lack of importance or contribution. Actually, the woman's role is prominently recorded in oral documentation as well as in biographical literature. They have a place, as well, in the *belles lettres* written about the early moshavot. However, it is almost impossible to find original source material which was written in the First Aliyah period by the women living in the moshavot (one exception will be discussed below, in section C.). It is also difficult to find research literature dealing with the lives of women and their roles in the early moshavot.

The tendency to minimize the relative contribution of women in the early settlement is undoubtedly a result of the nature of the existing society. Women's status was a function of the concepts and values which the settlers brought with them from abroad, where Jewish society was generally religious, traditional, and patriarchal. The status of women in conservative Jewish society was predetermined to be a subordinate one (Bernstein, 1987:10–14). As a result, an original document of any sort which deals with the women of the First Aliyah and their lives, is unique.

The source itself consists of two letters sent by the wife of one of the settlers of Zikhron Yaakov, shortly after she arrived in Israel in the year 1889, to her sister-in-law in Vilna. It is characteristic of the period, that neither the name of the author nor any information about her has survived. The only available information relates to the male members of the author's family; her husband, Shlomo Kalman Kantor, an engineer who immigrated to Israel from his native Russia toward the end of 1886 and settled in Zikhron Yaakov; her eldest son, Eliyahu, who followed his father to Zikhron Yaakov a year later, and the younger sons, David and Betsalel, who arrived in Israel with their mother from Kovna, Russia, toward the end of 1889.

The father, Shlomo Kalman, first studied at the Workers'

School (the Arbeiter Schule) of the Baron's administration in Zikhron Yaakov. Later, he settled in the moshava as one of the public employees of the Baron. He took part in surveying land bought by the administration, in addition to other responsibilities (four of his letters, from the years 1888–1896, are preserved in the Central Zionist Archives in Jerusalem—listed below as "CZA"– CZA, File Number A9/101/11).

The eldest son, Eliyahu, followed in his father's footsteps: during the years 1887–1889, he was a student at the Workers' School and an agricultural worker in Zikhron Yaakov; afterwards he worked as a foreman for the administration. As such, he was in charge of paving roads, constructing the new administration building, making additions to the winery of Zikhron Yaakov, draining the Tantura swamps, etc. Eliyahu specialized in surveying land, and was the head surveyor of JCA (the Jewish Colonization Association) in the Galilee region, in the early part of the twentieth century (Aaronsohn, 1985:499–500; Samsonov, 1942:237). The two other sons, David and Betsalel, were students at the elementary school of Zikhron Yaakov when the letters were written. Nothing more is known about them, or about their mother, the author of the letters presented below.

The letters were originally written in Yiddish, the language used by the immigrants from Eastern Europe, which was commonly spoken in the moshavot. A copy of the letters in alcohol–it is not clear whether this is a photostat or a copy of the original—is located in the Padoba collection at the CZA, File Number A9/92/14. These are private letters, not meant for publication, which were written by a woman to her friend and relative abroad. Nevertheless, they were published shortly afterwards in the Russian-Jewish paper *Hamelitz*, translated into Hebrew. (The first letter was published in Vol. 29, issue 253, dated December 2, 1889:1–2; the second letter was published in issue Number 132, Vol. 30, dated June 27, 1890).

Each of the letters was published by itself, again, in Hebrew, with several omissions and without any notes of clarification. The first was published in *The Book of Zikhron Yaakov*, edited by A. Samsonov (1942:203–4), and the second in *The Book of the First Aliyah*, edited by M. Eliav (1981, 1:180–81). This chapter will present both letters together; for the first time, without any omissions except for one paragraph which does not pertain to the moshavot and is located at the beginning of the letters: it will include notes whose purpose is to clarify references made in the letters (the notes relating to each letter will follow immediately after the letter it-self). In addition to the publication of the unabridged documents, an attempt was made to try to maintain the spirit of the original sources by translating them into language as similar as possible to the old-fashioned, vernacular of the letters themselves.

B. Letters From an Anonymous Woman Settler

Document A:

Letter from the Wife of Kalman Kantor, Zikhron Yaakov, October/November 1889.[1]

. . . And we reached our place, on *Erev Shabat*, (Friday evening) after dark, and we entered the guest house. During Shabat, I managed to look over the house which had been given us. It was a walled house with three rooms and a cooking shed, as well as a large barn for the animals, but I didn't like it because it was outside of the town, in the new colony,[2] even though it was only a ten minute walk to town; and the air wasn't very good there.

So I asked to get a house in town, and, fortunately, we found an available house of this sort in town, and it was given to us. The house is actually smaller than the first one, because it's missing one room, and it's at the edge of the colony, at the entrance to the town; but the air is very, very good there, because it overlooks the sea[3] and the area is inhabited by people.

Also, anything one desires which is sold in town is brought there by way of the end of the street, and as a result, we are the first to see the merchandise. The Arabs bring all sorts of things to sell: milk, eggs, chickens, wood, grapes and different kinds of fruit.[4] And everything is sold cheaply: ten eggs for 7 kopecks, a chicken for 30 kopecks—and there are lots of these—a log (a liquid measure) of milk for 3½ kopecks,[5] et cetera.

So far we have nothing, because we have not yet gotten settled down completely, but if God pleases, we will see the time when we will have a lot of possessions . . . It is absolutely true that after the *Pesach* (Passover) holiday, please God, the Baron will come to visit the colonies.[6] New houses will be built then, and we will be given another house which will be larger than the one we now have.

And during the winter, we will be able to live comfortably even in the house in which we are living right now, because it also has a cooking shed, and a large barn built of stones and plastered with mortar both inside and out, and only its windows are smaller than the windows in the house. Half of the barn we are keeping for the cow and the sheep and the horse, and the other half will be used for living purposes, if the house is too small. Many have already done this. Around the house we will make a garden. Our vineyard is far from the house, but it hardly makes a difference . . .

We won't be lacking for anything, even now. There is plenty of all the things which a person needs to keep alive. The Baron provides us with whatever is needed and required. We will be getting 54 francs a month, and E.[7] will also be getting 30 francs a month, and we are all living together, thank God, and we hope that with the proper attitude, our situation will improve in the near future. We don't have to pay fees for *shechita* (ritual slaughter of animals), nor do we have to pay for the synagogue, or tuition for schooling. The children are studying French, Arabic, and Hebrew in school, and they will be taught to sew with a sewing machine and all sorts of other handicrafts. There are four teachers at the school, and the children are taught dancing and singing as well. If, God forbid, someone gets sick—the doctor will treat him without charge, and medicines are also free and the midwife is available for those who need her without cost.[8] We have to pay bathhouse fees only.

After all this, I still yearn for Russia. The heat and the *Khamsin* (the desert wind), are very difficult for people from Russia; in the winter it is raining, and this is the best time of the entire year, when we are able to live well. The winter season here is full of different types of vegetables and fruit which grow on trees. Twelve apples for 7 kopecks, three liters of figs for 7 kopecks, three liters of raisins for 7 kopecks. For food, we serve compot and eat bread. It's possible to live well here if God grants health and strength!

When I came to town, the change in climate affected me badly, and on the fifth day after my arrival I got sick with malaria, God forbid, and I lay in bed for eight days. And even now I'm still weak and have little strength, but thanks to God, I have strength enough now to walk. D.[9] also got sick with malaria, and he too, thank God, recovered. Every foreigner who comes to live here from a faraway land has to drink from this cup, no one is spared. The change in climate has a bad effect. You mustn't drink water immediately after eating fruit which grow on trees, because it brings on the fever; also if someone drinks water while his body is still sweating—immediately the fever takes hold. You have to be very careful here.

We usually drink water here, mixed with wine or flavored syrup, or vinegar. The wine here is very cheap: 10 kopecks a log. Spirits are also cheap: 15 kopecks a bottle. The only thing that's expensive is beer, and it's warm and doesn't taste good. We have here geese, swans, turkeys, pigeons, and various other kinds of poultry, nothing is missing.

Our synagogue is very elegant; it's built like the synagogue for the neologics in K.,[10] but has even more paintings and decorations. The *parochet* (the curtain covering the ark), and the pulpit cloth are made out of red silk, finely made and embroidered with pure gold threads.

We also have a *hazzan* (a cantor) here, who conducts the choir on days of joy and happiness in our *moshava*. The Turkish governor came to visit last week in order to see the colony, he came accompanied by a large number of soldiers and army officials. He was honored greatly when he came, just like in Russia, when all the Jews would line the streets and greet him with songs and verse. A big banquet was made for him and his men, and they ate and drank and enjoyed their meal, and he left the colony very pleased.

My dear, beloved sister-in-law! don't be angry with me because I have made you read such a long letter; when I write, I feel as if we're sitting face to face and talking, because I still haven't forgotten the tears which you shed on the day we parted. Only God knows when we'll be able to see each other again. So, my deepest wish is that all of you not forget us, and that you write frequently, and let us know how you are and whatever happens to all of you, so we will know that we still have relatives in the faraway land, and won't start thinking that we were born amongst the stones of the field. Because my heart grieves mightily when I remember how we wandered so far away from our family nest, so the letters which you send us will be our only consolation. Write us as often as you can, just write.

We will be very careful to answer every single letter. Don't blame me for not writing until now. You'll understand that lately my heart wasn't into writing letters. In addition, I was sick, we shouldn't know from such problems again! I hope that in the near future I will be able to send you good letters and pleasant tidings . . .

I'm giving you regards from K.[11] Right now, with God's help, he is completely healthy; he doesn't know about this letter, and will write you himself shortly. E. (Eliyahu) sends regards. He is quickly learning to speak French and Arabic as if they are his mother tongues; he's a fine young man—if God wishes, we will have a lot of *nachas* (pleasure), happiness and pride, from him. S.[12] and D. (David) give you warmest regards . . .

Notes (Document A.)

1. The date of the letter is not known. The date listed is a result of my own estimate, according to the date the letter was sent from Vilna to *Hamelitz* (on Kislev 5750) for purposes of publication.

2. It should read "the old colony," and refers to the eastern hill of Zamarin, a former village of tenant farmers. This site was called in yiddish "olt Zamarin," as opposed to the "new colony" ("The town") of Zikhron Yaakov, which was set up to the west of Zamarin on a higher hill. It is not surprising that the family of Kalman Kantor, who was employed in the administration of the Baron de Rothschild, was first offered a house at Zamarin, which served as the neighborhood of the manor "administrators". (For a comparison with other recollections of Zamarin as to the difference between "up" and "down", see Buskala-Guttman, 1966:34.)

3. Indeed, the breezes in the western hill of Zikhron Yaakov were much better than those of Zamarin, which was lower and toward the east. It is worth remembering that "good air," as meant by the settlers then, referred to healthy air, i.e., air which was less prone to spreading malaria (literally, mal-aria, bad air). In those days, malaria was thought to spread through the air in microscopic particles called Miasmas.

4. The need to purchase basic foodstuffs from the Arabs of the area was a result of the type of farming characteristic of Zikhron Yaakov and the other moshavot. Their farms were based on growing cash crops (commercial agriculture) rather than the staples necessary for home consumption (subsistence farming). As a result, the Jewish settlers were dependent on the Arabs, as described here and elsewhere (see, for example, Buskala-Guttman, 1966:44). This dependency was the subject of a great deal of criticism. Notwithstanding this state of affairs, many of the farmers' wives supplied some of their household requirements from small vegetable gardens which they grew in their yards, as the author, herself, eventually does (see the next letter).

5. The kopeck was a Russian coin worth very little (one hundredth of a ruble). At that time, it was equal to about six Turkish grush, or about three hundredths of a French franc, which was the common currency in the moshavot (see note 7 below).

6. The author refers here to Baron Edmond de Rothschild of Paris, who took full economic responsibility for Zikhron Yaakov, and most of the other moshavot; this explains the connection between his visit and the timing of new house construction, which was to be funded by him. However, the Baron did not actually visit Israel until 1894.

7. Eliyahu, who completed his studies that year at the Workers' School at Zikhron Yaakov, began working for the administration at the basic wage paid starting workers (30 francs a month). This was in addition to the monetary support received by each family from the Baron, which was distributed according to family size.

8. All of these communal services which were provided at no cost to the settlers, were budgeted by the Baron and administered by his officials.

9. David, who was then a pupil in the elementary school of the moshava.

10. K. means Kovna. "The synagogue for neologics"—A synagogue with a more progressive service, as opposed to the traditional orthodox service. The author probably referred here to the placement of the *bima* (the pulpit) near the *aron kodesh* (the holy ark) (see Eliav, 1981, 2:202), and perhaps referred to the synagogue's many paintings and its luxurious interior decoration. The location of the choir, mentioned below, also belonged to the new customs which were introduced into the religious and cultural life of the moshava by the Baron's administrators. These innovations angered the traditionalist settlers.

11. Kalman, head of the family. For more details about him and his family see above, Section A.

12. The third son of the author was usually called by his middle name, Betsalel. Perhaps he had another name, which began with the letter "S".

Document B:

Letter from the Wife of Kalman Kantor, Zikhron Yaakov, February 28, 1890[1]

. . . We've already forgotten all of the troubles and problems which I wrote about in my previous letter; because, thank God, our situation is improving as time goes by. We have already grown accustomed to our work and the conditions of life here, as if we grew up and were born here. We have, thank God, a good and pleasant life. Our house is full of God's blessings, and our table has everything that a rich woman in Vilna has, nothing is lacking.

Every day I bring home a basket of eggs laid by my own hens; in the morning we drink good, fat milk from my cows; we have chicken every day for our noon meal, while over there we would only have such luxuries on holidays. For supper, we drink tea and eat bread with delicious butter. We have never been as quiet and tranquil, without worries, as we are today, and I have never imagined a life which is better than the life we have today.

We planted all sorts of vegetables in our garden; we've been eating green onions for quite a while; we've been eating roasted vegetables and tender radishes all winter. By *Pesach* (Passover) we will have, if God permits, new potatoes; and shortly the fruits will begin to ripen. We sowed wheat for eating all year round, as well as barley for our horses. We have a horse and wagon which cost 200 SR,[2] for taking trips and travelling whenever we need or feel like going.

We also planted a vineyard, and are happy to see its beauty and pleasantness. There is a wall of stones around the vineyard, so that the land is like a Garden of Eden laid out before us, while in the past it was wasted and desolate. We also have a grove of trees which provides wood for heating. We have to bring water and building stones by ourselves. Kalman performs all of these tasks with joy and happiness; and, may God be praised, he's very handy. Our garden has every sort of fruit tree, even apples and cherries; but most of the vineyard is planted with grape vines.

Now I'll describe our home: our house is the second house on the street when you enter the colony. It has three large rooms as well as a room for cooking.[3] We also have a large stable for our horses, a large yard and two large gardens. The whole valley surrounding us is covered with green—wheat, barley and vineyards. Facing our house is the sea in all its splendor and glory; the scenery is beautiful and very uplifting.

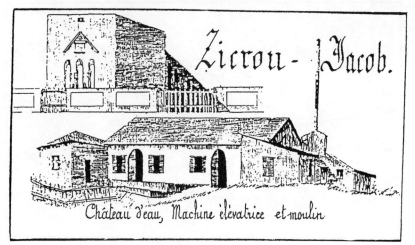

Figure 2. Zikhron Yaakov, water reservoir and well. Illustration by a senior official of Baron Edmund de Rothschild, 1899. Reproduced with permission of publisher from Sheid Eliahu, 1982. *My Memories of the Hebrew Moshavot.* Jerusalem: Yad Yitzhak Ben-Zvi, p. 108.

The air is clean and healthy. Everyone out walking passes by our house, all of the things brought into the *moshava* for sale pass by our house, so I buy everything cheaply without having to weary my feet going to the market to buy what I need. I've already learned to speak Arabic quickly, because everything is brought to my home and all of the sellers are Arabs. I also have nice household utensils as well as curtains for the windows, because we live like in the cities: we have a bit of luxury, but not too much.

All of us women wear white kerchiefs covering our heads. On *Shabat* I wear a nice kerchief, which cost me 3 SR, when I go to the synagogue. Our dresses are pretty and are sewn in the best of taste. Eventually, Zikhron Yaakov will become a bustling place, but actually it's already become a town. Soon, they will build ducts in order to bring water to the houses of the colony, and pipes and stoppers will be in every house.[4] Shortly, they will begin to excavate a wine cellar here, and soon they will build a railroad from Jaffa to Jerusalem and a railroad yard will be built in Zikhron Yaakov.[5]

Eventually, we hope that the face of the land will be renewed. In areas where jackals run, railroads will run full of pas-

Figure 3. Zikhron Yaakov, wine cellar. Illustration by a senior official of Baron Edmund de Rothschild, 1899. Reproduced with permission of publisher from Sheid Eliahu, 1982. *My Memories of the Hebrew Moshavot.* Jerusalem: Yad Yitzhak Ben-Zvi, p. 113.

sengers instead of desolate rocks—there will be hotels for tourists; in places where man does not set foot, people will work and engage in all sorts of handicrafts, day and night. My heart pounds inside to think of all of these pleasant hopes. If God has revived our precious land and turned the desolate desert into populated town, we pray that God will also turn all of the scorched and ravaged areas into homes for people, into vineyards and grapevines.

With all my heart, I wish that I could write you more, but I don't have enough time to write, because there is a lot of work to do today. In the morning, in the fifth hour, I must wake up in order to feed my household. Kalman goes to the field to do his work, along with ten Arab men;[6] Eliyahu goes to work in the gardens all day;[7] David and Betsalel go to school, where they learn Hebrew, French, Arabic, and how to read and write in all of these languages; and I am the only one who stays at home. Then I have to feed the hens, the geese and the ducks, the goats, the pigeons and the horse. After finishing all of this, I can rest; and in the evening I have to give them food once again.

I've also divided up the housework according to the days of the week: On Sundays I bake bread, on Mondays, I do the washing, on Tuesdays I prepare and ready the clothes which have been washed. Wednesdays are for sewing and mending torn clothes, and on Thursdays I bake *challah* (braided white bread), and cakes for Shabat, everything with pure olive oil; the price of a liter of the choicest olive oil is 12 kopecks, so that we use it almost in place of water. On Fridays I prepare everything and put up *cholent* (a slow-cooking stew of beans, potatoes, and meat) for Shabat. Shabat is a day of complete rest for us.

I will never lack work, and thank God, the household work is always on the increase. I wash the floors of the house by myself, and I clean all of the copper and bronze utensils every Friday until they shine; I even whitewash the walls of our house by myself. I also bought a sewing machine and I sew myself everything that I need. I have never known a better, more satisfying life than the one I am currently leading.

We live here in the shadow of the Baron, who feels the pain of his sons, may God be merciful on him, and we know no want. If a woman bears twins, then the Baron provides 4 SR a month for hiring a second wet-nurse and will also send her a second bed— but I pray that God will save me from this excessive blessing. Indeed, I don't have enough time to write of all the good and merciful deeds done by the Baron for us. May God reward him and his administrators as they have rewarded us . . .

Notes (Document B.)

1. The date on the letter reads February 14. This is almost definitely according to the Julian calendar, which was the accepted calendar in Eastern Europe, and was used by the author; in other words, February 28, according to the Gregorian calendar which we use today.

2. "SR" refers to silver rubles, Russian coins, then worth approximately 2.5 French francs or about 15 Turkish grush.

3. Compare the description of the house with its description in the previous letter. The basic dwelling unit of the Baron's administration (in Zikhron Yaakov as well as in the other moshavot), consisted of an entry hall which led to a kitchen, with two bedrooms on both sides.

4. "Ducts" refers to a system of pipes; "stoppers" refers to faucets. Running water was supplied to the houses of Zikhron Yaakov only in the middle of the 1890s. Until then, the settlers brought water from a public faucet in barrels, which they loaded on wagons. The faucet was located next to the reservoir of the moshava, which was built in 1891—it is possible that the author is referring to this.

5. The wine cellar was built, apparently, only in 1891 and its first section was dedicated in the summer of 1891 before the vintage. "Railroad yard" refers to a railroad station. The first railroad in Israel was actually laid down from Jaffa to Jerusalem in the year 1892, but since it had no branch lines it never reached Zikhron Yaakov or its environs. The plans mentioned here fit in with the wave of rumors which were widespread in the last decades of Ottoman rule, regarding plans to lay railroads throughout Israel.

6. The letter was written at the end of the winter of 1889–90, which was a period of intensive vineyard planting in Zikhron Yaakov. The planting was funded by the Baron, while his administrators supplied the seedlings and the wages for hiring ten laborers per day to work with each of the planters.

7. Eliyahu, the eldest son, worked at the time for the Baron's administration as an assistant gardener.

C. The Woman in the Moshava;
The Individual and the Community

The documents in front of us are personal letters, which were never intended for publication. This is a form of private document, which is both authentic and rare. In all likelihood, there are other letters of this sort in existence, which have not yet been discovered.

Another primary source written by a woman from the moshavot, the only other such source of its time currently known, consists of the letters of Nehamah Pukhachewsky (the writer known as "Nefesh") of Rishon le'Tzion. But this educated author was not typical of the women of the First Aliyah and her letters, which were sent to a public figure active in the *Hovevei Zion* movement, are not at all similar to the letters of the anonymous wife of Kantor, which were written to her sister-in-law and friend. (A letter of Pukhachewsky to M. Padoba dated the third day of *Hol Hamoed Sukkot*, 1890, was published in Druyanov, vol. C, 1932, Columns 324-5; the source as well as a letter dated 23 Tevet, 5750 (manuscripts in Hebrew), may be found in the CZA, File Number A9/92/10).

Nevertheless, the first letter of Pukhachewsky, which was written at approximately the same time as the letter of Kantor's wife, explains: "I have been so busy from the day I arrived, that I have not known the paths of Zion . . . And this is my answer to all of those who ask me seven times a day why I don't write anything from the Land of Israel . . . Because the Hebrew woman was not created in order to write and originate ideas. She comes and goes in darkness." (A letter from Rishon le'Tzion, the third day of Hol Hamoed Sukkot, (the 19th of Tishrei), 1890, in Druyanov, 1932, Column 324). This way of thinking, even if not expressly stated, underlines the approach of the wife of Kantor in her letters.

From this point of view, there appears to be a point in comparing the source in front of us with another type of authentic source of the same period: the literary works of women writers living during the First Aliyah. They themselves lived and wrote in the moshavot—Pukhachewsky, Trager-Barnett and Harari, who were mentioned above, as well as women writers living in Jerusalem at the time—Hemdah Ben-Yehuda, Ita Yellin, Hanna Builitin-Luncz and others (Berlovitz, 1984; Govrin, 1981).

As with the literary works of the women writers of the First Aliyah, the letters of the settler's wife also indicate "a concentration on the contents of family and home life . . . in the life experiences of the immediate surroundings" (Berlovitz, 1984:191). Indeed, the letters in front of us excel in live descriptions—the most detailed in existence of a private house, together with its furniture and yard, of the private agricultural plot which is attached to the house, and of foods, prices of goods, and the daily schedule of the members of the family.

However, it is interesting that several of the topics which were brought up in the works of the women writers of the time, are completely missing from the letters of the wife of Kantor: relations between man and wife, the difficulties of raising children, and liasons with neighbors. In contrast, topics such as communal events, life styles and ethnic traditions between old and new, have a central role in these letters. All of these topics have something in common—a departure from the writer's narrow, private existence to a broader, communal point of view. Thus, the source examined in this paper is different from the literary sources cited above. The broader point of view of the author is associated with a significant transformation which took place after her arrival in Israel.

In the few months which passed between the writing of the first and the second letter, the wife of Kantor experienced a sharp reversal of attitude toward the idea of settlement in the Land of Israel. At first, it was obvious that "this woman, who apparently was completely against this crazy undertaking of her husband, complains bitterly about her fate" (GLN, in the introduction to the first letter, *Hamelitz* 29, 1889:1). Accordingly, the topics of the first letter concern themselves with the hardships of the writer, with an emphasis on sickness and the pain of separation from her previous world. But her second letter reflects a new-found moderation, an attitude which is both idealistic and optimistic, almost enthusiastic. This time, the topics of public concern are more central to the letter: the status of education and other public services in the community, the plans for building and developing the moshava, the extensive involvement of the Baron de Rothschild in the new settlements, etc. Thus, this letter is the first source known mentioning early development projects which were completed only at a later date: the plan to excavate wine cellars in Zikhron Yaakov and the plan to supply flowing water to the houses of the moshava (see notes no. 4 and 5 to the second letter). Even though the public affairs mentioned are limited to the level of the local community, the references contained in the letters are able to reflect developmental processes taking place throughout the settlements: the development of the infrastructure of the settlements through the use of the most advanced technology available at the time, or the establishment of industrial plants to process the agricultural produce of the settlements, as part of the adaptation of a modern commercial farming economy. These were two of the basic principles which guided the work of the Baron de Rothschild throughout the settlements.

It must be emphasized that although the private letters are

able to describe events common to the Jewish settlement as a whole, the writer did not belong to a prominent family whose members were personally involved in the events described, as is the case with the women writers of the period. As a result, the candid letters of a simple woman settler to her sister-in-law constitute a testimony as to the personal involvement of the author, which is acutely expressed by her information concerning public affairs. In addition, it is also possible to learn from this source as to the nature of general information which was public knowledge, even though such information is expressed in terms of small talk and gossip . . . (Compare with the letter of a settler to his Rabbi, Zikhron Yaakov, January 1, 1883, Gaster Archives, London (manuscript in Yiddish), which was published in English by Aaronsohn and Ben Arieh, 1988:588–589).

Unlike most of the women writers of the First Aliyah there is no attempt here to deal with women's rights and the woman's role in society, or even an awareness of the writer's inferior status as a woman. It seems that the wife of Kantor accepted her role as homemaker and a wife with modesty but not with servility, and fulfilled her role with a sense of her own worth, without a feeling of passivity. It appears that the woman was satisfied with her status and accepted her role by being active. Her attitude does not necessarily indicate a lack of consciousness of other alternatives, but a conscious acceptance of the traditional inequality between men and women—a perception that apparently is indicative of the atmosphere then prevailing in the moshavot. The lack of desire to change the unequal relationship between the sexes was typical of the conservative society which existed in the first moshavot. The desire for a classless society, including the perception of equal status for women in the Jewish settlement, came to Israel together with Socialist Zionism, at a later date, during the Second Aliyah (1904-1914). The source examined in this chapter does not even deal with "feminist issues". Thus, the letters of the wife of Kantor do not attach any significance to agricultural work or to other ideological problems which occupied the thoughts of women throughout the world and which were critical issues for women of the next generation (compare with Bernstein, 1987:14–24; Etienne and Leacock, 1980; Sachs, 1983).

The lack of an ideological discussion in the letters of the wife of Kantor does not minimize their importance. The letters examined are neither literary sources nor official documents. Consequently, the education or the ideological and national consciousness of the writer are not very important. On the contrary, the ordinariness of the writer and the fact that she was one of many women who participated anonymously—and sometimes un-willingly—in the early settlement, enhances the value of the let-ters. This source is unique because of the information which it pro-vides regarding woman's daily life, roles and attitudes from the modest point of view of a common housewife.

The unique quality of this private source enables researchers to learn a great deal about the community as a whole. The legacy of this anonymous author seems to validate the quotation from the poem of the "national" poet of the period, written about the Hebrew women in general:

> Bake,
> Season,
> And prematurely end your season . . .
> (Y. L. Gordon, "A Mere Nothing")

References

Aaronsohn, Ran. 1983. "Building the Land: Stages in First *Aliyah* Coloni-zation, (1882–1904)." *The Jerusalem Cathedra*, 3:236–279.

Aaronsohn, Ran. 1985. *The Jewish Colonies at their Inception and the Con-tribution of the Baron Rothschild to their Development*. Doctoral Dis-sertation of the Hebrew University, Jerusalem (Hebrew).

Aaronsohn, Ran and Ben-Arieh, Y. 1988. "The Establishment of the Jew-ish Settlement in *Eretz Israel* and the Gaster papers," pp. 581–594 in *Jewish History, Essays in Honor of C. Abramsky*, edited by Ada Rapaport and Steven J. Zipperstein. London: P. Halban.

Berlovitz, Yaffa (editor). 1984. *Stories of the Women of the First Aliyah*. Tel Aviv: Tarmil Library (Hebrew).

Bernstein, Deborah. 1987. *A Struggle for Equality—Urban Women Workers in Prestate Israeli Society*. New York: Praeger.

Buskala-Guttman, Miriam. 1966. *Two Couches*. Tel Aviv (Hebrew).

Druyanov, Alter (editor). 1932. *Documents on the History of the Hibbat Zion and the Settlement of Eretz Israel*. Vol. C. Odessa: The Council of the Settlement of *Eretz Israel* in Odessa (Hebrew and other lan-guages).

Eliav, Mordechai. (editor). 1981. *The Book of the First Aliyah*. Vol. 1–2. Jerusalem: Yad Yitzhak Ben-Zvi (Hebrew).

Etienne, Mona and Leacock, Elinor (editors). 1980. *Women and Colonization, Anthropological Perspectives*. New York: Praeger.

Govrin, Nurit. 1981. *Roots and Crowns—Impressions of the First Aliyah in Hebrew Literature*. Tel Aviv: Papirus (Hebrew).

Sachs, C. E. 1983. *The Invisible Farmer—Women in Agricultural Production*.

Samsonov, Aryeh. 1942. *Zikhron Yaakov—A Chronicle of its History, 1882–1942*. Tel Aviv: Omanut (Hebrew).

Smilansky, Moshe. 1943–1944. *The Family of the Land*. Vol. 1, 2. Tel Aviv: Am Oved (Hebrew).

Women and Geography Study Group—IGB. 1984. *Geography and Gender*. London: Hutchinson.

2

Literature by Women of the First Aliyah: The Aspiration for Women's Renaissance in Eretz Israel

─── *Yaffa Berlovitz* ───

The Woman's Voice in the First Aliyah

In any consideration of the literary works by the women of the First Aliyah (wave of immigration), we must, at the outset, try to clarify what women were like during that period. This clarification leads us to potential sources (historical records, memoirs, diaries, anniversary albums, and the like), but the account which emerges is an extremely limited one. Contrary to the wealth of material dealing with men's endeavors, the description of women's activities is merely incidental. This comes about not only because a man's place in the early pioneering effort—as settler, founder, and builder—was given greater emphasis but also because his position as head of the family gave him the responsibility for everything that befell the family; whatever it was, it happened in his name. This outlook stands out, for example, in the anniversary album of Zikhron Yaakov, by Aryeh Samsonov (1942). In his roster of names, "And These Were Our Pioneers", the writer classifies the early settlers according to descriptions of their various tasks and accomplishments, to wit: "Those who were first to settle the land", "Those who could not bear the burden of their mission", "Those who succeeded and were privileged to raise a generation of sons and builders". And yet, in all these lists, not even once do we find a woman's name—almost as though, among all those people, there had been no women at all and the achievement of settling the land had belonged only to the men.

On the other hand, even when these documents do offer us some historical or biographical information about a woman (Hariz-man, 1958; Smilansky, 1950), her voice does not come through to us; we do not sense her opinions, her thoughts, her emotional reactions, and most important, her interpretation of that soul-stirring, historic event, the return to Zion. This lack, however, is complemented by the writings of the women themselves. Even though such works are few in number, and some were written at a later date (after the First Aliyah), it is they, nevertheless, which constitute the principal source for any inquiry into the essence of the First Aliyah woman; they alone can convey her voice most directly and most authentically (Luncz, 1919; Trager, 1923; Ben-Yehuda, 1940; Harari, 1947). Who was this woman, and how is she perceived in the historical setting of the period under discussion?

The Characterization of the Woman-Writer

The year 1882 marked a turning point in Jewish settlement in Eretz Israel (Palestine). Until that time, the link to Zion resulted in only scattered attempts at settlement, while from 1882 onward, these endeavors were carried out more regularly and more consistently. Despite financial difficulties, unfamiliarity with the country and a lack of agricultural know-how and training, Jewish colonies were being established one after the other (Rishon le'Tzion, Rosh Pina, Zikhron Yaakov), inaugurating the development of a new Jewish way of life. And in this ongoing pioneering venture, there is no question that women, too, were full partners. However, because the woman was still regarded in the traditional image of the help mate, her contribution to the settlement of the Yishuv (the Jewish settlement in pre-state Palestine) was taken for granted and not considered anything out of the ordinary.

Another reason for this attitude was the fact that a woman's participation was often the result of having passively followed her husband and was not the product of her own initiative and comprehension.[1] It must be remembered that immigration to Eretz Israel was taking place in the context of a dramatic ideological nationalistic change. For all that, *Hibbat Zion* (Love of Zion) was a movement which had only a small following among the Jewish masses of Eastern Europe—a following composed mainly of males. Where women were concerned, the situation was quite different. In the second half of the nineteenth century, most Jewish women in Eastern European "*Shtetls*" continued to fill their traditional roles (caring for home and family, and helping out with livelihood when necessary), while communal and national issues were far removed from their daily concerns. An additional factor was the very minimal education they received (reading and writing Yiddish plus the rudiments of arithmetic). This was of very little help to them in understanding the nationalist European state of mind and the Jewish idealists who were part of it, and who had been instrumental in creating this ideological Zionist movement. Therefore, it was not unusual that when a man who was a *Hovev Zion* (Lover of Zion) decided to realize his idealistic dream of Aliyah to Eretz Israel—leaving behind his well-ordered life and livelihood, and exchanging it for unknown surroundings in a distant and primitive country—his wife objected to his decision. Lacking in education and in ideological awareness, she simply could not understand what he wanted to do; if, in spite of it all, she did agree to follow her husband, it was often done out of submission and under constraint.[2]

Indeed, this involuntary Aliyah in her husband's footsteps often prompted outbursts of obstinacy and irascibility in the ordinary woman, especially in moments of crisis (see for example Trager, 1926). On the other hand, there were times when a reverse process was set in motion by crisis; when those very strains and stresses effected some sort of emotional transformation in a woman; from being stubborn and quarrelsome, she became dedicated to the country and its settlement.[3]

This dedication was expressed not only by the woman's work within the home and family, but also in the field and vineyard, where day in and day out, she had to cope with the hardship, the suffering, and the disillusionment that the new country offered. In the sort of life she led, the pioneering of a woman was no less daring than that of a man, especially when it took into account not only "woman's work" under extraordinary conditions (giving birth in the fields, caring for the sick without medical assistance, managing a household with only primitive equipment, and so on); but also what are usually considered male roles, or even confronting danger with great courage. Take, for example, Esther Greenstein. Unassisted, she forcibly removed an Arab bride's jewelry (as compensation for the damage done to her fields in Petah-Tikva by the wedding party), with the startled Arabs quickly arranging a "*sulha*" (a peace offering); or Ita Felman, who, after her husband's death, resolutely went on living with her children in their orange grove, working it and supporting her family therefrom; or Beila Eisenberg, who stationed the women of Rehovot around every unfinished new building, their aprons filled with stones, in order to prevent, with their very bodies, the razing of the building by the Turkish soldiers.

Nonetheless, despite these episodes of daring, women persisted in viewing themselves as merely doing their duties. Although the move from the Diaspora to the Homeland signified a new way of life (working the land and self-defense), and a new outlook on life (the pride of being a free people), there had been no change in how society regarded the woman. She remained of marginal importance and little consequence, just as she had been in the Diaspora. Once again, women were denied their rights (such as voting or being elected); once again, they were kept behind the scenes (unable to voice opinions in public); once again, it was men who made the decisions about any and all matters (public or private). And yet, it was just these women—on the one hand, so capable and so giving; on the other, uneducated, unappreciated, and lacking self-awareness—who formed the background for the ongoing development of women's literature, within the general framework of the contemporaneous literature. How did this come about?

In seeking to establish certain characteristics shared by the women who produced that literature, we must first point out that they had the advantage of being educated far beyond the levels of the average Jewish woman of the time—an education which included secondary schooling, vocational training, and even university study.[4] A further accomplishment which set these women apart from the others of the First Aliyah,[5] was a familiarity with Hebrew subjects (language, Bible, literature, and so on), not to mention the intimate knowledge of the principles of Zionism. Moreover, their devotion to the Zionist ideal was not the emotional aftermath of coming to terms with the country (as often happened in the case of the average woman). On the contrary, that ideal had been an integral part of their family education and concern; their fathers or husbands had been among the vanguard of the Hibbat Zion movement (as leaders, thinkers or activists) both in Europe and in Eretz Israel.[6] What also characterized these women—in this instance, not under the influence of the home, but rather as result of their very own outlook and development—was their cognizance of their own worth and of the vital roles they played, not only as daughters or wives of important men, but as equal partners in the social experiment taking place in the new country. Thus, though they too were denied basic rights and a voice in decision-making they found their own non-establishment ways to become involved and to render assistance: Nehamah Pukhachewsky of Rishon le'Tzion organized a "Hospice for the Needy" to serve transients and indigent laborers, which eventually developed into a society providing help to the ill and the destitute; Ita Yellin, in

Jerusalem, found employment opportunities for poor young women and arranged suitable medical care for the mentally ill; and Hanna Luncz ran a soup kitchen for the needy during the First World War. And these same women, in addition to their other activities, were engaged in writing—writing which was, in itself, part of their communal involvement. It was but another way to make their mark, as women, on the life which was taking shape in the country; it was also a way to speak out for those women of the First Aliyah who lacked the understanding or the daring to lay claim to the recognition due them. Therefore, if the overall writing of the First Aliyah (both journalistic and literary) dealt chiefly with the new land, the new society, and the new man, there existed also this specific writing by women (both journalistic and literary) which raised and argued the case of the new woman, as well.

These works by female authors began to appear in the last decade of the nineteenth century, with the writings of Nehamah Pukhachewsky and Hemdah Ben-Yehuda, and were followed by those of Miriam Gissin, Miriam Pfefermeister, Yehudit Harari, Elishevea Bassewitz, Hannah Luncz, and Ita Yellin.[7] Even when they continued writing past the time of the First Aliyah (1882–1904), or only began to write after that date, it is that period which is the common point of departure (whether they arrived in the country at that time or had been born there), and which is central to their writing (elements of the First Aliyah dominate their themes). For that reason, they fit the title of our study—as women of the First Aliyah. Even though in some cases, the theme tended to fade somewhat with the passage of time, their esthetic and ideological outlook on life remained that of the First Aliyah (in contrast to the esthetic and ideological outlooks of later waves of immigration). It is important to note that the appearance of women's literature in Eretz Israel at that time was surprising not only by virtue of its being written at all, but also because of its extent and scope. Considering how the Jewish woman was perceived in the Diaspora, the very fact that women were writers, and particularly writers in the Hebrew language, was a rare achievement. It is true that in the history of Jewish women through the ages there have been, at various times, writers and even Torah scholars.[8] However, each of these had been an isolated occurrence, a random event, with no follow-through or continuity. This was not the case with women's literature during the First Aliyah. As part of a labile community of fifty to sixty thousand Jewish inhabitants, who were living under the most difficult conditions, in a social climate which was neither open-minded nor encouraging on the subject of women, female writers appeared on the scene; and not only were there more writers as the years went by, but the work they produced did have continuity. From the time of the First Aliyah onward, women's literature in Hebrew was no longer a one-time affair; it continued to grow and develop, side-by-side with the growth and development of community life. While it underwent various metamorphoses and exhibited diverse manifestations, no longer was women's writing a sporadic and isolated event; it became part and parcel of a consistent literary corpus.

The Standpoint of Preaching in the Writings of Hemdah Ben-Yehuda

There were two areas of concern to the woman writers of the First Aliyah. One was the renewal of settlement in Eretz Israel and the second, the renaissance of women within the framework of that settlement life. In expressing the first concern, their writing concurred with all the clearly defined features which characterized the general literature of that wave of immigration,[9] regarding the second concern, however, a different picture emerges. Only in the literature by female writers was the dream of women's own renewal the recurrent theme. The male author also wrote about women as part of the new life and did this meaningfully and with feeling. However, the themes which interested him were either the conventional ones (the romantic tensions between man and woman, as in a love story—see Smilansky, 1934), or the ideological ones (woman as part of the overall social process of changing a community of settlers into a nation—see Barzilai, 1912; Jawitz, 1892). In either case, woman's aspirations were not to be found in what men were writing; in fact, they were not even part of the male consciousness. In our study, we shall focus upon this specific theme in women's literature: their aspirations for their own renaissance. In the works of First Aliyah women, these hopes were given expression via two different approaches: the standpoint of preaching and the standpoint of protest. In both cases, the result was a militant story, which demonstrated how the position of the woman settler was an inferior one; it was written, not only to illustrate the existence of such a condition, but also in the hopes of bringing about change. Thus, the militant story was meant to confront both the men of the community—who, as we have said, were not even aware of the problem[10]—as well as the women who, as a result of their conservative upbringing, did not discern any bias against them, but actually considered their situation to be the natural state of affairs and opposed any attempts to alleviate it (Trager, 1926).[11]

We intend to examine the way both these positions were presented in the works of two of the leading women authors of the period, with Hemdah Ben-Yehuda representing the standpoint of preaching, and Nehamah Pukhachewsky, that of protest. In considering Ben-Yehuda's work, we see that first and foremost, she was appealing to women, in an attempt to set them free of the constraints of the past and open their eyes to the new options of the present. However, a careful study of her stories and articles shows that her conception of renaissance was more relevant to the advancement of the settlers' overall concerns than it was to those of the woman as such. In other words, in the unique historic event in which they were taking part, the point of departure on the subject of women was first of all a national one, and only on second thought, was it feminist. Some years later, in an article she wrote in 1919, Ben-Yehuda apologized for this stand and explained that it had been impossible in the earlier years to fight for the liberation of women, while the nation itself was still not free: "While our people is enslaved, shamed and persecuted throughout the world, suffering from the tyranny of foreign rulers even within its own land, how can we liberate our women?" Consequently, there was only one hope—both for the good of the Jewish people and the good of the woman—and that was the national one: "We tried then, to arouse in her the feeling of nationalism, knowing that when its time came, then her moment too would come" (Ben-Yehuda, 1919). If later on (1919), Ben-Yehuda struggled to liberate the woman from the social periphery and establish her as an equal ("Only to lift the woman out of her degraded condition, to protect her rights, to prepare her for life in the community, to make her aware that her rights are equal to those of men in the same society" (ibid.), at the earlier stage, she had struggled to liberate woman from the national periphery and spur her on to equal involvement in the pioneering endeavor. Therefore, in considering how the dream of women's renaissance was manifested in female writing at that time, we discover that in Ben-Yehuda's works, this dream was equivalent to the rebirth of the nation. How did she portray women in the light of this rebirth? In Ben-Yehuda's opinion, there were two possible ways for the woman in Eretz Israel to contribute to

the advancement of the Yishuv. It could be: a) by helping to shape
a better society; b) by augmenting the existing community and reducing the threat of its decline. As to the first, she agreed with her
husband, Eliezer Ben-Yehuda, who maintained that in the last
analysis, it is the women who build the nation; for it is they who
raise and mold the next generation, having more say in this than
the men do. Obviously, in the early stages this influence is decisive, because that is when the very foundations are being laid for a
new nation and a new individual, when the influence of the woman
could determine the make-up, not only of the next generation but
of the entire nation-to-be. Here, E. Ben-Yehuda was stressing for
example, the major role women could play in deciding the future of
the Hebrew language in Eretz Israel (E. Ben-Yehuda, 1902). As
the driving force in its revival and renewal, he maintained that the
process of turning the passive, written tongue into a living, spoken
one could be accelerated only if women would speak Hebrew, as a
result of which the children would grow up with Hebrew as their
natural language.[12] Thus Ben-Yehuda lauded woman's importance
to the life of the nation; "It is they who are our true wealth . . . our
everlasting capital . . . which will bear fruit and yield a steady
profit, year after year, month after month, week after week and
day after day" (ibid.). Based on these ideas, Hemdah Ben-Yehuda
developed this theme, emphasizing her own conceptions and conclusions, to wit: if it is the woman who determines what
the next generation will be like, thereby prescribing the quality of
the future nation as a whole, then this responsibility requires her
to raise her standards (not only in the matter of the Hebrew
language, as maintained by Eliezer Ben-Yehuda, but in other, all-
encompassing areas of life). It is from this standpoint that H. Ben-
Yehuda reached out to the ordinary woman, preaching and teaching about what sort of woman she must become, in order to build
and mold a nation. This exhortation and edification was expressed
both in her journalistic works (Ben-Yehuda, 1903b) and in her literary works; through the use of rhetoric in her journalistic writing
and by exemplification in her literature.

    In these examples, Ben-Yehuda devised a model woman,
whose nationalism and education were her outstanding features. It
is important to remember that to Ben-Yehuda, education was not
merely the gathering of knowledge, but was primarily an outlook
on life, progressive and conceptual (it is well known that the concepts which helped lay the foundations of Hibbat Zion were drawn
from the philosophical outlines of the nineteenth century En-

Figure 4. Hemdah Ben-Yehuda (Central Zionist Archive).

lightment movement, among others). Naturally, Ben-Yehuda constructed a large number of her literary plots in line with these views, borrowing material from diverse aspects of women's lives in Eretz Israel. But the story lines always led towards one conclusion, the superiority of the educated woman, (ergo, the nationalistic one) both within the community and in her private life. Without any doubt, the stress laid on private lives and the presentation of education as advantageous to a woman, and an implicit guarantee of her personal success (which is Hemdah Ben-Yehuda's innovational addition to her husband's dicta) made her message more effective and enhanced her efforts to bring about change and progress for women through preaching and persuasion. A reader of her stories would quickly discover that an education is helpful in finding a suitable husband and assuring a happier married life; it even fosters profound romantic experiences. In her story "A New Dress" (1906), the Jerusalem doctor (who is going out with both Zila, the teacher, and Mira, the beauty) will choose the teacher, whose sparkling conversation captivates him more than any of the new dresses which beautiful Mira wears for his approval. In the story "Lulu" (1902), we meet a Yemenite woman, whose husband, a muleteer, has turned her out of their Jerusalem home. She runs off to one of the villages where she builds her life anew; she works and studies and marries a pioneer; and the more he teaches her, the more meaningful and vital her life with him becomes. And in the story "Under the Almond Tree" (1903a), Rachel, who is devoted to learning, falls in love with Yaakov, the laborer-intellectual. Although Rachel is married, Ben-Yehuda does not depict their short-lived "sin" in a negative way, but paints the picture of a relationship which encompasses not only emotional enrichment but cultural enhancement, as well.

So much for the first possibility outlined earlier (the new woman—the nation-builder). As to the second possibility (the new woman—augmenter and strengthener of the existing society), it is natural that in the initial stages of settlement, the body of settlers, still unsure of its way in Eretz Israel, was far from being a nation; it was more of a scattered community threatened at all times by the twin dangers of people leaving the country and of no new immigration. Ben-Yehuda demonstrated that the new woman, with her intellectual-nationalistic qualities, could be a very influential factor in those circumstances, as well. By becoming involved and by identifying herself with national ideals, she would contribute to the process of setting down roots in the land, to say nothing of the demographic increase of the Yishuv. This was in stark contrast to the woman who lived in the country against her will (with no attachment to Eretz Israel and its future settlement, as seen above); who would only encourage desertion of the country and weaken what already existed.

In "The Farm of the Rekhabites" (1903c), this critical issue is stressed by two settlers—Harbin and Ephraim—who are looking for all possible ways to increase the Jewish population of Palestine (Govrin, 1989a). Ephraim's way is to take to the roads, seeking the lost Jewish tribe, the descendants of the Rekhabites, while Harbin makes his way to the Bedouin tents, trying to convert those nomads, not only into cultured people, but into Hebrews, as well. While the two men discuss and formulate their plans, it suddenly occurs to them that all of their efforts will come to naught if they do not find a solution to the problems of the women. In Harbin's view the delay in woman's renaissance in the country had not only hurt past pioneering efforts, but continued to corrode all that was good in it:

> While it has been a long time since I have discerned among the farmers any real fervor, sacrifice or even a strong willingness to

suffer hardship . . . why, among the women, I found not even one out of a thousand! And if many of the true Lovers of Zion never came to settle in Eretz Israel, you can be sure the women had a hand in that. And more than a few of those who did come and then went back after a year or even six months 'were only following their wives' . . . What use is an idea, what good is a deed, if the woman is opposed to it? (ibid: 16).

On the face of it, this appears to be a strong case against women, but that is not really so. Later on in the story, the two friends engage in a mutual confession, speaking, as it were, in the name of the Jewish men of Palestine, taking responsibility for women's shameful situation:

> How can we expect anything of our women . . . if we do not dedicate ourselves to their education . . . and we cannot deny that in our villages, we have left the women completely alone. Which of us has ever taught his wife anything or even read to her! No wonder that by the time she is married a few years and has become the mother of two or three children, not only hasn't she made any progress . . . but she has turned into nothing but a servant, forgetting even what she knew before . . . Did we ever try to improve her situation? Did we arrange any sort of communal shelter for the children, where a mother could safely leave her child (in order) to attend meetings, to read, to listen, to speak, to develop, to learn? It is we, we who are to blame (ibid.: 21–23).

It should not be forgotten that in that era, such an admission of guilt could have been written only by a woman, because in the climate of the times, men felt no guilt whatsoever for women's lack of idealism. On the contrary, when a woman with nationalistic awareness tried to become involved and express her opinions publicly, she found herself muzzled by the men and even ridiculed (as described by Nehamah Pukhachewsky, below). The above mentioned confession, therefore, is not so much a realistic representation as a portrayal of the ideal so desired by the author herself.

In summing up the way Hemdah Ben-Yehuda created her literature, we find that in her stories about women, we must distinguish between two different genres: the militant-story and the local-color-story. The latter is a realistic, mimetic narrative, which aims at giving the reader (especially the one in the Diaspora) a close look at a gallery of Palestinian Jewish women of many different types: those from the "old" and "new" Yishuv, of Western and Oriental origin, from villages and cities, and so on (Ben-Yehuda, 1900, 1910, 1940a, 1940b). When we consider the militant-story, a different picture emerges. Since, as noted earlier, it is a story written for the purpose of exhortation and its main thrust is didactic, it does not necessarily present reality as it is, but rather suggests what it should be and occasionally even invents it. This method of writing often aroused criticism which attacked Ben-Yehuda's work as misleading. It was felt that while she ostensibly dealt with the existing reality of Eretz Israel, for all practical purposes, she was portraying it in a non-realistic way, to the point where it could be taken as a myth. It should be added, however, the Ben-Yehuda's militant-story is a myth only in retrospect, for that was certainly not her original intention. What she wanted was to recount the romantic Zionist dream, which she herself was living in her daily life. In other words, the militant-story is actually the way Ben-Yehuda applied her yearning and her dreams to the living reality, seeing in it not only the day-to-day hardships and suffering but also the immediate realization of the dream; not only the ordinary woman who is, but also the longed for new woman-to-be.

The Standpoint of Protest in the Stories of Nehamah Pukhachewsky

As mentioned above, the literature of the women of the First *Aliyah* was written not only from the standpoint of preaching, but from the standpoint of protest as well, and it is the latter which is represented by the writing of Nehamah Pukhachewsky. As soon as she arrived in the country (1889), Pukhachewsky began dedicating herself to the renaissance of women in settlement life; not satisfied with merely raising the issue in writing, she also strove to carry it out in actual practice (Govrin, 1989). And yet, there appears to be a dichotomy between her public struggle and her literary offerings. Publicly, she was forceful and firm, supplying answers and suggesting solutions; in her literature, she was perplexed and pensive, only raising questions which had confronted her. Furthermore, in her writing, as opposed to her public efforts, she was very restrained, the protest of her characters compressed into a somewhat sad and hopeless internal dialogue which had difficulty in breaking through to the outside.

The main body of Pukhachewsky's work has been gathered into two collections of stories: "In the New Judea" (1911) and "Life in the Village" (1930); in both of these, the reader encounters a wide assortment of women (farmers, laborers, domestic workers, kibbutz members). In the first collection, however, the stories deal mainly with women in the Oriental Jewish milieu (notably, those of the Yemenite community). If we question why this was so, we must turn for an answer to the ingathering of the Jews in Eretz Israel from both the East and the West. The literature of the First Aliyah (written, for the most part, by Jews of European descent) evinced considerable curiosity about the Oriental Jew. This re- sulted in more and more literary works which tried to fathom the nature of this unfamiliar Jew from the East—his life, his ways, and his customs. Pukhachewsky's interest focused on the Yemenite women in particular, not only because she knew them at close hand,[13] but even more, because both as a woman and as a product of Western civilization, she was deeply troubled by their commu- nity's marital customs. She could not understand how there could still be a group, part of modern settlement life, that allowed a man to take a second wife in addition to his first (particularly when she was going through some sort of crisis: mourning a child, unable to have children, becoming ill). In her first collection of stories, Pukhachewsky condemned this practice, emphasizing that such a woman was a victim not only of the man who considered her an object to be used for his family needs, but also of the Yemenite community which gave its approval to this practice. The female character as victim is presented on two levels: the plot level and the typological level. On the plot level, the development focuses on one specific incident, through which a male-female relationship is revealed, detailing the injustice done to the woman by the man. This incident is given two interpretations: that of the omniscient narrator and that of the dazed woman, who is helplessly drawn into an argument with herself. By moving backward in time through the chain of events and returning once more to the start- ing point in the present, her ruminations disclose an entire chapter in her life (Berlovitz, 1980: 138–141).

On the second level, Pukhachewsky makes a typological com- parison of the Yemenite woman and her husband. In this contras- tive confrontation, the character of the victim, despite her misery and misfortune, is shown to be superior; the author has endowed her with such traits that add quality to her persona, and only serve to detract from the character of the man in her life. These traits are especially evident in her amiable demeanor, which enables her to deal with both the Yemenite and the Ashkenazi environments. It is even more emphasized vis-à-vis the latter, for although that environment is incomprehensible to her (and at times, even hostile) she exhibits not only interest but a great deal of receptiveness toward it. Take, for example, Rumah ("Rumah") who is stirred by the musical sounds of the piano; or Aphiya ("Aphiya's Tragedy"), who asks her employer to teach her the aleph-bet, the Hebrew alphabet, although her husband has forbidden it; or Adayah ("After the Wedding"), who persuades her husband to try to save his life with an operation, even though the modern medical treatment is threatening and frightening to her. But the Yemenite man is different. Despite his position of authority and centrality in his native community, he seems to be wary of the Ashkenazi Jews around him and shies away from them. As portrayed by Pukhachewsky, he closes himself into the four corners of his home, rejecting any technological or cultural advances as heresies, holding on stubbornly to his old ways (among them his total domination in the matter of draconian conjugal laws). To be sure, against this oppressive domination, with all its painful and insulting implications, the Yemenite woman success in maintaining her proud bearing and this, Pukhachewsky believes, comes from her unique ability to make the best of things. As manifested in these stories, this ability does not derive from submission or weakness, but from an overwhelming vitality, which is the sum total of her affinity and love for nature and mankind. In spite of the despair that suffuses her (like Adayah whose husband deserts her because she is barren) or the loss she had suffered (like Aphiya, whose husband observes the Sabbath laws so scrupulously that he forbids her to call a doctor, after which she has a stillborn baby), in the end, she not only survives her crisis, but finds her consolation in it. Adayah recovers her strength for her husband's visits three times a week; Aphiya conquers her sorrow through the love she feels for the farmer's child she takes care of; and even Rumah, with all the bitterness she feels towards her late husband (who before dying, had imperiously commanded her to follow after him to the "eternal rest"), is able, on her deathbed, to find final consolation in the vineyards and fields that she glimpses through her window.

It is apparent, that by using this method of typological comparison, Pukhachewsky, out of the affinity she felt for the Yemenite women, wanted to be the voice for their muteness. She believed that after the radical changes they had undergone, coming from the old-world of Yemen to the new-world of Eretz Israel, these women were just beginning to understand that the way they were treated by men was not a feature of sacred tradition, but rather an expression of degradation and discrimination. On the other hand, believing that they still lacked the tools with which to explain this to the outside world (and possibly even to themselves), Pukhachewsky took upon herself the task of crying out their silent protest; in this manner, she could bring to bear all her reservations and grievances about discrimination against women simply because they were women.

We have already mentioned that the representation of woman's plight in the first group of stories pertained solely to the ethnic situation of the Yemenite women. It was only in 1923, more than ten years later (Pukhachewsky, 1923), that a parallel interpretation evolved, portraying the relationships between men and women settlers of Eastern European descent; most of the stories in the second collection (1930) were devoted to the Ashkenazi woman. As we shall see, her predicament is shown to be even more problematic and more entangled than those of her Yemenite counterpart. In retrospect, another question arises: why did Pukhachewsky put off frank discussion about the Ashkenazi woman until the 1920s? Had she been afraid, before that time, to reveal that the European Jewish man, for all his learning and progressive Western culture, had, where women were concerned, remained backward and inflexible? Was she ashamed to admit that though he had no trace of primitive tradition (as the Yemenite man did), it was precisely his civilized ways which helped him to oppress the woman with even greater sophistication? Either way, there is no doubt that Pukhachewsky had difficulty in facing up to that relationship, relevant to her own set of people. No longer the protester from the outside, being deeply involved, she had to wage her battles from within. How did Pukhachewsky register her protest in these stories?

Readers of the second collection get to know a female protagonist who is head and shoulders above any of the ordinary women we have previously described. Here is an intellectual and knowledgeable woman, skilled in one of many diverse fields (either professionally trained or self-taught) who has given up or reduced her activities in her chosen vocation in order to devote herself to a life of housework and farming (out of a profound belief in nationalism and in the dignity of labor). Such a woman is Sarah Zarhi (in "Sarah Zarhi"), who gives up a pedagogical career; such is Zehava Steinberg (in "The Farm"), who allows herself the luxury of reading Ibsen only when she is ill. And yet, in spite of her high standards and ideals, the man with whom she shares her life (be it husband, brother, brother-in-law) has no consideration for her and

takes advantage of her, harshly and offensively; he does not appreciate her efforts and always finds fault with what she does:
"'Naturally it isn't done right,' he answered in a rage . . . 'women's
work is always like that!'" ("Sarah Zarhi," in Pukhachewsky, 1930:
101); "Look . . . and heap abuse upon women and the way they do
things, spoiling and ruining everything" ("The Farm," ibid.:164);
". . . looks at the garden and says with faint ridicule: 'woman's
work!'" ("Loneliness", ibid.:197).

It is no surprise, therefore, that the heroine of Pukhachewsky's
stories is a bewildered woman. She cannot understand why she is
treated the way she is—on the personal as well as the social
level—for after all, she, unlike the ordinary woman, well knew
that joining her man in coming to the country meant the promise
of a whole new life. On the other hand, she makes no attempt to
resolve this misunderstanding frankly and as an equal. Quite the
contrary. We meet a woman who, for all her education and intel-
ligence, has a very poor self-image. In that respect, she is portrayed much the same as her Yemenite "sister"—submissive and
mute; in dealing with a man, she not only ignores his coarse behavior but even tries to pacify him, to lay the blame upon herself
and to justify his cruel disparagement of her (Sarah Zarhi excuses
her husband because he is ill; Zipporah Drori excuses her brother
because he is an orphan). But to her great astonishment, the more
forgiving she is, the more aggressive he becomes, and the more his
aggression grows, so does her bewilderment; her entire life is con-
founded. In her predicament, she tries to explain to herself (unlike
the Yemenite woman who lacked the ability to do this) exactly
what man's role is, in a male-female relationship; she seeks the
answers, not only from her own experiences, but from those of her
beloved literary heroines (in the works of Maupassant, Balzac,
Chekhov, and others). However, although she finds more and more
examples, the solutions are still beyond her reach, and like Sarah
Zarhi she is left troubled and perplexed:

> How will this all end? . . . It is not the hardship of a life of toil
> which leads to failure, because she is willing to make do with very
> little and ungrudgingly accepts whatever comes her way. There is
> only one thing she cannot overcome: the treatment of women—
> Slave and Woman, it is all one and the same. Except that the
> slave has found some liberators, while woman has found none.
> Woman, woman! What a shameful name to bear . . . for what
> purpose did nature endow her with this quality of submitting to a

Figure 5. Nehamah Pukhachewsky (Central Zionist Archive).

fate more bitter than gall? Why must she hang her head and bear her burden in silence? (ibid.: 97,116).

Indeed, one of the basic questions asked over and again by Pukhachewsky's heroine (sometimes of herself, sometimes of other women) is: Why is woman so passive? Why doesn't she rebel against men? In a conversation Zarhi has with her neighbor, Mrs. Dolitzky, a stormy discussion on the subject ensues. At its conclusion, however, they are left, once again, without any solution; with more doubt than certainty.:

'in my opinion, woman herself is to blame for her troubles. She would be able to improve her life, if she only knew how to go about it. For example? . . . First of all, we must unite and devise a specific plan for improving our lives. Those emancipationists, who keep themselves outside of family life, will never succeed; it is only the married women who will. They are the ones who must and if they want to, they will also be able to force their husbands to acknowledge that a woman too is a human being; this will erase the stigma of slavery which she bears . . .'

'Not true' . . . replies Sarah, 'it is precisely the married woman who is not able to fight back; her love and devotion prevent her from showing any opposition . . . We need unity, you say? Why, there are women from forty different countries already joined together to defend their rights, but with very poor results. Who knows which generation will one day achieve liberation?' (ibid.: 109).

At this point, it should be mentioned that Pukhachewsky's doubts about the renaissance of women in Eretz Israel—as both a nationalistic and a feminist act—only serve to emphasize how naive was Ben-Yehuda's grasp of this complex issue. For while Ben-Yehuda believed that the solution lay in a woman's acquisition of an education and in her nationalistic involvement, Pukhachewsky clearly felt otherwise. It was not enough for a woman to be educated and open to new ideas; neither of these had succeeded up to then in freeing the woman or society from the fixed image of her— as inferior and secondary to the male. So with all woman's awareness (as depicted by Pukhachewsky) of the prejudice against her, of feminist action throughout the world, of the need to find her own *modus vivendi*, she still lacked the temerity and daring to go against the traditional conventions which she grew up with; to stand erect and proud, like the new woman she so aspires to be. This was the source of her feeling that she was trapped between her weaknesses and her wishes, and this, too, was the source of the self-reproach which undermined all her confidence in her own worth: "I stayed by the window, torturing and berating myself . . . I alone am to blame . . . it is I who am wicked and evil . . . what an insignificant creature I am" (ibid.:161–3).

This feeling of nullity became even more acute when evoked on public occasions. Somehow, in her private life, the woman could attribute her insignificance to certain personal stipulations between herself and the male, but it was in the public domain that she revealed the prevailing legality of these stipulations, which was: she was rejected by men for the simple reason that she was a woman. Here is what Zipporah Drori, a farmer, writes in her diary:

Many of the leading figures of our settlement assembled for a general meeting and I decided to go to the meeting place. The people's representatives were gathered to discuss a burning issue and to pass judgment on it . . . I became very stimulated by the discussion and put my name on the list to reply, but when my turn came, they would not allow me to speak. Their reason was that I was only a guest at the meeting and not an official participant. Grievously offended, I wondered: have I no status whatever in this group into which I force my way and demand the right to discuss its issues? Cannot a poor, wretched soul like me contribute anything to this 'complicate mechanism' that is 'the settlement of our land'? Yet, on the other hand . . . a woman has no rights whatsoever, so by what authority does she push herself into the group to express her opinion? That is nothing but impudence on her part! A woman's place is in the kitchen, behind the stove and not among the chosen delegates of the people! (ibid.:185–86).

And it was upon this point that the main thrust of Pukhachewsky's protest was based—a protest that condemned the new male not only because he dominated and exploited the woman in their private lives, but even more, because he undermined her every attempt to free herself of the conventions of the past, to improve her status and assure her equal rights—for these, after all, were the declared principles of the national revival. Thus, in summarizing the militant-story as Pukhachewsky wrote it, we may generalize and say that if in her earlier works, the target of her protest was the Yemenite male, and in the later ones, the Ashkenazi male—for all intents and purposes, the depiction of the man was the same in both cases. In other words: the harsh treatment of women was neither an ethnic nor a cultural issue, but rather an essentially existential one. No matter what she was (primitive or enlightened, ignorant or knowledgeable) and no matter what the surrounding society was (conservative or liberal, backward or progressive), a woman was always rejected and deemed inadequate and insignificant.

We cannot ignore the fact that the later stories were increasingly concerned with this pessimistic conclusion. While in the earlier tales, Pukhachewsky believed that the problem was a purely social one and that the right kind of social struggle would bring about the desired results, in the later stories, this positive outlook became moderated. It was here, as we pointed out earlier, that Pukhachewsky's writing can be seen as divorced from life. In her real world, she continued to fight for the woman of the Yishuv on any terms, while in her literature, woman's plight remained a matter of existential introspection—as if only by a miracle of sorts was

there any hope of bringing about the longed-for changes. As Zarhi
expressed it: "Will there ever be a change for the better? And nature—which creates for every living creature some sort of protec-
tion against its attackers—will it some day give woman too the
means of defending her honor? Or will her life always be a groping
in the dark, with no exit?" (ibid.:103).

Conclusion

This article sets out to show how the aspirations of the First
Aliyah women (for renaissance, for rights, and for equality) can be
perceived through their literary works. It must be emphasized that
to date, there has been no thorough or comprehensive study of this
literature—neither from the ideological or esthetic point of view
nor from the standpoint of content.

This omission can be attributed to two factors:

A. Feminist criticism, as part of general literary research, is still
far from prevalent in Israel, and since this body of work has been
explored for the most part by feminist critics (that is, has been
reread in line with woman's parameters), it has not aroused the
interest of scholars—not the females among them, and certainly
not the males.

B. It has been accepted as fact by historical research that the first
women to take a stand for equal right in Eretz Israel were the
pioneering socialist-Zionists. According to this contention, it was
only with the start of the socialist-Zionist immigration (in the Second Aliyah: 1904–1919) that the subject of women and their status
was raised, and it was only then that the "working" woman, (as
opposed to the "farming" woman) began to consider the issue, from
its social as well as its publicistic and literary aspects (see Bernstein, 1987).

Additionally we hope with this article to accomplish the following:

A. To recommend that this neglected literature be reconsidered,
based on rereading according to feminist criticism;

B. To counter the historical convention which regards the women
of the Second Aliyah as the trailblazers. It is true that if we consider their actual deeds and achievements, they made far more progress than that of the First Aliyah predecessors. However, if we
consider the concept per se, the dream of woman's renaissance in
Eretz Israel, and the first halting steps in that direction, these as

indicated above, had existed even earlier, during the time of the First Aliyah. In other words, what I have tried to demonstrate through their literature is that the feminist awareness of those pioneering First Aliyah women was the direct outcome, not of socialist ideologies, but of Zionist ideologies. For it was national regeneration, along with migration from an old country to a new land, which awakened these women (or some of them, at any rate) to the opportunities for women's regeneration. And if at first they were willing to follow the male lead, devoting most of their energies to the realization of the collective Zionist dream (see above, Ben-Yehuda, 1919[14]), they gradually became aware of their own particular problems and increasingly felt the need to give expression to the aspirations for their own renaissance.

In conclusion, it is interesting to note that to the women of both the First and Second Aliyah, their part in the feminist struggle (be it shared hopes or active participation) was linked first and foremost to some other ideological struggle. This situation is far from unique and is a recurrent theme in almost all the chronicles of women's striving for liberation. It almost seems as if women, lacking self-confidence and feeling on the sidelines of society, are afraid to acknowledge that they too are an "oppressed minority", and it is only as a result of their involvement in other revolutionary struggles that they gather the courage to wage their personal battles. Thus were the first suffragists in the United States spurred on in the 1880s by the social and economic changes; thus, the women active in the Populist and Socialist movements in Europe at the turn of the nineteenth century demanded rights of their own, and thus too, the Jewish women in Palestine sought to achieve their own liberation along with the rebirth of Zionism taking place at that time.

Notes

1. The sources also mention a number of converse examples, like that of Golda Miloslawsky, whose husband did not want to immigrate to Palestine—only in 1885, after he had died, did she take her children and settle in Wadi Hanin; or the case of Batya Makov, who left her husband and came to Rehovot with her children in 1890.

2. Aliyah during this period was, in the main, the immigration of families. This was not the case in the Second and Third Aliyah, for example, when the immigrants were mostly young unmarried men and women. The

women therefore, were not followers but had come to Palestine of their own volition.

3. A case in hand is the story of Feiga Lehrer, who immigrated to Eretz Israel in 1883 with obvious dissatisfaction. Settled in an abandoned and desolate farm in Wadi Hanin, she and her husband went through terrible suffering and loss (the death of two of their children) as well as great financial distress. But it was this suffering that bound Feiga to the country; when her husband wanted to sell part of their land in order to alleviate their hard-pressed condition and bring additional settlers to the area, it was she who opposed his plans "because she had already come to love her land" (Smilansky, 1943).

4. N. Pukhachewsky had graduated from a Russian Gymnasium; H. Ben-Yehuda had been a student of chemistry in Moscow; Miriam Gissin, Miriam Pfefermeister, and Elisheva Bassewitz were teachers; Yehudit Harari had been trained in educational science in France and Switzerland; Hannah Trager was a professional nurse; and Hannah Luncz had done editing and printing. In addition to these writers, there were other educated women in the early settlements. This was especially evident in the colonies (Rishon le'Tzion, Rehovot, Gedera) whose founders had come from Russia, were less orthodox, and were intellectuals and professionals (in contrast to those who had emigrated from Poland and Lithuania).

5. The average woman of the First Aliyah was from Eastern Europe although there were, of course, women from other parts of the world. Besides the dominant European Aliyah, there was also immigration from Yemen, not to mention the women who were native to Eretz Israel: members of both the Sephardi and Ashkenazi communities of the "Old Yishuv".

6. H. Trager—the daughter of Zerach Barnett (one of the founders of Petah-Tikva and Neveh-Shalom); I. Yellin—the daughter of Y. M. Pines (active in Hovevei Zion and a prominent member of the Jewish community in Eretz Israel); H. Ben-Yehuda—the wife of Eliezer Ben-Yehuda (the father of modern Hebrew and a leading member of the Yishuv; N. Pukhachewsky—the wife of M. Z. Pukhachewsky (one of the first agricultural instructors); M. Pfefermeister—the wife of Yeshayahu Peres (a leader of the Yishuv in Jerusalem); and H. Luncz—the daughter of A. M. Luncz, the noted scholar who did pioneering research in Eretz Israel studies.

7. N. Pukhachewsky (1869–1934) and H. Ben-Yehuda (1873–1951) were the principal writers among First Aliyah women; M. Gissin and M. Pfefermeistr wrote children's stories; E. Bassewitz (1855–1932) reported from the Galilee (mainly from Metullah); I. Yellin (1868–1943) wrote a two-volume autobiography; H. Trager (1870–1943) composed memoirs, stories and articles (in English); Yehudit Harari (1886–1979) wrote short

stories; an autobiography, and a popular history of the Jewish woman from Genesis till the present, and H. Luncz (1892–1987) wrote short stories and a biography of her father.

8. There were women who taught the Talmud, like Rashi's three daughters (twelfth century); Hava Bachrach (sixteenth century) was noted for her learned commentaries; and Beila Horowitz (seventeenth century) composed a book of prayers for women (Tehinnot). Among the women of culture writing in the nineteenth century were the Hebrew poet Rachel Morpurgo (Italy), the author Grace Aguilar (England); and Emma Lazarus (United States), poet and translator.

9. The literature of the First Aliyah, including what women wrote, was characterized by: a) informative-explanatory works (to motivate more people into participating in the pioneering enterprise in Eretz Israel); b) impressionistic-romantic works (to describe the attitudes and experiences of the new life in the promised land).

10. In 1903, representatives of all factions within the Yishuv convened in Zikhron Yaakov in order to establish, for the first time, some sort of autonomous Jewish governing body in Palestine. Among other things, there was a suggestion to give women the vote, but this was rejected by a decisive majority (Kaniel, 1987:203). It was only after the First World War that the feminist struggle gained momentum both among workers' parties and the general public that some of the colonies allowed women to participate in the local elections; and that, in Rishon le'Tzion, Nehamah Pukhachewsky was elected, by a large majority, to the village council (Idelovitch, 1941:522).

11. In her memoir "Votes for Women", Trager (1923:133–35) describes an incident which took place in Petah-Tikva in 1886, when young women fought to get the vote and their own mothers came out against them.

12. During the First Aliyah, Hebrew was not yet spoken in Eretz Israel.

13. The first Yemenite families reached Rishon le'Tzion (where Pukhachewsky lived) in 1909. She helped them in acclimating themselves to the place, offering a great deal of care and assistance especially to the women. A street was later named for her in the Yemenite neighborhood.

14. In this article Ben-Yehuda confessed that fifteen years ago (1904), she met in Paris one of the leaders of the movement for women's rights— Dr. Keta Schürmacher. Dr. Schürmacher asked her to establish a branch of the movement in Jerusalem and to include in its activities Moslem and Christian women. Ben-Yehuda turned it down, saying that the Jewish women in Eretz-Israel had to help first their own people, and then care about women's rights.

References

(All items are in Hebrew)

Barzilai, Yehoshua. 1912. "Daybreak". *Ha-Shiloah*, 26:139–157.

Ben-Yehuda, Eliezer. 1902. "Our Possessions." *Hashkafa* 3, 19:145.

Ben-Yehuda, Hemdah. 1900. "The Very Same Birds." *Ha-Zevi* 16.

———. 1902. "Lulu." *Hashkafa* 3, 4:28; 5:36; 6:44–5.

———. 1903a. "Under the Almond Tree." *Lu'ah Eretz Yisrael*, edited by A. M. Luntz, pp. 15–29. Jerusalem.

———. 1903b. "The Advancement of Hebrew." *Hashkafa* 4, 11:81–82.

———. 1903c. "The Farm of the Rekhabites." *Hashkafa* Vol. 3, Nos. 12–14, 16, 21–23.

———. 1906. "A New Dress". *Hashkafa* 7, 91: 4–6.

———. 1910. "Kadish." *Lu'ah Eretz Yisrael*, edited by A. M. Luntz, pp. 137–148. Jerusalem.

———. 1919. "Our Day Has Come." *Do'ar Ha'Yom* 2, 30 September, p. 2.

———. 1940a. "What We Live For." *Hed Yerushalayim*, 27:2.

———. 1940b. "The Tale of a Turkey." *Hed Yerushalayim*, 42:3–4.

———. 1940c. *Eliezer Ben-Yehuda: His Life and Work*. Jerusalem: Ben-Yehuda Publication.

Berlovitz, Yaffa. 1980. *Nehamah Pukhachewsky—The New Way, Eretz Israel Literature as First Settlers' Literature*. Doctoral Dissertation, Bar Ilan University, Ramat-Gan.

Govrin, Nurit. 1989. "A Soul from Rishon le'Tzion is Yearning," pp. 114–171 in *Honey from the Rock, Studies in Eretz Israel Literature*. Tel Aviv: Publication of the Ministry of Defense.

———. 1989. "Finding the Rekhabites—Hemdah Ben-Yehuda," ibid. pp. 45–52.

Harari, Yehudit. 1947. *Amid the Vineyards*. Tel Aviv: Dvir.

Harizman, Mordechai. 1958. "The Trials and Tribulations of the Women of the Yesud," pp. 24–28 in *The Brave Pathfinders of the Huleh*. Jerusalem: The Local Council of Yesud Ha'Ma'ala.

Idelovitch, D. 1941. *Rishon le'Tzion*. Rishon le'Tzion: Mercaz Press.

Jawitz, J. 1892. *The New Year of the Trees—Life in Eretz Israel*. Warsaw.

Kaniel, Yehoshua. 1987. "Religion and 'Community' in the Outlook of the Immigrants of the First and Second *Aliyah*—1882–1914," pp. 329–338 in *Shalem* 5, edited by J. Hacker, Jerusalem: Yad Ben-Zvi.

Luncz, Hannah. 1919. "My Father's Life." *Lu'ah Eretz Yisrael,* pp. 320–355.

Pukhachewsky, Nehamah. 1911. *In the New Judeah.* Jaffa: Atin.

———. 1923. "Loneliness." *Ha-Tekufa,* 20:117–148.

———. 1930. *Life in the Village.* Tel Aviv: Hedim.

Raab, Yehuda. 1957. *The First Furrow.* Tel Aviv: Zionist Library.

Samsonov, Aryeh. 1942. *Zikhron Yaakov.* Tel Aviv: Omanut.

Smilansky, Moshe. 1934. "The New Teacher," "The Story of Love", pp. 38–72; 73–176 in *The Collected Works,* Vol. 1. Tel Aviv: The Farmers Association.

———. 1943. Pp. 224–225 in *The Family of the Soil,* Book I. Tel Aviv: Am Oved.

———. 1950. "Our Mother," pp. 25–26 in *Rehovot* (1890–1950). Rehovot: The Local Council of Rehovot.

Trager, Hannah. (1923). *Stories of the First Pioneers in Palestine.* London: George Routledge & Sons, Ltd. (English).

3

Yemenite Jewish Women—Between Tradition and Change

─── *Nitza Druyan* ───

Women's diversified role in the history of Palestine at the turn of the twentieth century has been given considerable research attention of late, and the findings have already succeeded in shattering a few myths concerning both the function and the status of women in those early pioneering days. In contrast to the old image of equality, happiness and fulfillment, history now reveals a different picture of their dreams, aspirations and emotions. Jewish immigrant women in Palestine in the early 1900s were not equal partners in the mission of *"yishuv u'bniyat Eretz Israel"* (settling and building the Land of Israel). Thus, they were generally not able to assume authoritative and directive roles within the sociopolitical, pioneering groups that eventually dominated Israeli leadership (Shilo, 1981; Izraeli, 1981; Bernstein, 1985, 1987; Blum, 1980; Druyan, 1985a).

It is in this context that Yemenite Jewish women in Palestine are introduced as a group between tradition and change. They are considered here as active members of the community, viewed primarily in relation to their participation in public life. Their position in the Yemenite community in Palestine is compared both with their former traditional status in Yemen and also with immigrant women from other countries of the Jewish diaspora. Their situation was studied a few years after their arrival in Eretz Israel, when the first generation of immigrant women was easily defined and located.

The first Aliyah from Yemen in significant numbers was made in 1882 and coincided with the East European "First Aliyah". Additional waves of Yemenite immigrants arrived in Eretz Israel in the early 1890s and 1900s. By the year 1914, fully one tenth of the Jewish population of Yemen had made Aliyah, an unprecedented percentage, as compared with other diasporas. On the eve of the First World War, they numbered about 5,000 in Eretz Israel. Of these, some 3,000 lived in Jerusalem, about 1,100 in agricultural settlements (moshavot) and about 900 in Jaffa. In 1914, Yemenite Jews were about six percent of the Jewish population in Palestine (Druyan, 1981; 1982a; 1983a; 1985b).

In Yemen

The one description that was always associated with the Yemenite Jewish woman was, "*kvudah bat melech p'nima*", "She is honored as a princess within the confines of her home." The Jewish community of Yemen was extremely conservative, both in its day to day life style and in its Sabbath, holiday and other ritual celebrations. Accordingly, tradition required that a woman's life in that land would be carefully circumscribed from infancy to maturity. Little was left to personality or initiatives, so she had almost no avenue of individual expression or development in her cultural life, although she was allowed involvement in occasional women-only activities, such as committees for poor brides or for assisting new mothers. The women did not have any role in decision-making within the extended family, they did not participate in community social events or other public affairs, and of course, a Jewish woman could not even imagine a vocational occupation in Yemen (Kapheh, 1961; Katzir, 1976).

From infancy, the Yemenite girl had an extremely rigid schedule, both on a daily basis and in her life cycle as the years progressed. She was not taught to read or write and had no other formal religious or secular instruction. Nevertheless, she was the recipient of a very structured education. From a very early age (four or five years old), she was taught all aspects of housework in combination with the religious obligations that she would need later in life: for example, dietary laws, separation of challah, salting and koshering meat, ritual immersion of utensils, forbidden foods, blessings for meals and candle lighting, dress codes and personal modesty and the precepts concerning the monthly cycle. These numerous and quite complicated instructions were taught orally, as obligations, without any discussion of the philosophical or historical background. The woman associated strict observance of these *halachot* (religious Jewish laws) with "*yir' at shamayim*" (love of G-d) and did not challenge them.

The daily routine of the woman in Yemen was strenuous. She

had to rise before dawn to fetch water and prepare the "gisher" (Yemenite coffee), grind flour, and bake and have breakfast ready when the men returned from the prayer service in the "kanis" (synagogue) at sunrise. By the time a girl was about eight years old, she participated in all of the daily household responsibilities: cleaning, washing, cooking, sewing, etc. She was engaged to be married often before she was twelve years old, and she was not able to choose her future husband. Marriage to older men was quite common as was polygamy, particularly because the practice of levirate marriage (a religious obligation to marry the wife of a brother who died without issue) was encouraged among Yemenite Jews even into the twentieth century. Immediately following her wedding, the bride moved to her mother-in-law's house where she joined the pool of female workers at the lowest possible status.

The wedding was definitely the highlight of the woman's life in Yemen. This was the time when she was the center of attention and a few weeks before and after the wedding, she was put on a pedestal and exempted from chores. Today, the picture of the Yemenite bride is regarded as the image of the Yemenite woman, although, ironically, it is not at all representative of most of her life. Similarly, a new mother was also given a few weeks to relax from her hectic routine, and her friends would arrange a ladies-only celebration in her honor.

Yemenite jewelry, known for its beauty and delicate filigree, is probably the most popularized of Yemenite art forms. In Yemen, jewelry was one of the luxuries enjoyed by women, for whom possession of a few pieces was important in that it served as a status symbol. However, the wedding costume and its jewelry was not owned by each bride, but belonged to a wealthy member of the community who rented the ceremonial outfit repeatedly. This custom was carried over to many Yemenite communities in Israel.

Questions that inevitably arise from the above descriptions often appear in the chronicles that detail the social history of Yemenite Jews: Were the women happy? Were they satisfied? In addressing these questions, one must consider whether this lifestyle allowed even the Yemenite men "happiness", or if it was part of their expectations. The common response usually parallels the traditional view that perceives the women as happy and satisfied in a world whose order was unchanged and unquestioned, with well defined roles for them.

A different picture emerges from the women's oral poetry. Since the women of Yemen were illiterate, their special oral poetry serves as an important historical source for describing their lives, aspirations and disappointments on the personal, as well as the more complex family and communal level. Their poetry, in Yemeni-Jewish, was only recently compiled and translated (Gamlieli, 1975, Hebrew translation; Caspi, 1985, English translation), and it reveals internalized expectations that were inconsistent both with the mundane role prescribed for them by traditions of generations, and with their smiling image and festive dress at weddings. Although the treatment and status of women depended also on the particular household and the internal family relationships, some generalizations can be made. Most women were weak from hard work and somewhat bitter, knowing there was no escape from their destiny. Their songs tell of sorrow and sadness and express yearning for a life of gentleness and love. For example, some of the names of their chants are: "I do not want an old man", "The Suffering of Love", etc. The following are two verses from the song "I Do Not Want an Old Man":

> I do not want an old man
> Nor his money
> I wish to have a young one—
> To play with and to kiss!

> I do not want an old man
> A broken scythe handle is he,
> I wish to have a young one—
> To squeeze all the bones in me.

A complementary picture emerges form the popular, orally transmitted literature, also compiled only within the last three decades (Noy, 1966; Seri, 1968). The oral literature, also recited by women, presents the normative images rather than women's own feelings. The "ideal" Jewish woman in Yemen was submissive, reticent, and graciously accepted her secondary and inconspicuous place in the family and the community. If a woman appeared to be bold, outspoken, independent and the least rebellious, she was portrayed as unfaithful to her husband. Such a woman was always depicted as sure to bring disgrace and disaster to herself and family.

Immigrants in Eretz Israel

A turning point, leading to a gradual change in the status of the women, occurred with the immigration of Yemenite Jews to

Eretz Israel/Palestine. Strangely enough, at the time, neither they nor the community at large expected, or desired, such a revolution. In fact, this was one of the reasons why the Yemenite community could not and did not adapt too easily to life in Eretz Israel (Druyan, 1982b; 1983b; 1986). For Yemenite Jews, immigration to the Holy Land did not mean a break with religion, old customs or cultural heritage, but rather an opportunity to observe the commandments even more strictly in the sanctity of Jerusalem. They tenaciously clung to their traditional folkways and therefore also expected the status, honor, function, and place of women to be as it was before. The Yemenites' aspirations that their Aliyah would serve as a religious redemption, as it is said, "rejuvenate our days as of old", completely contradicted the secularist ideology brought by Zionists from Eastern Europe (Druyan, 1985c).

In fact, the Yemenite immigrants confronted quite an unexpected reality, different from their dreams of maintaining their traditional ways. Conditions arose that removed the women from the framework for which they had been trained and were accustomed. It became evident soon after their arrival, both in Jerusalem in the 1880s and 1890s and in the agricultural colonies in the early 1900s, that the "old world order" could not survive, simple because often enough only the women in the family could find the employment that provided a meager subsistance. Under such circumstances, the men faced a major upheaval: employed women were gradually gaining self-confidence because of their income. They also became more socially sophisticated, acquiring knowledge in the ways of the world that the men lacked altogether.

How did the Yemenite community react to this major change? The following two documents demonstrate the social response and also provide examples of the primary sources available for the research of women in Eretz Israel.

A. In 1902, a ruling by the Supreme Sephardic Rabbinical Court in Jerusalem stated: Warning! All Sephardi and Ashkenazi heads of household are forbidden to employ Yemenite women as domestics unless their husbands acquiesce (Ratzabi, 1967:326–27). The court explained that it was responding to an official complaint, by the Yemenite Council of Jerusalem, which was not able to solve the issue on its own. It seemed that those working women, upon returning home, began to request the same treatment that they observed between husband and wife in their place of employment. When conflicts arose, many women even opted to sleep where they worked. Husbands complained that it was too costly to divorce

Figure 6. Yemenite women in Rehovot (Central Zionist Archive).

them and remarry, and therefore a remedy had to be found. On the other hand, the court also showed some contemporary sensitivity to women's rights, in that it forbade the marriage of girls not yet twelve years of age and it discouraged arrangements whereby young women would be given as brides to elderly men.

This appeal to the high court and its ruling demonstrated a desperate attempt by Yemenite men and the religious establishment to try and force the women to conform to their traditional roles. However, not only did the reality in Jerusalem exhibit a general disregard for this anachronistic decision, but even the rabbis of the court had to acknowledge, in the latter part of their announcement, that the status of Yemenite women was indeed changing.

B. Family and communal coercion were often applied to keep the women "in line" regardless of social and economic developments. The fascinating story of Shoshanna Bassin highlights the extent of physical abuse heaped on a woman who dared oppose the old structure.

> I was born in 1901 in the province of Sa'ada in Yemen. Most of the people in my village were Arabs. There were only about 20 Jews . . . The women used to weave baskets from reeds that grew near the river. We lived in a big house with my father's parents.

In 1909 we came to Eretz Israel. We had relations who lived in Jerusalem that had made Aliyah about a hundred years ago . . . We were a few families from the province of Sa'ada. It took us six weeks to reach the city of Aden on camels. There, we were delayed . . .

The voyage by boat was very long having docked repeatedly at various ports; there were also mechanical failures . . . At long last we reached the shores of Jaffa. We were met by people from the Zionist Office and we were brought to Rehovot. There, we made temporary shelters from straw.

My mother worked at farmhouses doing laundry. My brother, Shalom, was born shortly after we came, but my mother continued working while I had to take care of him. Shalom died when he was three months old, and I was sent to work. My job was to rock a baby's cradle and to clean the mistress' house. When my work was not satisfactory I was hit. I was so young and short that, in order to reach the sink to wash dishes, I had to stand on two crates. My pay was a meal! If the baby cried, I was ordered to take him for a stroll. I soon learned to pinch the baby so that I could spend more time outdoors. But, I was caught, dismissed from my job and hit by my parents. This stigmatized me as a bad worker and I could not find another job. I sat dejected on the steps of Rehovot's nursery school. The teachers took pity on me, invited me indoors, paid my tuition and provided me with a knapsack. This was the only year in my life that I was fortunate enough to spend in a formal education program.

One day in my childhood, my father was given a job as a sheep herder and as a ritual slaughterer in Ben Shemen. We moved from Rehovot and lived in a very small hut . . . My brothers Avraham and Shlomo lived with us and there hardly was any room for beds for all of us. My father would have me accompany him when, at 4:00 a.m. each morning, he herded the sheep at midday. In the afternoons I worked as a domestic and my salary was collected by my father. My mother worked in the laborers' communal kitchen. A few years later I worked with the adult laborers, in gardening and in the bakery, but I was paid at only half their rate.

In Ben Shemen, I helped the teacher's wife in household chores, and in return I was secretly taught to read and write (my father objected). . . . On the other hand, my mother was more sympathetic, but she had to be careful because my father ruled with an upper hand . . .

My mother's life was very difficult. She worked very hard all of her life and was never allowed to voice an opinion in the household. My father even wanted to marry a second wife. I was a young girl, but seeing my mother's grief prompted me to go to my father's bosses, the Zionist officials, who threatened to fire him in case of polygamy. My father protested, but in the end submitted to their will.

I did not participate in the social life; my father forbade it. Once, after persistent begging, he allowed me to go to a meeting, but I was shut out and told that I would not understand the goings on. A music teacher in Ben Shemen befriended me and made me part of the youth choir. He promised my father that I would associate only with girls. My participation in the choir was the only highlights of those years. I still remember the songs . . .

My boyfriend, Kalman, came to Ben Shemen in 1918 and we were soon romantically involved. He learned agriculture abroad and worked in the experimental station. In the evenings, he was in charge of the library. He secretly loaned me books to read that we later discussed. We had to meet secretly because I was afraid of my father. Kalman met him occasionally while working and found an opportunity to tell him of our love and his desire to marry me. This happened after my father heard from Yemenite friends that I rejected their company. My father did not answer Kalman, but when he returned home he beat me severely. I was sick for three days. My mother warned me of my father's wrath, but I informed her candidly that I was leaving home . . .

Shoshanna Bassin suffered numerous incidents of physical and verbal abuse by male family members. She was forced to leave Ben Shemen temporarily, but she did eventually rejoin Kalman.

A few friends told my father that Kalman and I would be married and he is invited to the ceremony. He was very angry and said that he would prefer to attend my funeral. On my wedding evening, my father and a few members of my family sat "*shiva*" in mourning . . . (Bassin, 1971).

Careful examination of the heroines in the literature portraying Yemenite Jews in Eretz Israel, reveals a similar strong character among Yemenite women. The authors, Mordechai Tabib and Haim Hazaz both describe the women's extraordinary strength and their ability to cope with hardship and suffering. In their writings, the women are regarded much more favorably than their male contemporaries (Tabib, 1961; Hazaz, 1973).

Shoshanna Bassin's experience demonstrates the upheaval in the lives of the Yemenite immigrants. Particularly for the women, a path opened allowing them to break away from their former con-straints. In Yemen, there was no other Jewish "host society" that could have absorbed women refugees had they opted to leave their traditional framework. In Eretz Israel, an exit from their social confinement was indeed forming in those days, but Bassin's account clearly points out that in her generation, there were many obstacles that made that avenue more theoretical than practical. The few women who succeeded in changing their lifestyles at the turn of the century, soon found out that their new milieu was at the end of a one-way road with no return.

In addition, one must remember that domestic work was almost the only occupation available for Yemenite women outside their community. However, even though these jobs were menial and certainly did not represent upward mobility on the socio-economic ladder, the different environment the women encountered on a daily basis introduced them to an entirely different existence outside the limits of their ethnic background. It was often the daughters of this generation of immigrant women that fulfilled their mothers' aspirations of breaking away, by gaining an education, leading a more modern lifestyle, and improving their standard of living.

Between Tradition and Change

Was there actually a revolution in the lives of Yemenite women in Eretz Israel at the turn of the century? There is evidence, from religious court documents and numerous letters found in archives, that these women were under considerable stress (Druyan, 1981; 1982a; 1983b). On one hand, their economic involvement outside their homes was physically demanding and emotionally draining, on the other hand, no less aggravating was their status at home. a discrepancy widened between their financial contribution to the livelihood of the family and the subordinate role that their fathers and husbands tried to maintain for them. The men strove to retain their exclusive authority in all decision-making, and did not hesitate to use extreme measures to that end.

The communal organizations continued to be the domain of men only. Yemenite men did not leave the women (young, old, married or single) any avenue of participation, even in charity activities. All philanthropic pursuits in the Yemenite *kolel* (religious community) in Jerusalem were exclusively in the hands of men, even the funds for poor brides or the committees that loaned

dishes and other eating utensils for use at communal social functions. The same was true in Tel Aviv/Jaffa and the agricultural
colonies (Druyan, 1981). Thus, the change in the women's economic
role was not translated into any reform in their social status
within Yemenite circles. This situation did not exist, interestingly
enough, among the Yemenite families who emigrated to New York
City in the 1920s and 1930s. Very much influenced by the American environment, Yemenite women in New York organized a number of charitable societies in which they served as leaders and rank
and file participants (Druyan, 1989).

The absence of Yemenite women from any aspect of public life
in Eretz Israel was very much in contradiction to the position of
Eastern European pioneering women among their peers in the labor movement. These young women were certainly not regarded as
equals in performing agricultural work, but in spite of the traditional kitchen chores assigned to them, they were not banned from
the realm of communal and public activities. In fact, many capable
women chose that avenue to fulfill their Zionist aspirations, and
because of the public image they acquired, they were eventually,
but mistakenly, thought to have had an equal partnership with
their male comrades.

However, many more differences existed between Eastern European and Yemenite women immigrants, most pronounced in the
case of the pioneer women of the Second Aliyah. Of course, there
were contrasts in literacy and education in general but also, for
Eastern European women the change in their traditional role had
already begun in their land of origin. Furthermore, the Eastern
European women, unlike the Yemenite women, declared their rebellion in the act of leaving their families to journey and settle in
Eretz Israel. Yemenite women in urban and agricultural settings
were religious and mothers of young children, while their counterparts, even at the same age, were single, without familial responsibilities, secular and highly motivated by nationalistic ideology.
Frustrated Yemenite women could not have left their community
to join with Eastern European women in their endeavor to secure
recognition for their participation in the labor Zionist enterprise,
although they shared some of the negative consequences of their
gender role. The religious and socio-cultural gap was far too wide to
be bridged in the first generation of immigrants in the early 1900s.

Moreover, when the pioneering women of the labor movement
realized that their hopes to take part as equals in the political ac-

tivities of the Zionist enterprise would not be satisfied, they chose two alternative directions. There were those who publicly revealed their deep disappointment by complaining in letters, newspaper articles, and at meetings. For example, there were continuous letters to the editor of *Hapoel Hatzair* by Sara Malkin, Tehiya Liberson and others in the years 1912–1914. Others expressed their tremendous energy via public activities such as education, social work, media, political activism, public relations, etc. Women such as Rachel Yanait Ben-Zvi or Manya Shohat excelled in those functions and found their fulfillment in them. On the other hand, the Yemenite women at the turn of the century, could not form a protest movement. They lacked a coherent awareness of their changing status and its translation into a collective demand to correct their unjust conditions. They were still in their frustration stage which was manifested in more personal than communal avenues. Yemenite women also lacked the self confidence that they could bring about a change for themselves. Rather, they concentrated their efforts to improve their daughters' fate. In addition, leadership was sorely missing from their ranks. This is particularly obvious when one compares them to women of the Second Aliyah period, many of whom were charismatic, articulate and endowed with eloquence.

The Labor Movement that was to assume the leadership of Eretz Israel emphasized its compelling ideology: building the land via a Jewish labor force. Issues concerning the status and equality of women were not at all priorities on the agenda. Therefore, if the women from their own countries of origin and their roles were pushed to the periphery of the socio-political arena, so much more so were Yemenite women and their special plight. Thus, the Yemenite woman was not yet an integral part of the revolution occurring in Eretz Israel in the pre-First World War years, even if intuitively it was part of her aspirations. In the first generation after immigration, she indeed experienced a radical change in her outlook, in her actual economic position and in her household. She also aspired to change her status within the community and sometimes realized that there were ways to break her ties with tradition, but it was only her daughter or granddaughter who was able to become part of this revolutionary trend. However, the history of the second and third generation of Yemenite women in Eretz Israel, in their struggle for equality and fulfillment of their intellectual potential, is no longer within the purview of Yemenite Jews.

It becomes an integral part of the history of Jewish women of our times.

References

Bassin, Shoshanna. 1971. "Memoirs," pp. 325–331 in *The People of the Second Aliyah*. Vol. 3, edited by Nahman Tamir. Tel Aviv: Mifaley Tarbut Vehinuch (Hebrew).

Blum, Shlomit. 1980. *The Women in the Labor Movement in the Second Aliyah Period*. M.A. Dissertation, Tel Aviv University (Hebrew).

Bernstein, Deborah. 1985. "Woman Pioneers and Laborers in the Second *Aliyah*, Hopes and Disappointments," pp. 145–163 in *The Second Aliyah 1903–1914*, edited by Mordechai Naor. Jerusalem: Yad Ben-Zvi (Hebrew).

———. 1987. *The Struggle for Equality-Urban Women Workers in Pre-state Israeli Society*. New York: Praeger.

Caspi, M. Mishael. 1985. *Daughters of Yemen*. Berkeley: University of California Press.

Druyan, Nitza. 1981. *Without a Magic Carpet*. Jerusalem: Yad Ben-Zvi and Hebrew University (Hebrew).

———. 1982a. *Pioneers of the Yemenite Immigration, 1881–1914*. Jerusalem: Shazar Center and Israel Historical Society (Hebrew and English).

———. 1982b. "Yemenites in Jerusalem—Old or New *Yishuv*." *Proceedings of the Eighth World Congress of Jewish Studies*. Division B, The History of the Jewish People. Jerusalem: World Union of Jewish Studies (Hebrew).

———. 1983a. "The Immigration and Integration of Yemenite Jews in the First *Aliyah*," pp. 193–211 in *The Jerusalem Cathedra*, vol. 3, edited by Lee Levine. Jerusalem and Detroit: Yad Ben-Zvi and Wayne State University Press.

———. 1983b. "The Natural Laborers, Yemenite Immigrants in the Agricultural Settlements," pp. 195–210 in *Se' ei Yonah—Yemenite Jews in Israel*, edited by Shalom Seri. Tel Aviv: Agudat A'aileh B'Tamar and Ministry of Defense Publication (Hebrew).

———. 1985a. "We were not Suffragists—On Pioneer Women in the Second *Aliyah*." *Cathedra*, 35:192–193 (Hebrew).

———. 1985b. "Yemenite Immigrants in the Second *Aliyah* Period," pp. 131–144 in *The Second Aliyah Period 1903–1914*, edited by Mordechai Naor. Jerusalem: Yad Ben-Zvi (Hebrew).

————. 1985c. "On Zionism among the Jews of Moslem Countries." *Kivunim*, 28:85–92 (Hebrew).

————. 1986. "Eastern Jews in Jerusalem—Between Sectarian Tendencies and Imposed Segregation," pp. 105–110 in *Proceedings of the Ninth World Congress of Jewish Studies*. Division B. Vol. 3. Jerusalem: World Union of Jewish Studies.

————. 1989. "Back to the Diaspora: Yemenites in New York Between Two World Wars." Forthcoming in *Proceedings of Tenth World Congress of Jewish Studies*. Jerusalem: World Union of Jewish Studies.

Gamlieli, Nissim Benyamin. 1975. *The Love of Yemen—Popular Yemenite Women's Poetry*. Tel Aviv: Afikim (Hebrew).

Hazaz, Haim. 1973. *The Stone of Time*. Tel Aviv: Am Oved (Hebrew).

Izraeli, N. Dafna. 1981. "The Zionist Women's Movement in Palestine, 1911–1927: A Sociological Analysis." *Signs* 7, 1:87–114.

Kapheh, Yosef. 1961. *Ways of Life in Yemen*. Jerusalem: Yad Ben-Zvi (Hebrew).

Katzir, Yael. 1976. *The Effects of Resettlement on the Status and Role of Yemenite Jewish Women: the Case of Ramat Oranim, Israel*. Ph.D. Dissertation, Anthropology Dept., Univ. of California, Berkeley.

Noy, Dov (editor). 1966. *Stories of the Jews of Yemen*. Haifa: Museum of Ethnology and Folklore (Hebrew).

Ratzabi, Yehuda (editor). 1967. *Come Hither Yemen*. Tel Aviv: Afikim (Hebrew).

Seri, Rachel. 1968. *The Holy Amulet–Folktales from Yemen*. Haifa: Museum of Ethnology and Folklore (Hebrew).

Shilo, Margolit. 1981. "The Women's Farm of Kinneret, 1911–1917: a Solution to the Problem of the Working Woman in The Second Aliyah". *The Jerusalem Cathedra*, 2:246–283.

Tabib, Avraham. 1961. *Dirt Road*. Tel Aviv: Am Oved (Hebrew).

Part II

Women of the Labor Movement

The women of the labor movement, the pioneering women of the Second and Third Aliyah (the halutzot) arrived imbued with nationalist and socialist aspirations, expecting that in the new Jewish workers' society they would be full and equal partners. This was expressed most eloquently by Yael Gordon, one of the leading women pioneers of the Second Aliyah:

> We want equality and emancipation for women, which will enable them to fulfill their roles both as mothers and as effective individuals in society. This must be our aim, especially in this young society being formed in Palestine out of the desire of the [Jewish] people to preserve its character and its "self" through work and creation. The young Jewish women who came here want not only to fulfill their national roles as daughters of our nation, but also to find themselves, the "self" of the woman-person, who has no more fitting place in the world in which to find the roots of her soul and to give it expression than in the workers' sector of our land (quoted in Bernstein, 1987:35).

The women of the Second Aliyah were the first to transform their personal frustration into collective protest and their protest into organized action.

The difficulties met by the pioneers, men and women alike, led to original and creative solutions, such as the establishment of communes, collectives, the kibbutz and moshav, the General Federation of Jewish Labor—the Histadrut, and so forth. The particular difficulties faced by women, even within these new institutions, led them to find additional solutions of their own, such as the women's training farms and the Women Workers Movement. Many of the articles in this section deal with these creative attempts.

The collective in Sejera, established in 1907 by Manya Wilbushewitz Shohat, was one of the earliest attempts at devising a new pattern of life. The collective was composed of twelve men and six women. They leased land from the agricultural training farm in Sejera for one year and cultivated it collectively, all work being shared by men and women alike. To the surprise of many, by the end of the year they had fulfilled the conditions of their contract and showed a small profit as well. As Manya wrote years later, "this was the happiest year of my life . . . we felt that we were creating a basis for collective work for the future, for ourselves and our children after us." Despite their success the collective disbanded at the end of a year and its members continued in related pursuits.

The collective in Sejera had a special significance for the women workers of the period. It was the only place where women enjoyed full equality with men in a mixed collective during the Second Aliyah. It would appear that Manya's own leadership together with the relatively high proportion of women, enabled them to achieve their goal—full participation in communal life and labor.

The achievements of women in Sejera on the one hand, and their exclusion from agricultural work in the later collectives on the other, led Hanna Meisel, a young agronomist, to devise a new route for the entry of women into agriculture: a training farm for young women where they would acquire the skills for the type of agricultural work most suitable for women's particular abilities. Meisel's aim, according to Margalit Shilo, was to enable women workers to combine their desire for independence, self-fulfillment and creative labor with the skills they needed as helpmates and homemakers.

The women's training farm was established in 1911 by Lake Kinneret (the Sea of Galilee). It was managed by Hanna Meisel and run jointly by the young women in training. It continued to serve as a place of training, a source of mutual support and a place of work during the hard years of the First World War until it finally closed down due to lack of funds in 1917. The women's farm in Kinneret, claims Shilo, above all else gave the women direction. They acquired the skills and with them, the assurance that they could be productive and autonomous. To do this, the young women established their own community. Only then could they begin to change the prevailing image of women taken over from the traditional Jewish society.

While Reinharz and Shilo write of the initiatives of two outstanding women, the diaries introduced by Deborah Bernstein and Musia Lipman, give us insight into the intimate experience of two young women, unknown women pioneers, themselves members of collectives. The diaries tell of their aspirations and their inability to fulfill them, of the dilemmas they faced and the ways they tried to resolve them, of their heartache and above all, their loneliness. This highly personal form of writing, the diary, reveals the interpenetration of the public and the private spheres in the lives of both women. As Bernstein and Lipman point out, "the private and the public were indivisible—love, work, self, the collective to which they belonged, the movement in which they participated, the land to which they came, were all part of their painful search for meaning, for integration of self."

The two diaries convey the image of very different women. The first, soul-searching and consumed by doubt and despair, arrived in Palestine in 1912 and left in 1914. The second, whose diary was written between 1925 and 1937, appears to have pushed her own queries aside and to have substituted them by an all encompassing dedication to the goals of the movement. Two ways to resolve the hardships, private and public, which they both faced.

The voice of another woman comes across in Nurit Govrin's article on Ira Jan, a painter and writer who immigrated to Palestine from Russia in 1907. Jan has been remembered primarily as the inspiration for the love poetry of the national Hebrew poet, Haim Nahman Bialik, rather than for her own creative work. One side of this work, Ira Jan's writing is discussed by Govrin. Ira Jan was not formally a member of the labor movement yet she was clearly affiliated with that camp. "One senses", says Govrin, "that the writer is essentially a socialist thinker, well versed in practical politics, emotionally involved, an insider, ready to fight for her beliefs". This fight, directed primarily against the established, middle-class leadership of the Yishuv, of the Zionist Organization and of Jerusalem in particular, is the main theme of her writing. Ira Jan's social critique against inertia, suppression of truth, decadence and lack of leadership comes across loud and clear, as does her own sense of loneliness and her sensitivity to the loneliness of others. Jan died shortly after the end of the First World War, having lost her health, her daughter and her paintings during the war years. A proud and determined woman, alone in spite of her many friends, she wrote close to her death, "I do not regret that I was born, but life is a thing of beauty only for the elect and I was not among them. I accuse no-one, especially since I did have beautiful, wonderful moments."

The chief response of Jewish workers to the difficulties they faced was to organize, to form political parties, workers' associations, mutual aid organizations and later the over-all institution of the General Federation of Jewish Labor—the Histadrut. Women followed a similar course, they organized. Initially they organized together with men, but as soon as they became fully aware of their special problems and of the inadequacy of the joint, male dominated organizations, they formed their own organizations as well. By far the most important of these was the Women Workers' Movement (WWM). The Movement was born at a meeting of young women workers in 1911, but it was formally established only in 1920, shortly after the establishment of the Histadrut which showed little concern for women, their representation and their problems. And yet, the women workers were dedicated Zionists and socialists and committed members of the Histadrut. Their own movement strove to be both affiliated and autonomous, to involve the labor movement as a whole in women's problems and yet to retain control of women workers' institutions and initiatives. The inevitable tension between affiliation and autonomy is the central theme of Dafna Izraeli's study, in which she analyzes the formative phases of the WWM. Izraeli argues that the inability of the WWM to retain its autonomy diverted it from its struggle for greater equality and transformed it over time into a social service organization which institutionalized and thus reinforced the categorical treatment of women.

The kibbutz, with its communal ownership of property, communal labor, services and life style can be seen as the most radical innovation of the labor movement. And yet, even there, argues Sylvie Fogiel-Bijaoui, equality was never achieved despite the radical transformation of the family and the collectivization of many of its functions. "It is surprising", says Fogiel-Bijaoui, "that within such a revolutionary framework, which openly stressed sexual equality, sexual inequality persisted." Two factors explain this seeming contradiction, according to Fogiel-Bijaoui. The first was the fact that the division of labor in the kibbutz was based, from the start, on the principle of productivity and profitability. Men, more capable of hard physical labor, were assigned to agricultural work which was considered the most productive and prestigious. Women, on the other hand, were assigned to the services and to peripheral agricultural branches, considered less productive and less prestigious. The second factor was the prevailing concept of maternity which saw the woman as the natural parent and motherhood as basic to the nature of all women. Thus, Fogiel-Bijaoui concludes, at a very early stage of development of the kibbutz, "after the birth of the first children, the unequal division of gender roles created from the very beginning by the principle of economic profitability, was legitimated by the definition of parental roles instituted within the communal settlement. From that point on the economic logic of profitability and the social definition of parental roles were to reinforce each other."

While Fogiel-Bijaoui discusses the transformation of the family in the kibbutz, Deborah Bernstein examines the working-class family in the urban setting. The structural change of the family which did take place in the kibbutz did not affect the towns. The traditional functions of the family were maintained, as was the traditional division of labor between male provider and female homemaker. Attempts at establishing a new type of family were made, claims Bernstein, a family which would be based on a partnership of spouses, companionship and shared commitment rather than on economic dependence and separation of spheres. And yet the circumstances which could have enabled such a family to emerge did not exist. "No economic, political and social system was created to make possible such family organization, no changes in image and identity vital for a full partnership between men and women took place." The tension between the aspiration of women to become full and active participants in their new community and the need for them to devote themselves above all to homemaking, remained unresolved.

4

Manya Wilbushewitz-Shohat and the Winding Road to Sejera

Shulamit Reinharz

In 1907 on the Sejera training farm in the Lower Galilee, Manya Wilbushewitz implemented a socio-economic plan on which she had been working for several years.* Her goal was to organize a group of Jewish workers in a way that would enable them to support themselves in agricultural labor, without exploiting anyone and without being dependent on charity. Her hope was that if her project succeeded, it could become a model for other groups of Jews in Palestine and eventually a model for large-scale settlement and employment. Whether or not her group at Sejera actually achieved that goal is a matter of continuous debate (see Frankel, 1981; Near, 1983). The purpose of this chapter, however, is to focus on the origins of her ideas and the winding road she took to put them into practice with the men and women at Sejera.

Manya Wilbushewitz was born in 1880 on an estate in Western Russia, in an area called Lososna, close to the town of Grodno. Manya's father was wealthy, deeply religious, and unlike many of

*For help in preparing this chapter, I would like to thank my husband, Jehuda Reinharz, as well as the members of my feminist research methodology group, Dina Abramovitz, Deborah Bernstein, Ruth Grushka, Michael Hermann, Thelma Nason, Henry Near, Moshe Mishkinsky, Joanne Seiden, and Zohar Wilbush. I would also like to thank Pergamon Press Ltd. for permission to reprint sections of my article, "Toward a Model of Female Political Action: The Case of Manya Shohat, Founder of the First Kibbutz", *Women's Studies International Forum*, 1984, Vol. 7, No. 4, pp. 275–287. The translation from Hebrew to English is my own. My next project on Manya Shohat is an edited collection of her correspondence and speeches. This will appear first in Hebrew (Yad Ben-Zvi) and is a joint endeavor with my husband.

his contemporaries, interested in technology. His land on the banks of the Neiman River included a grain mill that employed scores of peasants. Manya's mother was not interested in religion. She had received a secular education and fought her husband's plan to have their sons educated as rabbis. Manya was the eighth child of this conflictual marriage. None of her older brothers and sisters were to remain on the estate in roles intended by either parent. Instead, each pursued an ideological path ranging from joining the terrorist Social Revolutionaries, becoming a Tolstoyan peasant, emigrating as a farmer to Palestine with the *Hibbat Zion*, or obtaining a superior technical education and becoming an engineer in Palestine. Several eventually committed suicide when their feminist, romantic, or social ideals disappointed them.

Manya's family mirrored the contradictions of Jewish life in late nineteenth century Russia. At the same time as restrictions on Jewish occupation, education and travel were lifted allowing for a certain amount of assimilation into both the educated and revolutionary Gentile groups, Jews also experienced a backlash of antisemitism which provoked religious retrenchment, emigration, Zionism and socialism. In her childhood, Manya first was profoundly religious and then equally committed to Russian peasants. At the age of fifteen she ran away to the city of Minsk to become an industrial laborer. There in her brother Gedaliahu's factory, she organized a strike of the five hundred workers against him, protesting the excessively long work day. This was to become the first of her numerous efforts to improve the working conditions of industrial and agricultural laborers.

In Minsk many young Jews, similar to Manya, had converged. Their first-hand confrontation with class exploitation and political oppression led them to form divergent political groups. Among the most important was the Bund, founded in 1897, whose purpose was to pursue a revolutionary solution to the oppression of Jewish workers, in conjunction with the Russian socialist revolutionary movement—vis-à-vis both the Czar and the bourgeoisie. Competing with the Bund was the *Poalei Zion*, or socialist Zionists, who advocated gradual emigration to Palestine, while also trying to improve the economic condition of Jews still in Russia. A third set of groups was the terrorist Social Democrats and Socialist Revolutionaries who attempted to overthrow the Czar. Finally, the Hibbat Zion groups believed in immediate settlement in Palestine, but did not have a socialist orientation.

Manya befriended people in all of these groups and absorbed

aspects of each ideology. The action she chose to get involved in, however, was the establishment of clandestine evening study clubs, where workers were taught basic literacy, history, economics and socialism. She also joined a relief effort in the Tartar region bringing economic and medical aid to peasants suffering from the drought and cholera. One consequence of the latter experience was her encounter with the "mir" or Russian communal system which she believed represented a form of social and economic justice. As a newly committed socialist, she set up an urban collective upon her return to Minsk. Collective, she believed, provide "the proletariat with the means of its struggle" (Shohat, 1932:22)

Manya's political activism, inevitably led to her imprisonment and intensive interrogation at the hands of the Russian secret police. Through a curious relationship in prison, she became engaged in a cooperative effort with Sergei Zubatov, the head of the Moscow secret police, to establish a political party which would protect Jews from harassment as long as they limited themselves to labor issues and did not pursue a revolutionary strategy. Manya Wilbushewitz and Sergei Zubatov were successful in establishing the Jewish Independent Labor Pary (JILP) in June 1901 and quickly achieving many of its goals. But growing unemployment soon weakened the position of the JILP among Jews, and disenchantment by von Plehve, Minister of the Interior, with Zubatov his underling, brought a swift end to the party. Zubatov was sent into exile and von Plehve agitated the Russian masses against the Jews, culminating in the traumatic Kishinev pogroms of 1903. At this point Manya, too, began to contemplate violence and joined a terrorist cell.

For the first time in her life Manya left Russia, her purpose being to gather funds in Berlin for her terrorist group. Recognizing the danger his sister was courting, her brother, Nahum, intervened and through a ruse, brought her to Palestine on January 2, 1904 at the age of twenty-four. With her arrival she became one of the first members of the Second Aliyah, composed mostly of radicalized young Russians who came to Palestine between 1904 and 1914. Shortly thereafter, Manya learned that her terrorist group had been infiltrated in Russia and its members executed. With this tragedy she no longer felt capable of effective political action in Russia and instead directed her attention to labor issues in Palestine.

Palestine presented Manya with a new set of circumstance. In the three months since her brother, Nahum, had been in the country, he had befriended Olga (a midwife) and Joshua Hankin who for the previous three years had been involved in attempting to purchase large tracts of land for the Jewish Settlement Association (or ICA). Nahum had been sent by their brother, Gedaliahu, an engineer like himself, to conduct a survey of Palestine's geography and natural resources in order to lay the foundation for the development of industry. This information was to be used to plan capital investment and create durable circumstances for Jewish immigration. Manya accepted Nahum's invitation to join him on a six-week horseback study tour with four other individuals. The first was Joshua Hankin's brother, Mendel, who served as Arabic-speaking guide. The second was Sophia Zevnegorodska, a young woman who had recently arrived from Russia accompanying a large group of children from the Belkind School orphaned by the Kishinev pogroms. She brought these children to a school at Shefiya near Haifa where Manya's future husband, Yisrael Shohat, lived temporarily. Two Arabs were hired to assist the group. Participation in this trip transformed Manya into a Zionist, although seeds for this transformation had already been planted by her earlier family life. Manya felt an attachment to the landscape, especially to a section called the Hauran where she believed many Russian Jews could find refuge if an appropriate economic base were developed. The following is one of her many descriptions of the experience:

> We rode on horseback every day for 10 hours. We would change horses. We passed all the Arab places in the country, from Dan to Beer-Sheva, and in Trans-Jordan. The trip lasted 6 weeks. I became tied to the land with a deep love, an unusual love, which filled my entire soul, mind and emotions. This love has remained with me always, and it burns in me now. It was as if a tie had been renewed between us that was 2,000 years old. The beauty of the country and its natural environment had a strong influence on me (Shohat, 1904:5).

This ideology of resettlement, new to Manya, reflected the basic Zionist position that Jews should "return" to Palestine. However, Manya's Zionism unlike that of most Zionists of the time, had four special attributes—activism, large scale dimensions, self-labor, and collectivism. Whereas the World Zionist Organization at the time favored negotiations with world powers for a charter permitting mass settlement, Manya favored immediate "infiltration" of Jewish settlers. Since the number of Jewish settlers at the time was small, Manya's plan for hundreds in the Hauran was grandiose. Moreover, her idea that settlers should work the land themselves rather than be landowners, and her promotion of self-sufficient collectives, were viewed as extreme socialism. The settlers already in Palestine did not rely on their own labor, nor did they live collectively. Rather, they depended on Jewish philanthropy and Arab labor.

Self-labor and collectivism reflected Manya's conception of Zionism not as a transplanting of Jewish life from Russia to Palestine but as a transformation of the Jewish community so as to become "ideal". Manya's efforts are noteworthy in the sense that she conceived of her plans before implementing them. Her ideas were rooted in her experience with Russian collectives combined with the socialist ideology she had adopted there concerning urban and rural class exploitation. At the end of her trip Joshua Hankin introduced her to ICA officials to whom she presented her ideas about settling the Hauran, which they promptly rejected.

Not easily dissuaded, Manya next accepted Joshua Hankin's suggestion that she undertake a survey of the First Aliyah settlements so she could better address the criticisms of the ICA officials. At the same time, she hoped to supply him with information he needed to convince the ICA to purchase land in the Jezreel Valley (Wilbush, 1974:10). In the tradition of Russian youth and American and British reformers who collected statistical data on local working conditions, Manya set out to study the twenty-three Jewish rural settlements of Palestine then subsidized by the Paris-based Baron Edmund de Rothschild.

> I decided to clarify for myself, what does this new land really mean to me? I saw only agriculture. And where was the proletariat? My plan was to travel throughout the settlements and do a statistical survey in which I had expertise. I prepared statistical tables and I filled them out. (Later, these papers were taken from me). I was absorbed in this statistical study for a year (Shohat, 1904:5)

Although Manya's economic study focused on the cause of the communities' perpetual annual deficits, it also included questions about the relations between employers and employees and between Jews and Arabs. One farmer described how Manya went about her study: "She attacked me with questions about the expenses and income of my farm, about Jewish labor and Arab labor, about the relations of the two groups in the country, and she even wanted to know if Arab men and Jewish women fell in love with one another,

and if this could bring the two peoples closer together . . ."
(Smilansky, 1947:696). From her survey Manya concluded that the
economic arrangements of both the First and Second Aliyah groups
were senseless and discouraging. Her observations about the settlements were as follows:

> After I thoroughly studied the economic situation of the Baron's
> ICA villages, I reached, in 1905, the firm conclusion that the sys-
> tem of agricultural settlement, which the officials of the Baron
> devised, was bankrupt in every sense of the word. As early as
> 1881–1882 a pioneering, wonderful, idealistic type of person came
> to Palestine, capable of minimal independent work. And now, af-
> ter they spent 25 years in the country, we found them completely
> reliant on the ICA officials, lacking any faith in their enterprise,
> and employing Arab workers. They were all bitter and hopeless.
> They all believed in the Uganda option. Their sons did not con-
> tinue in the farms and left the country because they could not
> stand the work regime that was established by the officials
> (Shohat:1961:8).

One might question the objectivity of her findings—after all, she
was already a committed socialist looking for the proletariat. Yet,
Henrietta Szold, certainly not a socialist, came to the same conclusion after her first visit to Palestine in 1909, as described by biog-
rapher Joan Dash:

> Disillusion lurked in Zikhron Yaakov, which was ugly and plan-
> less, where everything seemed sad and neglected and some un-
> happy instinct had produced the look of a Russian village, squat
> and narrow and turned in on itself. The hired overseers of the
> Rothschild colonies, she learned, were dishonest and took no real
> interest in the settlements; the man who managed Zikhron lived
> in Haifa. It was common gossip the overseers seduced the young
> school teachers and married them off later on, when they were
> tired of them. Miss Szold had noticed many Arabs living in the
> villages. They were workmen, she was told, Jewish workmen
> were too expensive. So the Jews of the Rothschild colonies, who
> were pensioners of the Baron, living on his bounty, paid Arabs to
> do their work and complained about the Baron's administration
> (Dash, 1979:5).

In the rural settlements of the First Aliyah, Jewish men and
women carried out traditional family roles. The women remained
at home and employed Arab women to help care for the children,
while the men managed the farm and employed Arab laborers to

work it. Because of this arrangement and political antipathy on the part of the First Aliyah the new immigrants of the Second Aliyah had difficulty finding work. Unemployment was related to the underdevelopment of the economy and the preference among the First Aliyah employers for Arabs who demanded lower wages than Jews. Arabs were able to accept lower pay because their families had food-bearing land and had extensive experience in a low-income standard of living. Second Aliyah immigrants, on the other hand, were landless, without family support, and had no farming experience. Despite these work arrangements, the farmers of the First Aliyah were always in debt. And Jewish town dwellers in Jerusalem, Hebron, Safed, Jaffa, Haifa and Tiberias did not fare much better. They survived on minor trade and foreign charity that Manya felt could not lead to economic development.

Having hypothesized that new collectivized agricultural settlements could be self-supporting, and that the towns and First Aliyah settlements offered no viable alternative, Manya presented her ideas to Yisrael Shohat and his brother Eliezer, two very young, penniless Poalei Zion members from her hometown of Grodno. The Shohat bothers had arrived in Palestine only two months after she did, but they came as committed Zionists with their ideology already in place. In response to near starvation, Yisrael, Eliezer and a few friends formed a workers' commune in Petah Tikva. When Manya visited them, the commune was very contentious. (Later, Yisrael and Eliezer Shohat were to become leaders of two competing workers' Zionist parties—Poalei Zion and *Hapoel Hatzair*). In addition, its members were striving to defy civilization and live at the lowest possible standard of living. Whereas Manya felt a higher standard of living and culture were desirable, they wanted to reduce their standard of living to what they perceived to be the level of the Arabs. She rejected their idea as utopian and unattractive, while Yisrael rejected her collectivist idea on the political grounds that in order to become part of the proletariat they must avoid exclusivity. Cooperatives, he contended, foster group pride and dull class consciousness. Eliezer, in turn, opposed her idea on the grounds that the new immigrants were not yet ready for collectivism and failure would doom the idea forever (see Shohat, 1930:6; Shohat, 1961:8). In addition, Yisrael was engaged in a different project altogether—to develop an organization which Jews could use to protect themselves and their settlements from physical danger. He believed a mobile group of workers should be created which would both defend Jews and work the soil.

Such a system was the only means, he believed, by which Jews could actually take possession of the land, since it was the principle on which Arab claims were based even after the land was purchased by Jews. From Manya's perspective, she was left no allies—both the ICA and her fellow socialist Zionists opposed her. As it turned out, by 1907 Manya was able to bring both groups together.

A true believer in collectives, Manya's first step was to form a carpenters' cooperative in Jaffa based on her Russian experience both in carpentry and in urban collectives. She "raised a loan for them and worked out its rules on the basis of the Russian Artel Movement which had a communal foundation. The cooperative lasted only three months because when (she) left . . . internal dissension broke out and the cooperative fell to pieces" (Shohat, 1932:22). This experience may also have taught Manya the importance of developing skills to foster good group relations and settle labor disputes, skills she was to later use repeatedly. For example, in early 1905, when Joshua Hankin involved Manya in his work of purchasing land in the Jezreel Valley, a conflict arose between the Hadera farmers and Hankin concerning 1,500 dunams which the farmers claimed Hankin had promised them. Manya was chosen to settle the dispute. Although she decided against Hankin, he accepted her decision and immediately implemented it.

Intent on moving forward with her idea of agricultural collectives, Manya decided to travel to the ICA offices in Paris in the summer of 1905 after one and a half years in Palestine. Supported by her statistical evidence, she hoped to convince the Baron and the ICA to buy the Jezreel Valley. She also wanted to broach the idea of agricultural collectives in the Hauran with Meyerson, the head of ICA. As an intellectual with several books of philosophy to his credit, she thought he might grasp the significance of collectives. Decidedly unenthusiastic about her socialist plans, the Baron gave her permission to attempt settlement in the Hauran, but he gave her no financial backing. While in Paris, she also turned to the internationally known Zionist, prolific writer and physician, Max Nordau, but his reaction was worse; he listened to her detailed lecture for 1½ hours, filled with numbers and calculations, and when she was done—he remained silent. When she inquired why he was silent, he answered by saying that he was weighing whether or not to suggest she see a physician (Smilansky, 1947:696)

To Manya the idea of an agricultural collective was vital but admittedly vague. To remedy this problem, she took advantage of her stay in Paris to study the concept, drawing on the resources of a relative, Ivan Wilbushewitz, employed as the head of a journal that published studies about the French colonies. With his help, she also obtained governmental material concerned with Algeria and Tunis. However, she soon learned that information on agricultural management in these underdeveloped areas was oriented toward exploiting and exporting natural resources. More relevant to the Jews who sought to develop Palestine was the history of religious communes and utopian experiments. At the end of her studies, she concluded that there were no models for the settlements she envisioned, and that related models had all failed. Although her conviction about the value of collectives did not falter, her research yielded no economic blueprints for collective societies.

Manya then travelled from Paris to Basel in July 1905 to attend the 7th Zionist Congress which resolved to obtain Jewish settlement rights in Palestine but to keep actual settlement limited. When she returned to Paris from Basel, she was approached by Meir Kagan, a friend from the former JILP, who asked her to abandon temporarily her Palestine project and turn her attention to the Jews still in Russia. Specifically, he asked her to try to raise funds in Paris and America to purchase arms that could be smuggled into Russia for Jewish self-defense. Manya turned again to the Baron, who gave her fifty thousand francs, on condition that his name not be mentioned. She also obtained ten thousand rubles from the twenty-eight-year old Reform rabbi and honorary secretary of the Federation of American Zionists, Dr. Juddah Magnes, whom she had met in Basel. Altogether she raised 200,000 rubles from wealthy individuals and at mass meetings of Russian socialists and immigrants in Paris. With this money she went to Liege, Belgium to purchase revolvers which she hid in her clothing and brought to Russia surreptitiously. Manya distributed these guns and ammunition to Jewish defense groups. On one trip she was cornered by a member of the secret police, and to avoid being killed, killed him. To dispose of the evidence, she shipped his body in a trunk to a fictitious address. Manya remained in Russia and participated in self-defense efforts during the pogroms of 1906, but felt she had to do more. For three months she was a member of a terrorist group "to exact vengeance on the leaders of Russian anti-semitism" (Shohat, 1932:23). In the spring of 1906, the group was infiltrated and its members arrested. Manya avoided detection, escaped from Russia, and returned to Palestine via Constantinople in late 1906.

Not having received settlement funds from the Baron or convinced Palestine settlers to join, Manya decided to take another
route, and travelled to the U.S. in early 1907 to seek funds and
settlers, to continue her study of collectives, and to persist in her
fund-raising efforts for Jewish defense in Russia. At that time Socialist Zionism was very young in America, the first group having
been formed in New York only in March 1903 under the name
National Radical Verein Poalei Zion. Only in December 1905 after
the Kishinev pogrom, did they hold their first national convention.
In its program, the Socialist Zionists declared that normal social,
political, and economic development of Jews could not take place
without a land of their own, and that land should be Palestine.
However, they demanded that any Jewish state should be based on
socialist principles, with the workers owning land and the means
of production (Urofsky, 1975:103). American Zionists were very
small in number at the time, and even those who joined one of the
many splinter organizations believed that Zionist aspirations
would be fulfilled only in the distant future. Those drawn to Poalei
Zion were immigrants living in urban ghettos where they struggled with their own poverty or tried to move out into American
society. Thus it is not surprising that even ". . . in America,
[Manya's] mission was only half successful" (Smilansky, 1947:647).
Smilansky also points out that Dr. J. L. Magnes introduced her to
wealthy American Jews. These people were willing to contribute
money for self-defense in Russia but rejected the idea of the collective.

During her half year in the U.S., Manya was able to convince
Magnes to visit Palestine, and after he later immigrated, the
two of them worked extensively to promote peace between Arabs
and Jews. While in the U.S. Manya also met Henrietta Szold,
twenty years her senior, who described Manya as an extraordinary
woman, "a warm, palpitating and yet Tolstoian personality" (Dash,
1979:82). Despite the good impression Manya made, her idea of
collective settlements was seen as so fantastic that she was unable
to find investors or joiners. For a while she lived in a New York
commune, but much of her time was spent briefly visiting communal settlements such as the Dukhoborian who had immigrated
from Russia to Canada. These groups inspired her. "I saw that it
was possible to create and advance communistic colonisation, although in place of religious idealism, we would have socialist idealism" (Shohat, 1937:56).

Manya returned to Palestine via Paris in August 1907 without

having raised funds for a collective and without any specific blue-
print to meet the needs of the Hauran. On her return, she travelled
part of the way by ship with Chaim Weizmann who was making
his first trip to Palestine. Together they stopped in Alexandria
where she addressed Zionist groups, from there they travelled to
Beirut where they were quarantined. Like most others who met
her, Weizmann was struck by her charismatic personality, and
Manya was to find in Weizmann an approachable political leader
for years to come (Weizmann, 1949:124).

Throughout her journeys, Manya sought principles on which
to base her agricultural collective. She concluded that to avoid
the creation of a class society, the collective should be based on
the abolition of private property. "We, the first socialist Hebrew
workers in the country, who brought with us radical opposition to
any private property, couldn't even imagine that from private
property a national society would develop for the Jewish people
that wished to free itself in Palestine. And it was obvious that the
settlements of Rehovot and Hadera did not satisfy our soul or cap-
ture our hearts" (Shohat, 1961:8). Second, to avoid competition between Arabs and Jews, the collective should not attempt to take
over existing Arab employment. "Before me the decisive question
stood very sharply: either we came to Palestine in order to remain
forever in the status of proletariat, begging at the doors of the
farmers who under no circumstances wanted us or our labor; or we
came here to create for ourselves a different form of settlement,
sympathetic to our values" (Shohat, 1961:8). Third, to avoid exploitation within the collective, the members should be free to leave,
unlike in the Russian mir where there was a supervisory class of
elders. Fourth, to assure a high cultural level, there should be limited work hours and evening study groups. Finally, as an alternative to landowning or working for landowners, the collective should
lease public lands. At that time, the *Keren Hakayemet* (Jewish National Fund) was starting to purchase lands, starting from the assumption that the Land of Israel should be the property of the entire people, and not of individuals. "And thus, I seized upon the
idea of integrating the Keren Hakayemet ideas with the principle
of tenant farming, as it was practiced among the Arabs" (Shohat,
1961:8).

This leasing plan derived from a particular form of Arab labor
she had seen. Similar to tenant farming (Shohat, 1937:55), this arrangement was also a variation of the system developed in Russia
after the freeing of the serfs. This plan allows the farmer some

independence even without owning the means of production. Specifically, the tenant farmer receives as a loan from the property owner, tools, land, seeds, animals and living expenses. When the harvest is in, the tenant farmer pays back to the owner ⅘ of what has been earned. This covers the loan, gives the owner a profit, and leaves the farmer with a profit for his own purposes. These terms are even more beneficial to tenants if they are organized as a voluntary collective. Thus, a socially and financially successful system could be established without much initial investment.

At first Manya considered the idea of an integrated collective consisting of Arab and Jewish members, but she then determined that this would be impossible (Shohat, 1929:619). Unfortunately, Manya did not explain why she wanted to form an integrated collective in 1906, nor why she felt it was impossible to do so. The story of the relations between Arabs and Jews in Palestine before the First World War is complex (see Mandel, 1976). Jewish ideology was not hostile to Arabs, nor did Jews come to Palestine with the intention of displacing Arabs. Arab nationalism had not yet emerged and Arabs were benefitting from Jewish settlements both in terms of employment and markets for their goods. Thus there were "generally close and good . . . day to day relations between peasants and settlers" (Mandel, 1976:31). At the same time, however, there were land disputes between the new Jewish colonies and Arab farmers who had lived on the sold property. These disputes led to Arab marauding and violence against persons and property. Manya's desire for Arab Jewish cooperation was unusual in the context of the Arab-Jewish relations of the period, but not unusual in light of her commitment in Russia to Gentile peasants despite their hostility to Jews. In later years, Manya went on to become actively involved in creating organizations to promote Arab-Jewish friendship and co-operation. Most of these efforts were unsuccessful and unpopular.

Upon her return to Palestine in August 1907, Manya contacted Dr. Hillel Yaffe asking him to convince the Zionist groups or the ICA officials of her idea of agricultural collectives. According to her report, Dr. Yaffe answered that "there is no hope whatsoever for your plan. You will not find people who believe in such a thing. The Keren Hakayemet has no money for this type of experiment, nor would they understand it; and the Baron will under no circumstance agree to your idea. There is only one place, Sejera, which has the objective conditions for this type of experiment, but Krause will not dare to try it even if he is convinced of its value, because he'll lose his job if it becomes known in Paris" (Sohat, 1961:8). She then turned to Joshua Hankin, who, to her surprise, became convinced of the value of the idea. He, in turn, persuaded Manya of the value of trying out her plan in Sejera rather than in the Hauran. He also agreed to present her case to the young agronomist, Eliahu Krause, the manager of the Sejera farm, who was also his brother-in-law, and after much hesitation, Krause agreed to try to implement Manya's idea on his responsibility, even though it endangered his own position (Smilansky, 1947:696). With this agreement in her pocket, Manya turned again to the two workers' parties—Poalei Zion and Hapoel Hatzair—to get volunteers for her collective in Sejera.

In Jaffa at a meeting of Poalei Zion on September 29, 1907, Yitzhak Ben-Zvi and Yisrael Shohat set up a secret group called *Bar Giora*, building on the idea that Yeheskel Hankin and Michael Halperin had suggested already in Russia, and that Alexander Zaid was dreaming of in Palestine. This idea was that the Jews of Palestine would create an organization to defend themselves. Those present at the meeting—Yisrael Shohat, Yitzhak Ben-Zvi, Yisrael Giladi, Yeheskel Nissinov, Yeheskel Hankin, Zvi Becker, Alexander Zaid, Moshe Givoni and Komrov—discussed the need to set up a group of shepherds and a group of guards. At this point, Manya contacted Yisrael Shohat. He realized he could use her proposed settlement as a site on which to train a cadre of Jewish guards. He agreed to contribute his men, but did not tell her of his larger scheme (Shohat, 1961:8). As can be seen in the events to date, Manya was a pragmatist. Her socialist zeal did not deter her from seeking funds from capitalist philanthropists, nor did her commitment to particular principles prevent her from seizing the opportunity to implement something similar. All of the elements of such an opportunity had just presented themselves. She had a site, a plan and a group of volunteers.

Sejera

Sejera was a community in the hills of the Lower Galilee, consisting of two parts: one section, founded by the ICA in 1889, was a short street with closely set small private homes on each side, and garden plots in front, resided in by Jewish families from Kurdistan and Jewish converts from Russia. The other section, on slightly higher ground, consisted of a walled yard in which there were sin-

Figure 7. Manya Willbushewitz-Shohat (Central Zionist Archive).

gle rooms resided in by individuals who came to work under Eliahu Krause's direction. The purpose of the farm at Sejera was to train Jewish farmers in self-sufficiency. Its manager, Eliahu Krause, was a progressive Russian Jew only two years older than Manya (see Michaeli, 1973). Some people who trained on the farm (e.g., David Ben Gurion) went on to live with and work for the families in the other part of the settlement. The students and farmers grew wheat and barley, and raised poultry and cattle. Those in training had to be accepted personally by Eliahu Krause and approved by the Paris office. While in training, they received a monthly wage.

Joshua Hankin and Manya Wilbushewitz arrived at Sejera just as Krause was assessing the farm's financial situation and discerning that the year would end in a deficit as had the previous years. In response to her request and Hankin's recommendation, Krause signed Manya on as a worker at Sejera. She was to work half-days in the dairy section, and half-days as a bookkeeper. Sometimes she also participated in the plowing, walking in the furrows behind a horse (Smilansky, 1947:696). In addition, she helped Krause in his dealings with other workers. For example, Yitzhak Nadav remembered that the following year when he came to Sejera and wanted to work as a builder,

> I turned to Manya Shohat, who was the [central organizer] of the place, in the employ of ICA, with the suggestion that I get the work on the same conditions received by Arabs, or even worse conditions. Manya turned to Krause, and was able to get his agreement, on the condition that he give us only small jobs on an experimental basis (Nadav, 1986:14).

When she first arrived, Manya obtained from Krause the right to form a collective from among some of the trainees already on hand and additional ones who would come. The workers in the collective would pool their expenses, would make joint decisions about how their work was to be done, and would not hire others to work for them. In all three ways, the collective would be different from the work arrangements both of the other trainees and of the settlers in the other section of Sejera. The collective members would also pool their wages in order to establish a fund to provide shelter, clothes and food for new workers who would go where work was needed for a period of two years. In this way the collective would begin to participate in the task of settling the land. As it turned out, the collective also enabled people to work who could not engage in physical labor. Thus, Yisrael Shohat, suffering from chronic asthma, functioned as the treasurer of the grain mill of the farm (Paz, 1947:363).

Twenty years after the collective was disbanded, Manya wrote a memoir about the way it functioned:

> According to the contract we drew up with Krause, we got to work in the fields and the dairy shed on the conditions of an Arab tenant farmer. We could use both the livestock and drygoods and seeds, and we were supposed to give him a fifth of the harvest. We got a place to sleep, but it was an awful place, and also an advance. We worked independently, on our own complete responsibility. We were responsible for organizing our own work. Krause used to sit with us once a week and advise us, as an expert, how to plan our week's work, in order to determine what our situation was and to help prevent mistakes. We asked him to give us lectures in agronomy. The workers there before us did not have a kitchen. The collective arranged a communal kitchen which some of these other workers also used. The relationship between these

other workers and ourselves was very good. Despite that fact,
they didn't believe that we would complete our year without a
deficit, and they did not join us (Shohat, 1929:620).

Manya's idea was that in addition to their learning farming, these
young Russian Jews could also learn how to organize a farm; they
could acquire the skills to set up their own settlements and become
independent of foreign philanthropy. She was able to entice the
apprentices with the guarantee of a full year's employment and a
remote place in which to engage in their efforts to set up a self-
defense group. In October 1907 the experimental collective was established. Krause had agreed to a collective composed of eighteen
people who would take responsibility for the fieldwork. This number was soon reached by drawing on people already on the farm,
the *Bar Giora* group, other members of Poalei Zion, and newcomers. Some of the members were Poalei Zion people who had
functioned as a collective of day laborers in Rishon le'Tzion and
then for four months in the "Jerusalem stonecutters commune".
When that collective broke up, one member, Kayla Becker (Giladi),
received a letter to join her friends in Sejera which she did. A bit
later she was joined by her sister, Zipporah, and her friend, Alexander Zaid (see Giladi, 1937:135, and Nadav, 1986). Thus, those
already in Sejera experienced the formation of the collective as a
gathering of friends, relatives and political allies. Strangers were
immediately identifiable as "not one of us".

> In one of the meetings [in Sejera of Bar Giora] there was talk of
> our members in Jerusalem and of the need to bring everyone to-
> gether here. With great excitement we waited for them. And one
> day, while I was resting next to the wagon in the fields, Mendel
> Portugali came up to me and told me that they had come: Alex-
> ander Zaid, Yeheskel Hankin and Gabriel, a person I had not yet
> heard of. We were surprised that Zipporah Zaid had not come. And
> only after a few days did I discover that "Gabriel" was none other
> than Zipporah, who had dressed in men's clothing, so that Arabs
> would not be able to recognize her on the road since they went on
> foot from Jerusalem along the length of the Jordan. We too wore
> black trousers at work in order to prevent the Arabs from under-
> standing that we participated in the night watch (Becker, 1947:
> 511).

Ultimately, the collective numbered six women and twelve
men. The women were the two Becker sisters, Kayla (who married
Yisrael Giladi) and Zipporah (who married Alexander Zaid); the

three Shturman sisters, Esther (who married Zvi Becker), Sara (who married Moshe Krigser, later Amiad) and Shifra (who married Yisrael Betzer); and Manya Wilbushewitz (who later married Yisrael Shohat). The men were Zvi Becker, David Beldovsky (later Ben-Galeel), Gershon Mentkovits (later Ben Zur), Yisrael Giladi, Levi Gefen (later replaced by Meir Hazonovitz), Yehuda Zeldin, David Yisraeli (formerly Rubin), Pik, Saadia Paz, Joseph Shapiro (replaced by Moshe Givoni, formerly Yozubar) and Yisrael Shohat (see Shapiro, 1961).

It is important to note several points about the members of the collective that contributed to its success: most already had experience in collectives; many were related to one another; and all were of the same political persuasion, some having known each other already in Russia. Many of the members were to fall in love with each other during the year (e.g., Esther and Zvi Becker) or culminate their previous romances and marry (Zipporah and Alexander Zaid). The lack of children at this stage made life somewhat easier for the collective. And although there were numerous violent conflicts with neighboring Arabs, these were on a small scale compared to the military problems that would later arise.

When negotiating with Krause for the establishment of a collective, Manya was adamant that it include women. She finally was able to convince Krause to accept women as full members even though in the rest of Palestine women were not given the same employment opportunities as were men (see Maimon, 1960; Bernstein, 1987; Shilo, 1981; Izraeli, 1981).* Manya believed that in addition to being unjust to women to deny them the right to do physical labor, it was also unfair to the Jewish community because working-women could contribute to a "healthy Jewish future" (Schama, 1978:172). Under Manya's influence, Krause developed the reputation of being fair to, and supportive of, women. Krause was even willing to take on women workers when there was a waiting list of men. Thus when Shifra Shturman arrived in Jaffa at the age of twenty-two with her parents, three brothers and three sisters (Chizick, 1947:720), she was met by people who told her:

> There was only one little place, Sejera is its name, under the management of the agronomist Krause, in which there is hope for a young woman to obtain work [in the Galilee]. I went there and afterwards my sisters Ester and Sara came, and my brother

---

*Shilo and Izraeli are reprinted in a shorter version in this volume.

Haim. One has to say to the credit of Mr. Krause, that he accepted female workers despite the inclinations of the administration of the ICA, and when it came to writing down the names of workers would substitute a male name for the female worker so no one would know . . . Sejera was the first place open to women's work and there the idea of the movement of women workers started to blossom (Betzer, 1947:504–506).

Shifra was the first woman at Sejera. She later was joined not only by her sisters and Manya and the other women of the collective, but also by Lea Meron, Haya Sara Hankin (for a description, see Hankin, 1937), Bilha Horowitz, Hanna Meisel (for a description of her important role at Sejera, see Krigser, 1947), and others. These women, while not members of the collective, worked in close contact with them. Kayla Giladi shared Shifra's feelings of relief to be able to work at Sejera:

In those days there was no possibility for girls 'of our type' to find any kind of work. Not even as a servant in a private home. Krause was the first and only one who helped us learn to become competent in agricultural branches. He had a clear vision that agricultural settlement was not possible unless the wife (or woman) was also involved in it. In practice, we were equal in all the work with the boys . . . Krause used to be proud of us, and when official visitors would come, he would bring them to the fields to show them the unforgettable picture of Jewish girls, wearing pants, ploughing behind the oxen (Giladi, 1981:62)

Krigser also mentions being shown off by Krause (1947). In his memoirs, Saadia Paz also expressed pride in the opportunities for women in the collective, but he interpreted it differently.

During the year in which the collective existed, we were able to convince the director that women should be allowed to have temporary jobs in the farm, and could thus learn farming. Our objective was to establish a settlement of guards, which would require that the men would leave from time to time to guard in various places, as permanent or temporary guards, and thus the wife could fill the husband's role when he was away . . . (Paz, 1937:518).

Many social movements involve a change in dress. The collective in Sejera was no exception. The women wore pants and other articles of men's clothing for practical reasons. Alexander Zaid wrote that the practice started after Zipporah came to Sejera dressed this way, and that Zvi Becker sewed the outfits for the women (Zaid, 1947:171). The women also carried arms (Zaid, 1947:172). Every morning before breakfast they cleaned their oxen and prepared for their work in the fields. The women were also responsible for the kitchen (Giladi, 1937:136). In the evenings the men and women of the collective gathered to prepare the next day's work and to study. Krause taught them about modern agriculture; Manya lectured on socialism; Yisrael Shohat discussed the affairs of the day; David Ben Gurion (not a member of the collective but also on the farm) gave Hebrew lessons, and a local Arab taught them Arabic (Shva, 1969). The collective established committees with specific functions, such as setting up the work assignments, and created ad hoc groups to settle disputes among members or with Krause.

The social relations among members and between them and Krause seem to have been excellent. The men and women of the collective admired Manya, Yisrael and Krause, who in turn admired each other and the members of the collective. Kayla wrote about Manya and Yisrael:

> Yisrael Shohat seemed to me to be a kind of Sheikh among his friends, and they were all under his personal influence and listened to him, even though they were all close to one another . . . I became a good friend of Manya Wilbushewitz, who was very strong, and her idea was that all women should be strong and could thus take part in all the difficult and dangerous work which men do (Giladi, 1937:136).

Shifra wrote about Manya: "Manya brought with her enthusiasm, and lively social and cultural life" (Betzer, 1947:505).

Manya had the same influence on Ester Becker.

> Manya was unlike the other women, both in her appearance and in her personality. She captivated me. Manya had enormous power of persuasion. She was the center of the life of the place. She approached everyone as a sister, as a mother. She was courageous in her nightly guard duty, and in riding on a wild horse. She had enormous initiative, she had a feel for new ideas, and actualized them in her life (Becker, 1947:510).

Despite the success of the collective, its contract was not renewed after its year had expired. Most of the men had other preferences, and the ICA refused to continue with the experiment. Thus they developed the Jewish guard organization, Hashomer. Some of the members stayed on, while most moved elsewhere. Five of the women stayed behind to train the newcomers and to take on other jobs (Giladi, 1937:139). Zipporah Zaid, for example, cooked meals for Alexander Zaid and Yitzhak Nadav because when the collective left, the communal kitchen was shut down. At the time, Yitzhak, Zipporah and Alexander lived together in a cave near the village, which Alexander felt was necessary so that they would achieve pure simplicity (Nadav, 1986:15). Yisrael Shohat was opposed to the women becoming guards, although he was persuaded to accept two (Zaid, 1947:174). Krause continued to give the women complete autonomy in managing the work and responsibility for training the newcomers, a situation which aggravated the newly arriving men.

It must be acknowledged that because Yisrael Shohat had brought his Bar Giora men to Sejera, he was as much the collective's leader as was Manya. During the experimental year, he convinced Manya that the idea of Jews assuming guard duty responsibility in place of Arabs was more important than continuing the collective agricultural experiment. Thus they established the Jewish guard organization, *Hashomer*. At the end of the contract period, Yisrael argued that the group was so small that it could not go on to Hauran to establish its own settlement, nor could it stay at Sejera which was a training farm. Moreover, Krause's superiors in Paris informed him that Manya could not stay at Sejera since she was a socialist. Thus, despite Manya's success, the group did not renew its agreement for another year with Krause. Manya and Yisrael became lovers at Sejera and in mid-May 1908, they married. Manya believed that only monogamous marriage complied with "the laws of nature". Rejecting free love, Manya was known for advocating freedom within marriage (Ben-Yocheved, 1937:389). Many couples followed Manya's and Yisrael's path and married. In subsequent years, most of these couples had children. Manya became instrumental in developing forms of collective childrearing although she was not successful in convincing the men of Hashomer to give women the same roles as men in guard duty.

Just as Manya had predicted on the basis of her studies, the Sejera collective fulfilled the conditions of their contract with Krause, repaid what it owed, and made a small profit. Her experiment vindicated her belief that a collective agricultural economy was a viable means of Jewish settlement in Palestine given the conditions that existed in Sejera. In addition, the collective model demonstrated that workers did not have to live in degrading conditions and could sustain a cultural life. The group's simultaneous success in establishing Hashomer, the guard organization, would become a focal point for the lives of most of the members for decades to come. Finally, the collective supported her conviction that women were as capable of agricultural work as were men. For Manya, at the age of twenty-seven, the completion of the contract ended her search to identify the ideal socio-economic conditions. It is not surprising that when looking back on that year, she wrote:

> That was the happiest year of my life. For all of us, those were beautiful days . . . We sensed that in the future our experiment would be used as a landmark for many of the workers who would go to the land of the Jewish National Fund to work on their own responsibility; we felt that we were creating a basis for collective work for the future, for ourselves, and our children after us.

The positive experiment in Sejera produced several important results according to Manya:

> [1] we overcame doubts about living, producing and working as a collective in Palestine and we forged a path for collective settlement; [2] in the course of the year the collective life and the common goals of the members in Sejera tied the members to one another deeply and permanently; [3] the collective framework made it possible for the members of *Bar Giora* to realize, to strengthen and further develop their self-confidence to establish Hashomer as a legal defense organization, that would train the population to defend whatever it had created, and to defend the whole nation. Only the Hauran plan we were not successful in realizing (quoted in Ben-Zvi, 1976:66; for a discussion of the group's relation to Hauran, see Zaid, 1947:173.)

Interestingly, in her list of achievements at Sejera, Manya did not mention the other victory—the demonstration of women's ability. This omission is remarkable because after Sejera, when the group was transformed into Hashomer and some women went on to Um-Juni (later Degania), the women became extensively dissatisfied with their roles. In the next agricultural collectives (i.e., early *kvutzot* and kibbutzim) women were excluded or confined to kitchen and laundry work (see Betzer, 1947; Izraeli, 1981). Because of these problems, Hanna Meisel established a separate training farm for women at Kinneret in 1911 (Shilo, 1981) and women workers organized by holding national meetings starting in Merhavia in 1914. Thus, Sejera has a unique place in the history of Jewish women in Palestine and in the history of socialist experiments. The ridicule of women by men was largely suppressed at Sejera during the collective period because of Manya's personal charisma, Krause's values, and the sheer number of women which made them a substantial portion of the group. In the next collectives (kvutzot) established by groups at Degania and Kinneret, these factors were missing (see Betzer:1947).

The evolution of Manya Wilbushewitz's thought and action until 1907 thus took many different paths, which was characteristic of young Russian Jews of her time. Her supportive siblings, personal courage, close relations with a wide variety of people, perseverance, and charismatic personality may have made her even more open than others to the currents of contemporary thought. Although she went on to accomplish many similarly creative goals, her creation of the first Jewish agricultural collective in Palestine became a key factor in the creation of a strong socialist component of Israeli society. The role of a woman in laying the foundation for the subsequent development of kibbutzim, and the special role of women in Sejera are two of the many overlooked aspects of this period.

References

Becker, Ester. 1947. "From the Life of a *Shomer* Family: My Entry into the Guarding of Sejera," pp. 509–520 in *The Book of the Second Aliyah*, edited by Bracha Habas. Tel Aviv: Am Oved (Hebrew).

Ben-Yocheved. 1937. "Dvorah Dreckler," pp. 386–393 in *The Hashomer Anthology*. Tel Aviv: Archive and Museum of the Labor Movement (Hebrew).

Ben-Zvi, Yanait, Rahel. 1976. *Manya Shohat*. Jerusalem: Yad Yitzhak Ben-Zvi (Hebrew).

Bernstein, Deborah. 1987. *The Struggle for Equality: Urban Women Workers in Prestate Israeli Society*. New York: Praeger.

Betzer, Shifra. 1947. "With the First Ones in Um-Juni and Merchavia," pp. 504–506 in *The Book of the Second Aliyah*, edited by Bracha Habas. Tel Aviv: Am Oved (Hebrew).

Chizick, Hanna. 1947. "Haim Shturman," p. 720 in *The Book of the Second Aliyah*, edited by Bracha Habas. Tel Aviv: Am Oved (Hebrew).

Dash, Joan. 1979. *Summoned to Jerusalem: The Life of Henrietta Szold.* New York: Harper & Row.

Frankel, Rafel. 1981. "Ideological Variations in the Forms of Collectives in the Days of the Second *Aliyah.*" *Katedra*, 18:112–117 (Hebrew).

Giladi, Kayla. 1981. "Jewish Girls Plough with Oxen," p. 62 in *The Beginning of the Kibbutz*, edited by Tsur Muki, Yair Zevulun and Hanina Porat. Tel Aviv: Sifriat Poalim (Hebrew).

Giladi, Kayla. 1937. "From Sejera to Kfar Giladi," pp. 135–146 in *The Hashomer Anthology*. Tel Aviv: Archive and Museum of the Labor Movement (Hebrew).

Givoni, Moshe. 1937. "The First Days," pp. 528–531 in *The Hashomer Anthology*. Tel Aviv: Archive and Museum of the Labor Movement (Hebrew).

Hankin, Haya-Sara. 1937. "Wanderings," p. 151 in *The Hashomer Anthology*. Tel Aviv: Archive and Museum of the Labor Movement (Hebrew).

Izraeli, N. Dafna. 1981. "The Zionist Women's Movement in Palestine, 1911–1927." *Signs*, 7:87–114.

Krigser, Sarah. 1947. "The Start of our Agricultural Training," pp. 506–509 in *The Book of the Second Aliyah*, edited by Bracha Habas. Tel Aviv: Am Oved (Hebrew).

Maimon, Ada. 1960. *Women Build a Land*. New York: Herzl Press.

Mandel, Neville. 1976. *The Arabs and Zionism before World War I*. Berkeley, CA: University of California Press.

Michaeli, Ben Zion. 1973. *Sejera, Its History and Personalities*. Tel Aviv: Am Oved (Hebrew).

Nadav, Isaac. 1986. *Memoirs of a "Hahosmer" Member*. Israel: Ministry of Defense Publishing House (Hebrew).

Near, Henry. 1983. "To Each, His Degania." *Katedra*, 29:63–78 (Hebrew).

Paz, Saadia. 1947. "The Collective in Sejera," pp. 363–364 in *The Book of the Second Aliyah*, edited by Bracha Habas. Tel Aviv: Am Oved (Hebrew).

Paz, Saadia. 1937. "Conquests," pp. 516–525 in *The Hashomer Anthology*. Tel Aviv: Archive and Museum of the Labor Movement (Hebrew).

Schama, Simon. 1978. *Two Rothschilds and the Land of Israel*. New York: Simon and Schuster.

Shapiro, Joseph. 1961. *Work and Land*. Tel Aviv: Am Oved (Hebrew).

Shilo, Margalit. 1981. "The Women's Farm at Kinneret, 1911–1917: A Solution of the Problem of the Working Woman in the Second *Aliyah.*" *The Jerusalem Cathedra*, 1:246–283.

Shohat, Manya. 1904. "Chapters from the Beginning. A. Seeking a way." Mimeograph. Yad Ben-Zvi Archives, Jerusalem (Hebrew).

———. 1930. "The Collective." pp. 3–7 in *Women Workers Speak*, edited by Rachel Katznelson Shazar. Tel Aviv: Moetzet Hapoalot (Hebrew).

———. 1932. "In the Beginning: the Collective," pp. 19–26 in *The Plough Woman: Records of the Pioneer Women of Palestine*, edited by Rachel Katznelson-Shazar. New York: Nicholas L. Brown, Inc.

———. 1937. "Guard duty in the land," pp. 51–56 in *The Hashomer Anthology*. Tel Aviv: Archive and Museum of the Labor Movement (Hebrew).

———. 1961. "The Roots of the Kibbutz Family." *Al Hamishmar*, 4.9.61:8 (Hebrew).

Shva, Shlomo. 1969. *The Daring Tribe*. Merhavia: Sifriat Poalim (Hebrew).

Smilansky, Moshe. 1947. "First Meetings," pp. 691–697 in *The Book of the Second Aliyah*, edited by Bracha Habas. Tel Aviv: Am Oved (Hebrew).

Urofsky, Melvin. 1975. *American Zionism from Herzl to the Holocaust*. New York: Garden City, Anchor Press.

Weizmann, Chaim. 1949. *Trial and Error*. New York: Schocken Books.

Wilbush, Nahum. 1963. *Expedition to Uganda*. Jerusalem: Zionist Library (Hebrew).

Wilbush, Nahum. 1974. "The Routes of My Life: Autobiography of Nahum Wilbush," pp. 9–18 in *Haroshet Hamaaseh: Anthology of the History of Industry in Israel. Memorial Book for Nahum Wilbush, Pioneer of Innovative Jewish Industry in Palestine*, edited by Shmuel Avitzur. Tel Aviv: Melo, Ltd. (Hebrew).

Zaid, Alexander. 1947. "The First Days," pp. 165–178 in *The Book of the Second Aliyah*, edited by Bracha Habas. Tel Aviv: Am Oved Press (Hebrew).

5

The Women's Farm at Kinneret, 1911–1917: A Solution to the Problem of the Working Woman in the Second Aliyah*

—————— *Margalit Shilo* ——————

In 1911 something without precedent was created within the Jewish community in Palestine: a women's farm at Kinneret in the lower Galilee. It was open to women only, since the workers' farms in general were closed to them except for kitchen and domestic duties. It was typical: only Jewish male laborers, for the most part as yet unskilled, worked on the farm at Kinneret. But no one felt that this same privilege should be granted the young female pioneer who came to the land with the same purpose and aspirations as her male counterparts (Meisel, 1967:21).

The story of this farm is more than a description of one of the Zionist institutions that developed in the country during the period of the Second Aliyah. It spotlights a grave problem which has received scant attention till now: the problem of the "*poelet*", the female farm-worker.[1] What was her goal in life and how did she try to achieve it? How did her male co-workers relate to her? How did the settlement institutions view her, and what solutions did they suggest? A description of the founding and development of this farm sheds light on these questions and presents the main solution to the problem of the female worker of that period.

Increase in Women Farm-Workers

What was woman's place in the agricultural settlements? During the First Aliyah the settlers came with their wives, who be-

---

*This article first appeared in Hebrew, in *Cathedra*, No. 14, 1980. The chapter in this volume is a shortened version of the original one.

came housewives in the new settlements. Agricultural matters, however, were generally outside their concern, and during that period we know of few women farm-workers. Furthermore, these farmers did not give their daughters (nor in many instances their sons) an agricultural education. The women and girls of the settlements did not consider themselves to be involved in farming (Smilansky, 1909:11–12; Ettinger, 1919:1). Even the women of Jaffa and Ahuzat Bayit (later Tel Aviv) did not see employment outside the home as a challenge, and rarely went to work. When Sara Thon presented statistics about women's work in Jaffa, she pointed out that Jewish women should be educated and taught that work is not shameful (1910:1063). The tendency to hire outside laborers and to minimize one's own work, which was prevalent during the First Aliyah, was not fertile soil for the growth of women farm-workers.

The Zionist Movement granted women full equal rights. Nonetheless, the women created a separate framework for themselves within that movement—the Women's Organization for Cultural Activity in Palestine—which sought Zionist solutions to their special problems. The woman's image in the Zionist Movement was completely traditional; her place was in the home, the school, or the office (*Altneuland*). Among the dozens of Zionist leaders we find not one woman. Ussishkin's 1905 settlement plan for young men from Eastern Europe made no provision for the immigration of young women, other than those accompanying their husbands or fiancés. In theory there was equality, but in practice there was no change in their traditional status or functions.

Among the many accomplishments to be credited to the pioneers of the Second Aliyah in their development of the Jewish community in Palestine, the creation of a new female image—the working woman—deserves special note. Only with the arrival of the first young women of the Second Aliyah, women who were no different from their male colleagues in their longing to work the land, did the Jewish community become aware of the phenomenon of the woman farm-worker. In the nature of things a young woman had to fight doubly hard to make Aliyah. To leave her home called for twice the effort required by her male counterpart. It is against the background of these obstacles and the even greater difficulties she encountered once she arrived in Palestine, that we note the remarkable fact that almost every one of these girls was of a special calibre, having unusual fighting spirit and unique attributes which alone enabled her to break new ground.

Alongside the men who came for the most part as individuals, young women began to arrive. Their number did not exceed a few dozen in the first decade of the century, and only toward the end of the Second Aliyah, in 1911, were they a few hundred.[2]

The girls were young (16–17), just like the boys, and most were unmarried. All came from the same social background, they were born in Eastern Europe and grew up in the workers' parties. The circumstances they encountered in Palestine were not favorable, their living conditions were unbearable, a woman could not squeeze into the men's living quarters, but needed a corner of her own. That corner was not available because no one was concerned about it. The women's writings often mention the fact that in the summer they lived outdoors, while in the winter they found "refuge" in the storehouse or in the kitchen (Liberson, in Katznelson-Shazar, 1930:7–9). An almost total neglect of minimal hygienic conditions characterized the life of the workers in general and the women in particular. Only when the situation became completely intolerable, and the miserable living conditions exacted their toll in lives, did the workers realize that they must seek to correct it.

What image should the woman farm-worker choose to emulate? Should she be like the male worker, the Russian woman farmer, or the Arab peasant woman? It was during the Second Aliyah that the woman worker sought her identity and found it. These were the years in which a new and innovative figure was delineated: the working woman who saw farming as her life's work and was prepared to stand on her own. The archetype of this working-woman was Sara Malkin. Her struggle paved the way for all who followed in her footsteps (Malkin, 1946).[3] In her letter to Hapoel Hatzair (1912) she accurately described the dilemma which a young woman faced upon her arrival in Palestine. While in her young Zionist group, she had fought as an equal, alongside the men, for the right to make Aliyah and settle the land. However, upon her arrival, the equality vanished: the men went out to work the fields while farm-work was unavailable to women. Nor did finding routine but difficult farm work generally solve her problem, since she was then faced with a demand for physical labor beyond the capacity of the average woman.[4] Until the establishment of the women's farm at Kinneret, most of the girls earned their livelihood in sewing, housework, and services (Sturman, 1944:4; Malkin, 1947:491). The fundamental struggle for the right to be a full partner, and for equal rights to work the soil, brought with it a new concept of the woman's role. No longer did she see herself primarily as wife and mother, that ranked second, after achieving the goal of fulfillment through working the soil. This new purpose became of primary importance for the woman, and her traditional mission was relegated to a secondary place in the hierarchy of values.

The Attitude Toward Women Workers

The woman's desire to work the land met a major obstacle in the objections of those making the work assignments. They did not provide her with agricultural work, even of a kind that matched her ability. From the outset she faced the absolute refusal of the farmers to employ her. The farmers, opposed to Jewish labor in general, were not sparing in their opposition to women's labor and negated it in even sharper terms. They claimed that it was unethical to engage a woman in hard physical work. Their opposition was not specifically to employing a woman in the fields, but rather to her very freedom and her desire to live alone, to work with the men, to openly announce her equal status, and to lead, as it seemed to them, an immoral life. The actions of the young women, even more than those of the men, appeared to the traditionalists as an attack on their world view and a desecration of the Holy Land (Even-Shoshan, 1963:208–22). The farmers took care to keep their daughters away from the new, non-conforming pioneer women.

Nor did women's lot improve even when their male colleagues were distributing the work. Sara Malkin left Kinneret in protest against not being allowed to raise chickens (Dayan, 1935:60), while Miriam Baratz outsmarted the men. She learned how to milk cows from an Arab village woman and forced the members of the collective (*kvutza*) in Degania to allow her to milk (ibid. 56–57). Tehiya Liberson had better luck. After Sara Malkin proved that lack of suitable work leads the woman worker to leave the collective, she was given the privilege of clearing stones and doing chores in the barn (in Katznelson-Shazar, 1930:9). The men did invite the women to participate in their labor collectives, but only to manage the housekeeping (Baratz, 1948:52).

It seems that the male workers who adopted a new ideology and life style for themselves did not include the young women who came with them in their experiences. They viewed women as housekeepers who would take care of all their needs. The men who wrestled with difficult problems of survival paid no attention at all to the dead end in which the women found themselves. In Degania, in Merhavia, and in the workers' groups, the woman worker was not accepted as a member with equal rights, but as an unofficial member only (concerning Degania, see Even-Shoshan, 1963:213; concerning Merhavia, see E. Becker, 1947:517). This discrimination was expressed in refusing women the opportunity to do farm work, denying them the right to vote at membership meetings, and in paying them a lower wage than that paid to men. The latter, more than anything else, expressed the value placed on women's labor.[5] Even in the spring of 1914, most workers' settlements would employ women only in their traditional tasks; resentment was openly expressed by the women at their first conventions.

The women workers' first achievement actually occurred at the Jewish Colonization Association farm in Sejera. There is certainly nothing accidental in the fact that the first collective initiated by a woman was the first place where six young women were assigned farmhand's work, ploughing with oxen, which required great physical strength. Among the women who later remained at Sejera was Hanna Meisel who, as a result of her experience there, conceived the idea of the women's farm. The experience at Sejera was a breakthrough which proved that women must be given consideration, and that their ability cannot be treated lightly.

The turning point came with the recognition of the importance of labor not only for women, but for the entire agricultural economy. The shift in the structure of the farm and the transition from the exclusive cultivation of orchards, or field crops, to as mixed and varied a farm economy as possible—a process which began during the period of the Second Aliyah and was extensively developed at the Ben-Shemen farm—also contributed decisively to changing the perception of woman's place in agriculture (Even-Shoshan, 1963: 212).

Arthur Ruppin (head of the Palestine Office of the Zionist Executive, the first Zionist agency in Eretz Israel founded in 1908), frequently stressed the woman's importance to the farm economy. His approach was purely practical. One must lend a hand to women in order to further agriculture (Ruppin, 1968:108–111; Ruppin, 1912:6). In his report to the Eleventh Zionist Congress he stated unequivocally:

> We have been so busy till now training the male farmer that we have completely forgotten the female farmer. Nevertheless, it is impossible to dispense with her help. Many farmers cannot run an

orderly household nor improve their farm because the women do not know how to manage household affairs (Ruppin, 1937:56).

Hanna Meisel

The women's intense desire to take their place alongside men in working the land, and the growing recognition that women were essential to the agricultural economy, paved the way for setting up a special women's farm. It was Hanna Meisel (1883–1972), a person of strong personality, capacity for work, and understanding of others, who initiated the idea and carried it out (Harari, 1959:343–46; Dayan, 1967:233–39).

Meisel had studied agronomy in Europe, and was the first woman in the country with a higher education in agriculture. Upon her arrival in Palestine in 1909, she worked in Judea, and then went to the Sejera farm in Galilee, where she and two other women took charge of the vegetable garden. Hapoel Hatzair sent her as its delegate to the Eleventh Zionist Congress. She took an active part in the Women Workers' Convention held in Merhavia in 1914, and even was a member of the Galilee Workers' Committee. From the very outset Meisel strove to chart a new course for women—selective agricultural work according to their particular abilities.

Hanna identified both with Ruppin's view that woman's work must be encouraged in order to make things easier for the farmer and the farm economy, and with the women who saw their fulfillment and salvation only in agricultural work. She created a synthesis of both viewpoints: agricultural work that would be useful to the farm while satisfying women's yearnings and emphasizing their importance in their own right. As a result, unlike the women workers, Hanna stressed the need for household management and, in contrast to the Palestine Office of the Zionist Executive, she emphasized the woman worker's independence and the possibility of her maintaining herself without depending on men.

The Women's Organization

The Women's Organization for Cultural Work in Palestine was established in 1907 at the Eighth Zionist Congress at the Hague. Betty Lishansky, one of the heads of the organization, described its purposes in a letter: "Educating young women in Palestine and finding means of subsistence for them; establishing hospitals and training nurses; fighting the exploitation of women." (Letter of briefing to Warburg, 14 July 1911, CZA, L1/20, translated from German). The organization's most important accomplishment was the establishment of embroidery workshops—first in Jaffa, in 1908, and then in Jerusalem, Tiberas, Ekron, and Safed. Their purpose was to provide occupation for girls who were deteriorating in idleness, and to teach them a skill that would give them a livelihood; also to teach them to read and write Hebrew and give them a positive feeling about the country. The products of the workshops were sent abroad where they were sold by members of the Organization. The number of trainees grew steadily; in 1913 there were 400, of whom 90 percent were from Oriental communities.[6] The organization also undertook cultural work among the Jewish women in the Diaspora, Zionist propaganda, education of youth, and community work among women.

In addition to the crafts' workshops, the organization in Palestine helped to establish the first Jewish hospital in Haifa, headed by Dr. Auerbach, supported the *Shaarei Zion* Hospital in Jaffa, and helped found the women's farm in Kinneret. Sara Thon, wife of Jacob Thon, the assistant director of the Palestine Office, organized the women's activities in the country. Most of the members, especially the more active ones, were wives of men involved in the Zionist Movement. Sara Thon was the moving spirit; she expressed her positions vigorously, openly, and without fear.

The Establishment of the Women's Farm

After spending about a year in Palestine, Hanna Meisel returned to Europe where she spoke to various concerned parties about establishing the women's farm (7 November 1910, 13 December 1910, CZA L2/257 II). At the beginning of October 1910, Otto Warburg wrote to Ruppin, reporting on Hanna's visit and the budget proposal she presented. Warburg was favorably impressed with the idea and asked Ruppin to reach a decision. The proposal was for a farm for fifteen girls, with a barn, chicken coop, vegetable garden and fields, on an area of 100 dunams (25 acres). According to Hanna, the initial expense would come to 22,600 frances and the annual budget would be 6,000 francs (Warburg to Ruppin, 1 November 1910, CZA L2/21 I). While in Berlin, Hanna met with the representatives of the Women's Organization and got their agreement in principle to support the farm. It was decided that the Jewish National Fund would lease the land, with the Women's Organization bearing the rental costs and the ongoing expenses.

Hanna Meisel and her girls reached Kinneret at the beginning of April 1911 (first report was sent in March 1911, CZA L1/97). Unlike the original plan, however, a separate farm was not set up; the girls joined the Kinneret men's training farm which had been established three years earlier. They were a separate but dependent body, an arrangement that lasted about one and a half years as discussed below.

Why was the farm set up at Kinneret? Undoubtedly Ruppin was guided first and foremost by economic considerations. Kinneret had land with plentiful water where vegetables could be raised. Moreover, the Kinneret farm was in a difficult situation. A workers' strike had led to the removal of the farm's manager. The farm was not fully occupied and there was a desperate need to put it back on a firm basis. The women's farm which was to receive ongoing funding for its manager and workers, and which paid rent for the land, seemed to promise an improvement in the financial condition of Kinneret. Moreover, setting up the farm at Kinneret would bring about a noticeable saving in its basic expenses. Ruppin, who had been criticized for wasting money on the Kinneret (men's) farm, was reluctant to set up another large and expensive establishment, and preferred to set up a smaller farm that would first prove itself, and only thereafter function on a larger scale.

Goals of the Farm

Unlike the male workers' farm at Kinneret, which was established primarily to provide employment, and only secondarily as a center for agricultural training and as a model farm, the main function of the women's farm was to train women for agricultural work and for household management. Speaking about the farm at a workers' meeting in the spring of 1915, Hanna Meisel said clearly that she did not intend it to be an institution in which women would find work, but one which would provide an agricultural education to young girls who wished it (WWC, 1914:12–13). Unlike the men's farm which, it had been hoped, would be profitable from the outset, the women's farm was planned as a place that would not be self sustaining. Hanna Meisel stressed that an educational institution must be supported in order to cover the special expenses involved, and that it should not seek to produce profits (Meisel to Lishansky, 14 February 1912, CZA 2L/255). Since a student could not earn enought to support herself, each girl received a monthly stipend paid by the Women's Organization.

What image of the working-woman did the farm seek to create? Did its purposes change over the years, and was there agreement on this subject among all those concerned? Hanna Meisel did have a clear idea, although there were differing emphases in her talks to different audiences. Her primary goal was to create a farm woman with agricultural skills, especially in those farmyard activities suited to a woman, who was also to manage household affairs in a rational, orderly manner. Her aim was:

> . . . to educate Jewish girls to order, cleanliness, and system. I wanted the girls to learn vegetable growing, gardening, planting fruit trees and a few flowers, something about chickens and, as needed, to care for a cow. They should also learn cooking and sewing (Letter to Thon, 3 January 1912, CZA L2/255 I).

The farm reflected the goals of the founder: emphasis was placed on farm work, while household management took second place (see below). This concept gained the support of the Women's Organization and the Palestine Office; both groups were in favor of creating an image of a good, efficient woman farmer who would help the rural economy (see Thon, 1913:7).

A different view was expressed by the women workers whose fate the farm was trying to determine; but it was not heard openly before the farm was established. The rift that was created between them and Hanna Meisel as a result of their different outlook will be treated below.

The Organization and Management of the Farm

The farm functioned for only six and one-half years. From April 1911 to September 1912, it was part of the (male) workers' farm at Kinneret. Starting in October 1912, the farm became an independent operation. From the outbreak of the First World War in August 1914 until its end in August 1917, the farm felt the impact of the war.

The beginning was extremely modest. Hanna Meisel came to the farm with four girls who were soon joined by two others, and the farm work began.[7] Hanna was the instructor and work-manager for vegetable gardening, chicken-raising, the plant nursery, and the kitchen. From the outset, she focused on those occupations that she wanted to develop as areas of women's farming. For their work and supervision of the girls she received a monthly wage of one hundred francs from the Women's Organization in Berlin. Hanna and her girls lived in the nearby settlement of Kinneret. These first steps were considered a preparatory stage to setting up an independent women's farm in August 1911.

The girls worked both outdoors and in the house, and received half their salary from the Women's Organization and half from the Kinneret farm. Their salaries were not identical, varying from thirty to fifty francs a month (10 April 1912, CZA L2/255 I). The emphasis at the farm was on agricultural work but it was decided that on hot or rainy days the girls would work at sewing work clothes for the (male) workers. It was even suggested that the girls take care of the sick workers, but the Women's Organization objected, out of concern for the girls' health. After a while, it was decided to teach the girls dairy farming, and to train them to work in the plant nursery and in field planting. At first they ran a large community kitchen for themselves and the male workers. But due to various difficulties, and because of the desire for independence, it was decided to maintain a separate kitchen. During the winter season the girls were taught botany by Hanna Meisel. As more girls applied, the "graduates" were shifted to Sejera in order to make space for others to be trained at the farm. At Sejera they did farm work and retained contact with Hanna who continued to guide them (Meisel to Lishansky, 14 February 1912, CZA L2/255 I).

Even though the Women's Farm gained supporters during the first year, Hanna was not satisfied. She was dissatisfied, above all, with the inclusion of the women's farm in the men's farm in Kinneret (letter to B. Lishansky, 14 February 1912, CZA L2/255 I). Joel Golda, the director of the men's farm, did not like the idea of another (female) director at Kinneret and, from the start, there was neither community of interests nor common language between them (Malkin, 1912:14). Golda hoped to benefit financially from the girls, and the first dispute arose over their working wages; he wanted to pay them as little as possible (Meisel, 13 June 1911, CZA L1/20). Hanna did not spare her criticism of the disorder and lack of planning prevalent at the farm, and pointed out that it was impossible to educate girls for agricultural work in such a place (Meisel to Thon, 3 January 1912, CZA L2/255 I). In summing up the first period in the history of the farm she said: "It was a women' farm without a farm" (CZA A76 report translated from German).

The Period of Consolidation

The solution to the women's farm was found at Kinneret. After Joel Golda left the farm and the *Ha'ikkar Hatzair* collective[8] took over, the number of men living at the farm decreased considerably, and part of it was rented out to the girls. Hanna Meisel's dream was realized: the women's farm became an independent institution with an area for living quarters and its own piece of land. A wall was raised between the women's farm and the workers' farm to assure the girls' privacy (Meisel, 1 August 1912, CZA KKL 2/17 I). In the farm house, which had been built as Bermann's residence, the top floor was designated for the girls' living quarters and the grounds in front of the building were set aside as a garden in their care. In addition, they were assigned seventy dunams (about eighteen acres) of the farm's fields. It was about a half-hour's walk from the house to the fields.

The lease was drawn up between the Women's Organization which was financially responsible for the farm and Arthur Ruppin, the director of the Palestine Development Company. The rental was set at two to four percent of the estimated value of the property leased (CZA L2/77 I). Ruppin was, at one and the same time, a supporter of the farm concept and a person with a financial interest in its success, who was concerned with receiving income from the property whose owners he represented. The Women's Organization, which was carrying the main financial burden for the farm, had no professional knowledge of farming, and the full weight of the project rested on the shoulders of Hanna Meisel, who often felt herself alone and lacking adequate support.

The number of girls at the farm was not fixed and varied between fourteen and twenty-two. During the years of the farm's existence, a total of about seventy girls studied there (Meisel, CZA A76, report translated from German). Most of them immigrants from Eastern Europe; a few were from the *moshavot*, the Jewish villages in Eretz Israel founded at the turn of the century. At first they stayed at the farm for a period of one year; then, beginning in 1913, two years. With the increase in the number of women pioneers, the number of applicants to the farm grew.

The girls generally had little education, and some were even illiterate. They were of different ages. The director preferred to take girls of about sixteen years old who would fit into the learning framework of the farm more easily. The girls' salary remained as it was when the farm was started. Although a suggestion was made that they pay for their stay at the farm, it seems that this was never put into effect.

Life at the farm took on a routine of eight to nine hours of work during the day, plus study in the evening. Every evening the work schedule for the next day was planned jointly. In October 1913, a special teacher was appointed for household management.[9] Each girl gained experience in every area of farm work (Navratzky, 1914:311–20).

Branches of the Farm Economy

The farm's importance undoubtedly stemmed from the development of "women's branches" of agriculture which had, till then, received very little attention from Jewish farmers. From the start, the farm concentrated on these areas, sought new ways to expand them, and developed the special work systems needed for them. The men's work on the farm was minimal—ploughing and clearing rocks. The girls did the rest.

As the farm was becoming consolidated, a new branch of agriculture was developing on Jewish farms, the dairy barn. The small barn prospered under the women, and alongside it they put up a chicken-coop. The farm took pride in providing everything it needed for its own sustenance. Thus, Hanna Meisel achieved her goal with the establishment of a self sufficient Jewish farm.

Hanna's chief interests were the orchards and vegetable gardens. The farm specialized in raising various kinds of vegetables and in a highly developed nursery which provided hundreds of lemon, olive, almond, and eucalyptus seedlings for the area's farmers. The girls had to handle the sales as well, and some shied away from this "non-creative" task. But there were those among them who identified with the Russian peasant woman who brought her garden produce to the market. They also began the experimental planting of bananas, which had not yet been grown in the country (Krigser, 1947:508). Eucalyptus trees were nurtured to dry the swamp and improve the air. A decorative flower garden was another innovation.

Although household management was not one of Hanna

Meisel's favorite areas, and despite the fact that it was not considered "real work" (see below) by the girls, Hanna insisted on its being part of a farm economy that would provide all its needs in a rational manner.

The Pattern of Life

The shore of Lake Kinneret had a special emotional impact on the young people of the Second Aliyah. In every discussion of the pros and cons of the farm site, the lake's unique, almost mystical, effect on its residents was emphasized. "Lake Kinneret is not just scenery, not just a segment of nature—the destiny of a people is encapsulated in its name. From within it our past peers out at us with a thousand eyes. With a thousand lips it speaks to our hearts" (Rachel, 1960:199–200). Undoubtedly this exalted sentiment was fostered by the beauty of the place and the fact of its having nurtured several "firsts", the first Jewish National Fund study-farm for workers; the first collective—Degania; the first study-farm for women. The girls of the farm and, above all, Hanna Meisel were susceptible to the beauty of the surroundings and landscape (Meisel to Ruppin, 31 October 1912, CZA L2/255 I).

Many came knocking at the farm gates, so that it was almost always overcrowded (CZA 23/1634). The climate and the swampy land caused much illness. Much of the reports about the farm dealt with the girls' health, which improved or worsened according to the season of the year (31 October 1912, CZA L2/255 I; July 1913, ibid. 23 January 1914, CZA L2/258 I). To prevent this as much as possible, an attempt was made in 1914 to dry the swamp by planting eucalyptus trees (26 March 1914, CZA L2/77 II). The beneficial effect was immediate.

The security situation at the farm had its ups and downs according to events in the region generally. Since only girls lived there, those responsible felt a very special concern. In 1914, as the security situation in the region deteriorated greatly, special precautions were taken at the farm; the girls went out to the fields with an armed escort. The farm had to shoulder the special security expenses along with its neighbors (December 1913, CZA L2/77 II). There is no evidence that the girls shared in guard duty or learned to use arms. It would appear that for all of the aspirations to equality in matters agricultural, there was no such intention in the realm of security.

Hebrew was the language spoken at the farm. The girls were
even more zealous about this than the men, and influenced the
neighboring men's farm. Sabbath and holidays were marked by the
girls with outings and general recreation, but the lifestyle was free
of religious bonds. In spite of the criticism voiced by the Women's
Organization, the Sabbath was not observed and the Jewish holidays assumed a secular cast at the Women's Farm (report of A.
Bambus to S. Thon—CZA L2/254 II; Criticism of Women's Organization, Lishansky to Thon, 9 January 1914, CZA 2L/254 II).

In spite of the difficult external conditions, a positive atmosphere, of pleasure and satisfaction in creating a new pattern of life,
generally prevailed at the farm. Hanna Meisel continually emphasized the fact that the girls were diligent, showed ability, and
worked with happiness and love (14 February 1912, CZA L2/255 I).
The girls' recollections of their stay are filled with nostalgia; their
attitude to the farm and its founder was one of love and joy. It was
clear that one effect of a stay at the farm was a sense of spiritual
exaltation. The poetess Rachel expressed her felt sentiments of
that period in poetic language:

> We yearned for sacrifice, torture, prison chains, that we might
> sanctify on-high the name of our homeland . . . more than one of
> us shook with malaria on her meagre cot. Yet not for a moment
> did any of us lose the feeling of gratitude for her lot. We worked
> with exalted spirits . . . (1960:210).

Differences of Opinion

Alongside the high spirits and the sense of satisfaction there
were also differences of opinion at the farm. The women did not
always agree with what Hanna Meisel had determined to be the
path they should choose:

> Not everything was acceptable. We aspired to blur the difference
> between us and the men . . . and here it seemed as if someone
> wanted to impose special women's functions on us once again. It
> was not to our liking for the most part. What sort of future is it, to
> be farmers' wives? And, above all, who thinks about this in the
> bloom of youth, when hearts yearn strongly for great and as yet
> unrevealed things?! (Bluwstein, 1940:27).

At the first women-workers' convention held in Merhavia in
1914, Hanna admitted openly that there was a difference of opin-

ion between her pupils and herself about what the woman's goal should be. She saw before her the "question of the rural working woman," whereas the girls saw before them the "Jewish woman worker". The girls' negative attitude to learning household management stemmed from this difference in perception.

In spite of the encouraging reports that the girls were adjusting to Meisel's demands, it seems that their opposition did not cease. Shoshana Bluwstein put it in a candid, harsh fashion:

> The girls object [to home economics]. What sort of subject is that! All their lives women have worked in the kitchen. "Kitchen and children" has been the slogan throughout the generations. What did a woman see in her life? she never left the children's room or the kitchen . . . the kitchen is a bitter necessity, but to make a goal of it? (ibid.)

The girls' resentment of housekeeping was reflected in the neglect and disorder around them. No doubt this expressed their revulsion at the idea of "ordered life" and "domesticity".[10] Nonetheless, Hanna stressed that the girls who came to the farm must accept its authority. The girls were students for whom she was responsible—she admitted them and she dismissed them. But the girls suggested that they be more involved in setting farm policy and in deciding upon the admission of new girls. For all this, the girls did not harbor feelings of bitterness or rebellion. They looked upon Hanna as an "older sister" and felt affection for her. "We loved Hanna very much", as one of the women students wrote many years later.[11]

At the women-workers' convention in Merhavia, the comings and goings, the women who left the farm, were specifically mentioned. And yet, without a doubt, this constant coming and going must be seen against the "wanderlust" phenomenon which characterized the workers of the Second Aliyah and was an expression of their inner turmoil.

Criticism was leveled at Hanna Meisel by the Women's Organization as well, which felt that the farm was being run too loosely, without any discipline. As they put it, the farm should be suitable for the daughters of good families too, not only for Russian revolutionaries. In addition, the Organization was sensitive to the criticism of the religious circles (e.g., 16 May 1911, CZA L2/257 II; 30 January 1914, CZA A 148/37).

Hanna was not influenced by the Organization's criticism, but she did listen to the girls. In her plans for a new study-farm she stressed that the girls should also be educated for their mission as agricultural workers.

The Farm During the War

In August 1914, a new period began for the country. The First World War brought destruction to the Jewish community in Palestine, first by severing the country from its centers of funding in the Diaspora and then by expulsions, ruin, illness, and famine. The Jewish community was impoverished and over one-third was exiled or died.

During the war, and probably because of it, the stream of girls to the farm increased. The difficult conditions in the country were especially hard on the weaker elements of the population. The farm was a refuge for girls who no longer could earn a living in the Judean settlements. From the start, the Women's Farm was the place where the girls could find work, and with the outbreak of war this assumed greater validity (e.g., December 1916, CZA KKL2/171 I; 18 February 1916, CZA Z3/1473).

The Women's Farm was affected by the war from the very start. In a report dated August 1914, Ruppin emphasized, among other things, that the Palestine Office had informed the training-farms that they must reduce their expenses (CZA Z3/1457). Preserving what was, while marking time and worrying about providing for tomorrow's needs—this was the farm's guiding purpose during the three years till the war's end. In war as in peace, the farm's full burden fell on the shoulders of Hanna Meisel who worried not only about its continued survival, but also dealt with fund raising, and the special problems raised by the war (14 May 1915, CZA Z3/1473).

The number of girls at the farm remained as it was before, about twenty, plus two teachers who remained there: Hayyuta and Sara Bussel. The budget was a major problem. In September 1914, a letter came from the Women's Organization saying that it could no longer guarantee the farm's expenses (27 September 1914, CZA L2/77 II).

At the end of 1915, the number of girls went down to seventeen, then to fourteen. In 1916, the budget was reduced even more. A year later Hanna wrote that everything had doubled in price over the previous year (Meisel's report, 1917, CZA L2/77 II). She stresssed that the farm's special problems were aggravated because there was no institution in the country responsible for it, while the war made it especially difficult to be dependent on a distant organization. She expressed her opinion that it would be most desirable for the Palestine Office to take the farm under its wing. She repeated this request often throughout the war, but got no response. Neither was the Jewish National Fund willing to provide relief.

Natural mishaps were added to the war troubles. A plague of locusts in the spring of 1915 caused severe agricultural damage, even though at Kinneret and in the entire Galilee the damage was not the heaviest (Meisel's report, 10 January 1916, CZA L2/77 II). In the spring of 1916, the Jordan rose and flooded the farm's vegetable garden. In the winter of 1917, heavy rains inundated the fields (30 April 1916, 24 May 1917, CZA L2/77 II).

The sanitation situation also deteriorated. The girls who came to the farm during the war were generally younger and weaker than their predecessors and were harder hit by these problems. Friction developed between the farm and the neighboring collective of Kinneret.

The Closing of the Farm

Alongside the deliberations and efforts to maintain the farm, from time to time the possibility was raised of closing it. As early as October 1914, Hanna Meisel expressed her fear that this might be necessary (3 October 1914, CZA A 148/37). The fear was premature and, until January 1916, the Women's Organization continued its regular support. But from then on, closing was considered much more seriously.

In January 1917, deliberations about closing the place began once again, even though the farm was then valued even more. The additional year of war had aggravated the financial condition of all the parties involved. At meetings held at the Thon home in Jerusalem in the summer of 1917, Jacob Thon and Hanna Meisel again presented proposals to continue the farm, but the budget ran out. In the summer of 1917 the farm was closed (CZA L2/77 II). To prevent its deterioration, Hanna Meisel remained there with a group of fifteen girls and a budget from the Palestine Office. They lived there about three years.

Plans for a New Training-Farm

All the time the farm was operative, and even after it was closed, those interested in it continued to plan its establishment in

improved form and on a broader base. These plans were generally
accompanied by questions. Is there really a need for a special agricultural training-farm? Does the existing format educate the girls
properly and meet the agricultural and social needs of the country?
Is the farm's location in Lower Galilee an advantage or a disadvan-
tage? Where should the farm be established, and under what conditions?

The question of whether to teach young men and women agriculture in a special framework or on the existing farms, had already arisen before the establishment of the first workers' training-farm, but it took on a special nuance when it was discussed in
connection with girls. Young men, even those without agricultural
training, could more easily find some sort of work in the field. Every male worker, even if untrained, could do simple farm work that
mainly required physical strength. This was not true for women
workers. Almost any farm work that was physically suitable required some agricultural knowledge and skill. Therefore, a training-farm for women was not analogous to a similar institution for
men, it had to be considered differently. This was emphasized time
and again by Hanna Meisel, perhaps because she was not immediately understood (Meisel, 1922:5–6). It seems that the rejection
of her thinking about the training-farm derived from the failure to
understand the unique problems of women.

Two detailed programs for setting up a new training-farm for
girls were proposed by Hanna Meisel and Akiva Ettinger, an
agronomist sent to Eretz Israel by the Zionist Organization. Both
were intended to solve the problems that arose at the Kinneret
farm. Ettinger suggested a comprehensive school in which girls
with different needs would find their place within a variety of
frameworks under one roof. He recommended different courses of
study for the younger girls who would live in a dormitory, for the
older girls who would be non-resident students, and short vocational courses for housewives. He also proposed that this institution organize agricultural instruction in the settlements. According to him, one institution should formulate basic programs and be
a center for agricultural study. First and foremost, Ettinger was
guided by the recognition that such an institution would be much
more profitable and more easily adaptable to the various demands
made upon it. In practical terms, he felt it desirable that the
Women's Organization continue to carry the ongoing budget, with
the Jewish National Fund providing the land and the buildings. In
the spring of 1917 he felt that an institution housing sixty girls

would suffice to answer the settlement needs of Palestine (CZA KKL2/17 I). He paid no attention whatsoever to the specific problems and special needs of the women of the Second Aliyah, but cited various examples from European countries. In his writings he dealt with the problems of the settler's wife, but not with the problems of the independent female worker.

There is much greater depth in the writings of Hanna Meisel who, over the years, never ceased to think about this subject. Again and again she dealt with the key question; What is the purpose of the farm? One can discern that over a period of time there was a shift in her thinking. At first she felt that the woman should be educated to be a farmer only, that is, a farmer's wife; but when she realized that the woman worker had other aspirations, she adapted her idea to the new reality. In a pamphlet she wrote in 1920, she stressed that the farm is meant to impart agricultural knowledge . . . so that they can fulfill their obligations whether as working wives of working farmers, or as independent workers, as members of a collective of young men or women, or on a small farmstead of their own or belonging to someone else, or in any other form (Meisel, 1922:5).

Her words gave validity to the patterns of life which had gained acceptance in the decade since she had founded the farm. In addition, like Ettinger, she emphasized the importance of educating the woman for the farmer's household. Together with her understanding of the new life styles, she did not give up the traditional idea of the wife as a "helpmate" who supplements the farmer's work by caring for the auxiliary plot beside the house and rearing his children.

Meisel's understanding of the spirit of the Second Aliyah girls did not move her from her original positions; she merely expanded them. In contrast to the girls who aspired to create new lifestyles in which there would no longer be room for the stereotyped woman, Hanna Meisel thought about enriching woman's life—to be a woman and a mother, and also a modern, knowledgeable, skillful farmer.

The cooking courses that Meisel advocated were nothing but a training-farm where the emphasis was on home economics, and especially on managing a workers' kitchen. In other articles she included home economics in the curriculum of the agricultural training-farm. But the growing need for kitchen managers, and the girls' aversion to this work apparently created the need for another institution, set up from the beginning for this purpose. The traditional occupation which was like a "step child" in the eyes of the Second Aliyah girls, but which was indispensable, thus found its rightful place. Before they took the course, they had been unwilling, and had completely misunderstood its worth. After they finished the course, most of the girls approached the work with a complete change of attitude.

In 1917, Hanna Meisel already realized the need to train new educational staff for the future; she also wished to take further training herself. Her efforts bore fruit, though not immediately. In 1926 the girls' agricultural school in Nahalal was established, upon her initiative and under her direction. The re-establishment of the farm attests to the approbation it had earned. Among those engaged in Zionist activity its image was favorable and, at times, was accompanied by an aura of admiration and romance. It seems that all who visited the farm felt the positive spirit prevailing there. This was probably among the few institutions in the Zionist Movement from which its creators derived immediate satisfaction.[12]

Image of the Woman Worker

It is difficult to appreciate the full contribution of the farm to the change which took place in the image of women workers. We have already indicated that the idea of a woman engaging in agricultural work as the equal of a man was one of the innovations of the Second Aliyah. Neither the kibbutz nor the moshav—the two forms of settlement which developed the country's agriculture— could have survived in their current format without solving the woman's problem. The women's farm in Kinneret, above all else, gave the women direction. There they learned both agricultural practice and theory and so acquired the assurance that they could produce and achieve on their own. The acceptance of the woman- worker as a peer, with equal rights, came only after she proved her ability as an outstanding agricultural worker in specific branches of the farm economy. The ideological change in the perception of the woman worker came only after the change in her qualifications.

The male workers' society, which paid no heed whatever to the place of the woman, had functioned as if it were possible to set up an exclusively bachelor society, at least in the first phase of settlement activities. Degania rejected the first graduates of the women's farm who sought to join it, fearing that their skills were inadequate and that they would cause a deficit to the collective. The struggle to prove the ability of the woman worker led to a unique phenomenon. Alongside the single-sex groups of male workers aided by a very few women, there now arose single-sex groups of women assisted by men working only as "imported" labor but not as members having equal rights. The agricultural knowledge gained at Kinneret helped to form a new social unit.

> So what if the [women's] collective lasts for only a year, and on rented land? The essential things is not the farm but the collective itself. It is now clear to all how very illogical this temporary collective was from an economic standpoint, but at that time it was accepted and natural (Yanait, in Katznelson-Shazar, 1930: 89).

The girls uniting in a closed collective was a step in their progress toward the recognition of their ability by the agricultural establishment, and their acceptance as members with equal rights. It was a transitional form of settlement that was abolished when women were accepted into the workers groups with equal rights.

Hanna Meisel often complained that the settlement institutions did not properly value the farm's influence on women's place in the settlement of Palestine, and disparaged women's importance in the rural economy. She undoubtedly exaggerated so that her demands would be better received. Nonetheless, one can say, after careful examination, that while the Palestine Office openly declared how important women's work was, it still did not see fit to take the farm under its wing. Over and above the financial considerations, which undoubtedly bothered Ruppin, the traditional disparagement of women's work remained. Responsibility for the women's farm, like responsibility for the poor girls of Jerusalem, remained in the hands of the Women's Organization. There were grounds for Hanna's complaints.

Agricultural Advances

Together with women's entry into the agricultural economy, new branches were developed which were appropriate to their physical ability. Vegetable growing, which in large measure had been in Arab hands, became one of the areas taken over by women workers; although its physical requirements were not too strenuous, it demanded devotion and training. Thanks to the women's farm, vegetable farming enjoyed an unusually rapid growth. It assumed new importance during the war.

The serious food shortage caused by the war, and the general unemployment, which hit especially hard at women workers, were problems requiring immediate solutions. The formation of collectives of graduates of the Kinneret farm provided an answer to these problems. These collectives raised vegetables in Petah Tikva, Ein Ganim, and still later, at the farm in Kinneret. During the war there were six such groups in Judea and Galilee, involving 70 of the 89 women workers then in the country (Thon's memo, 28 August 1917, CZA Z3/1482). The farm graduates also helped guide amateurs in this venture.

The Farm's Influence on its Surroundings

Among the declared purposes of the farm at its founding was the intent to influence the farming settlements and especially the women who lived there, so that they would learn how to run and improve their farmsteads. Agronomist Akiva Ettinger reported that the Kinneret farm's influence had indeed been felt in the lower Galilee settlements. There had been an improvement in order and cleanliness, and a greater understanding of the importance of the area of land adjacent to the farmhouse which, in the nature of things, was given over to the farmer's wife (11 August 1914, CZA Z3/1457; KKL 2/17 I). This statement may seem overly positive, nonetheless, the women's farm did have both a direct and indirect influence in making farmers' wives aware that they could benefit and improve their farms. In time the idea took root among the agronomists and the workers' community that the farm belongs not only to the farmer, but to the entire family. "The womens' proper function is work and life in the general collective", according to Joseph Bussel, one of Degania's founders.

In evaluating the women's farm, one must note that of the seventy girls who participated, only two left the country. The rest remained and were involved in farming. One may also hazard a guess that the stability of the women, together with their knowledge of farming, contributed to the stability of the men, to their ties to the land, and to their sinking roots in one place.

The advances in agriculture and the enhancement of the women's image were two processes that greatly influenced one another, both immediately and over the long run. These processes led to the crystalization of new social forms and thereby exerted a far reaching impact on the history of the Jewish community in Palestine.

Notes

1. Should the wife of a *shomer* (Jewish security guard) be categorized as one of the women workers of the Second Aliyah or not? By origin, age and place of settlement in Israel, she would be viewed as a female worker, although her own view of her life's calling as a wife of a shomer excludes her from that category. Later on, however, beginning with the war period, she settled in a rural area with her husband and also engaged in farming. She is not dealt with in this article or included in the statistics cited.

2. Evidence to the number of women workers is limited, but clearly they were few. For the only research summary of the number of workers see Z. Even-Shoshan (1963:208–220). According to him in 1907 there were 14 women workers in Judea; they comprised 9 percent of all workers there. In 1909, six of the 165 workers in Galilee were women, that is, less than five percent. The 1912 count of the Workers' Committee of Judea totalled 522, including 30 women. The 1913 census of the Palestine Office counted 971 workers, with 194 women comprising about nineteen percent.

3. Hayuta Bussel, also of the women workers of the Second Aliyah, wrote of her after her death—"She was the first of the first, the strongest of the strong, the fighter among fighters" (Malkin, 1946:13).

4. There were occasions when girls did obtain work in the fields but left it after awhile because it was too difficult for them physically (see Thon, 1910:1063). Wilkansky, too, stressed that the women workers, limited to a few tasks, and capable of working for only short periods, could not work in the farm economy on a regular basis (1918:333–334).

5. At the Kinneret farm, the "cook" was offered higher wages than the male workers, but she refused to accept it.

6. Report of the Women's Organization scattered in different files of the CZA, among them—CZA Z3/1634; L2/76—minutes of the group; L2/254 I—correspondence on the workshops; L2/255 II; L2/257; L2/236—a report on the workshops.

7. The sources on the number of women workers are not identical. The first girls at Kinneret were Leah Meron, Hanna Chizick, Atara Kroll, Mina Zevin, Sara Krigser and Rachel Bluwstein, See Krigser (1947:507–508).

8. A small group of workers who came on Aliyah from the U.S.A.

9. The teacher was Alfreda Bambus, daughter of Willy Bambus, the well-known Zionist, who had been professionally trained in Germany. She

wrote detailed letters about the farm and even a report "A Day at the Women's Farm" (German) in the Six's Report of the Women's Organization (CZA A76).

10. The Berlin women complained vigorously that the Russian "revolutionary" girls were not suitable human material for the farm. (4 December 1913, 1 December 1914, CZA L2/254 I).

11. From the recollections of Tamar Shai, Yanait Ben-Zvi's sister, in a letter to the author.

12. Both the institution and Hanna Meisel herself won support and respect, as seen all through the discussion so far from Arthur Ruppin, the highest Zionist authority in the country, Jacob Thon his assistant, and his wife Sara Thon, the Woman's Organization's representative in Palestine, as well as from the German agronomist Abugen, who visited the farm in 1912 and the Zionist agronomist Ettinger, who visited it in 1914.

References

Baratz, Yoseph 1948. *Degania Alef.* Jerusalem: *Hever Hakvutzot* (Hebrew).

———. 1960. *A Village by the Jordan.* Tel Aviv: Ott (Hebrew).

Becker, Ester. 1947. "The Life of a *Shomer*'s Family," pp. 509–521 in *The Second Aliyah*, edited by Bracha Habas. Tel Aviv: Am Oved (Hebrew).

Bluwstein, Shoshana. 1940. *On the Shores of Kinneret.* Tel Aviv: Private Publication (Hebrew).

Dayan, Shmuel. 1935. *Upon the 25th Anniversary of Degania.* Tel Aviv: Shtiebel (Hebrew).

———. 1967. *With the Founders of the Settlement.* Tel Aviv: Massada (Hebrew).

Ettinger, Akiva. 1919. "Agricultural Education for Women." *Hapoel Hatzair* 12, 1:21–23 (Hebrew).

Even-Shoshan, Zvi. 1963. *The History of the Workers' Movement in Eretz Israel.* Tel Aviv: Am Oved (Hebrew).

Harari, Yehudit. 1959. *Wife and Mother In Israel.* Tel Aviv: Massada (Hebrew).

Krigser, Sarah. 1947. "The Beginnings of Our Agricultural Training," pp. 506–509 in *The Second Aliyah*, edited by Bracha Habas. Tel Aviv: Am Oved (Hebrew).

Liberson, Tehiya. 1930. "The First Years," pp. 7–10 in *Women Workers Speak*, edited by Rachel Katznelson-Shazar. Tel Aviv: Moetzet Hapoalot (Hebrew).

Malkin, Sara. 1912. "About Women Workers at Kinneret." *Hapoel Hatzair* 5, 11–13:14 (Hebrew).

———. 1946. *Sara Malkin*. Degania Alef (Hebrew).

———. 1947. "My Way in Israel," pp. 488–500 in *The Second Aliyah*, edited by Bracha Habas. Tel Aviv: Am Oved (Hebrew).

Mamshi. 1911 "On the Question of the Women Workers in the Galilee." *Hapoel Hatzair* 4, 4:4–6 (Hebrew).

Meisel, Hanna. 1922. "Agricultural Training For Women Workers." *Hapoel Hatzair* 15, 38:5–6 (Hebrew).

———. 1967. *Training Girls for Settlement: Kinneret and Nahalal*. Tel Aviv: Tarbut Ve'hinuh (Hebrew).

Navratzky, C. 1914. *Die Judische Kolonisation Palastinas*. Munich (German).

Rachel. 1960. *Rachel's Poetry*. Tel Aviv: Davar (Hebrew).

Ruppin, Arthur. 1912. "The Question of Agricultural Workers." *Hapoel Hatzair* 5, 5–6 (Hebrew).

———. 1937. *Thirty Years of Building in Israel*. Jerusalem: Schoken (Hebrew).

———. 1968. *Memoirs*. Tel Aviv: Am Oved (Hebrew).

Smilansky, Moshe. 1909. "The New *Yishuv*: 1-Galilean *Moshavot*." *Ha Omer* 3, 1:11–12 (Hebrew).

Sturman, Atara. 1944. "Years in Israel," pp. 3–25 in *Women in the Kibbutz*. Edited by Lilia Bassevitz and Y. Bat-Rachel. Ein Harod: Hakibbutz Hameuchad (Hebrew).

Thon, Sara. 1910. "Women's Labor in Palestine." *Die Welt*, 14:1063 (German).

———. 1913. "The Question of Women Agricultural Workers." *Hapoel Hatzair* 6, 23:6–7 (Hebrew).

Wilkansky, Yitzhak. 1918. *On the Way*. Jaffa: Central Committee of *Hapoel Hatzair* (Hebrew).

WWC. 1914. "The First Women Workers' Convention." *Hapoel Hatzair* 7, 37:12–13 (Hebrew).

Yanait, Rachel. 1930. "Stages," pp. 89–95 in *Women Workers Speak*, edited by Kaztnelson-Shazar. Tel Aviv: Moetzet Hapoalot (Hebrew).

6

Fragments of Life: From the Diaries of
Two Young Women

——— *Deborah S. Bernstein and Musia Lipman* ———

Introduction

A search in the archives turned up two diaries, fragments of
the lives of two young women. Both are, at one and the same time,
unique individuals, anonymous young women, and typical figures
of their time. Anya arrived in Palestine in 1912 and left less than
two years later, in 1914. We know little of her before and after her
period in Palestine, though her main whereabouts during this period can be charted[1] (Tsur, 1984:30–43). Anya came from Ber-
dichev, a well-known center of Jewish religious life in the Pale of
Settlement, to Palestine towards the end of 1912. She went directly
to Migdal[2] and moved on from there to Jerusalem, to Ben Shemen,[3]
to Kinneret.[4] She left the country on the eve of the First World
War. We do not know if she returned to Russia or moved westward.
The world was entering a period of vast turmoil and we have no
later information concerning her. R. has less of a clear identity. We
don't even know her full first name. We don't know exactly where
she came from, though we do know that she came from Russia and
actively experienced the Russian Revolution. R.'s writing is somewhat less fragmented than Anya's. Though she does not write regularly, her writing does extend over a much longer period of time
(from 1925 to the last entry in 1937), giving us some sense of continuity and somewhat greater insight into the ways she tried to resolve the dilemmas she confronted.

Anya and R. were both women pioneers, halutzot. They were
both searching for a sense of self, and acutely aware of their
search. For both the private and the public were indivisible—love,
work, self, the collective to which they belonged, the movement in
which they participated, the land to which they came, were all part

of their aching search for meaning, for integration of self, for sense of self. None of these components was simple, the integration of all, so deeply sought for, was the constant theme of their fragmentary writing, never really achieved by either.

Anya and R. come across, from between the lines of their diaries, as very different young women. Different in temperament, in style of writing, in their ways of dealing with their similar dilemmas. In temperament they strike the reader as being of an almost opposite nature. Anya, possibly younger than R.,[5] appears to be tossed about by her inner torment and search for sense of self. She appears deeply depressed, often at loose ends, crying out for a sense of control over her life, for support, for an outstretched hand ... R. also conveys a deep sense of loneliness but appears very self-contained and in control. She seems, above all, to be hard on herself rather than to cry out to others. She is far more steadfast, disciplined and decisive. No open questions, as for Anya, but instead crystal clear goals and priorities.

Their writing, the very style and language used, seems to reveal and reflect these differences. Anya's diary is fairly typical of the diary "genre." It is often fragmented, confused, or written in private code, which makes it almost inaccessible to the reader. It was clearly meant to be private, very personal in nature. It was written in Russian, her mother tongue. R.'s writing has a very different quality. In her style, as in her story, the borderline between the private and the public becomes blurred. Her writing touches upon very intimate matters, and is written as a diary. Nevertheless, it was sent by the writer to be published.[6] It is impossible to know at what point in the writing of the diary it was meant, by R., to be seen and read by a more general public. The diary was written in the awkward Hebrew of a non-native speaker. The style is often epigramatic, loaded with ideological pathos, strewn with capitalized words and stock pieties, generalizations about human nature and expressions of single-minded devotion to a well defined, unchallenged, ideological framework. Such linguistic style is in no way unique to R. but was highly typical of the pioneering activists. This is how they spoke, how they wrote, probably how they thought. The public took over the private, even in the diary.

The strategies adopted by these two young women for coping with their dilemmas also appear to be very different. The difficulties they both faced were immense. Trying physical conditions, strenuous manual labor, life within an intense and not very considerate or gentle collective, unrequited love and passion. Anya seems to fall apart. At least, that is the self she presents in her diary. A deep sadness appears to come across to her close friends, judging from a letter written to her included in the diary. Her yearning for her beloved Grisha-Tzvi Shatz, a romantic poet and writer ever in search of true love and intimacy (Tsur, 1984) is hinted in her diary. They were together for a time in the "intimate commune" in Migdal. A sense of closeness and gentleness is conveyed in their correspondence, included in the diary, but their paths clearly part early on. Anya is on her own. She is overcome by a sense of loss, by aching loneliness, by an inability to understand what is happening to her and she opts out. She does not opt out of life, as did some, but first she opts out of the collective and then out of the country.

R., on the other hand, appears to take the polar opposite route. She has a very clear idea of her goal in life—dedication to the cause and personal autonomy, shared with her beloved. When this goal is unattainable, as her beloved will not enable her to retain the sense of self so essential to her, she disengages from him and from the private sphere in general. Total dedication to the cause takes over. So does the public jargon. Twelve years later, quite clearly summing up for the general reader, she writes, "my love is dedicated to my child, to my work and to the Movement." The child is referred to at this point for the first time. No family or intimate relationship is mentioned or hinted at. One is left to guess that the child was her decision, her choice, brought up by her within the kibbutz.

In addition to individual differences, there were differences of timing, of the social context in which each of the young women had to function. Anya was of the Second Aliyah, an immigration of single men and women. The search for collectivity began, in most cases in Palestine, and was often disappointing. The loneliness was immense. A deep sense of loneliness can be felt even in the published writings of Sara Malkin (e.g., 1947:488–500) seen by her peers as the model of the determined agricultural worker and activist. The younger and more vulnerable expressed their loneliness more openly (Katznelson-Nesher, 1978:67–69). There was a preoccupation with suicide. Tsur has called attention to the relative frequency of suicide among the halutzim of the Second Aliyah (Tsur, 1976:33–44). Reference to such cases is made both in Anya's diary, and in Govrin's article (in this volume). The extent to which suicide was part of the experience of the Second Aliyah might be ascertained by the fact that the writings and letters of two young women, who committed suicide during these years, were included in the collection of writings edited by Rachel Katznelson-Shazar, published in 1930 under the title—*Women Workers Speak* (Katznelson-Shazar, 1930) and in English under the title *The Plough Woman* (1932, later edition 1975). There were no established, relatively stable support systems. Both men and women were always on the go, moving from one place to another. Anya belonged, at the start, to a small group who tried to establish a new collective form which they called the "intimate commune" (Tsur, 1984). Her own sense of loneliness was not eased by the supposedly intimate nature of the collective. Possibly the sense of loneliness was even more acute. She kept wandering, like others, and like many others, left Palestine. R. arrived thirteen years later, in 1925, to a changed social setting. In the meantime the Third Aliyah had taken place. The ranks of the pioneering immigrants had grown substantially and become far better organized. The Histadrut had been established, as had the Women Workers' Movement and its executive body the Women Workers' Council. There was the Labor Exchange to help find employment. There were women's farms and women's collectives (*havurot*). As a result, as Izraeli claims, the young women of the Third Aliyah felt less deprived than their forerunners. No doubt, life was not easy, but there was more to hold on to while trying to resolve the inevitable dilemmas.

The fragmented nature of these two diaries, fragments of time and fragments of experience, thoughts and above all emotions, appear to be typical of women's diaries in general. Springer and Springer (1986) point out that women's diaries tend to be written over short periods of time, during times of crisis or passage, while the form of the diary, argue Moffat and Painter, is analogous to women's lives—emotional, fragmentary, interrupted, private, restricted, daily, and concerned with self (1975:5). In both these respects Anya and R. share much with numerous other women who wrote their diaries and journals, at times to express their loneliness, by far the most frequently expressed emotion (ibid.), at times to obtain self-understanding (Baldwin, 1977:34), or as Anais Nin wrote, as "an escape from judgement, a place in which to analyze the truth of women's situation" (Nin, 1976:27).

Excerpts from the Diary of Anya, 1912–1914.[7]

Migdal.

October 30th, 1912

> It is so odd. Today I need to talk, to write a lot. But there is no one to talk or write to. There is no one close enough.

December 2nd, 1912

I live in Migdal now. We lead a curious life here. I do the same
work every day. It is very boring. In the morning, as soon as I get
up, I must stoke the stove, then boil the milk, peel the potatoes for
the stew and cook some soup, dairy or parve. Then I must do the
dishes and sweep the room. And rest for a while. Then the Sam-
ovar again, dinner, the dishes, fatigue and sleep. And the next
day, it's the same thing all over again. The hands are always
dirty. I wash them and feel sad because they are getting so rough.
I don't see a thing beyond our courtyard. There are eight of us
now, six men, one other girl and myself. One of our comrades died
last week.[8] He was simple, and gentle and open-eyed. Very sweet
and good, alive and practical, a young man of twenty-four or five.
We are not yet joined together. There are misunderstandings. We
are all so different. I am often ill with Malaria. The climate here
is not healthy. I gain weight and then grow thin suddenly. They
say one must hope for better times, but I do not believe all this.
The entire settlement, the entire region, is infected with Cholera,
and there is some panic in our room as well. It is late now, a
quarter to twelve. I must get up early tomorrow.

December 21st, 1912

Everything around is so odd and savage, and I am savage myself.
So many experiences, so much sympathy and antipathy. I cannot
tell about my feelings. My life. I wish there were someone here
with me, some person who would penetrate my soul and touch it
where it hurts most. A "soul expert" who would operate on me.
Afterwards I would feel reborn. I think it would have been a new
phase for me, a new life. All those layers of life that accumulated
there have rotted inside, and there are convulsions where new
experiences, so many of them, have stuck. Even the lives of ordinary people are made in such odd ways. There is something I need
to say, and it won't come out. Our comrade, Moshe, has died. He
shot himself to death. I often think of suicide. What a strange
moment in life. Can't any one of us think of suicide all of a sudden? In certain conditions, anyone can rape oneself. It is only a
mood. When one looks at the beauty of nature, the beauty that
nature itself creates, there are states when it just wouldn't let one
die. I think that I could never kill myself on one of those bright
warm mornings that nature gives us as a gift. When I go out into
the street and see the blue of the sky and the wonderful sunlight
around, when I feel the soft pure air, my feelings turn about—I
feel good, and I think that my life is still all before me. When we
live, we create something.

лиши я начинаю понимать и я все
соз наваѣ, что я не создана для такой
жизни, я не то и тогда я начина
думать.

21 февр.

Как ни страшно, но не могу
определить своё состояние, и
куда больше тянет меня
ведь страшно подумать, что
каждый шаг мой сделан
сделан не по желанию, а
почему-то сама не знаю почему.
Вот уже третья неделя,
как работаю но помню, каза
лось, что лучше, что чище, что
привлекательнее ни окружа
ющей тебя природы. Прямо
страшно становится, когда
смотришь вокруг себя, глаз
своих не веришь, что я
... эту неоглядную,

Figure 8. A page from the diary of Anya (Labor Archive).

мне как-то страшно твой
думаешся и ?? перерыво?
?но ?исьмо ?и??. ?ев?
?о?ию ?ка?

Вторник ?/VIII 9?г.

Как много ?о?но было
сказать о ?изни своей за
??? год ?! Ми?ал, ?е
??одно ????? восклик
?у?ь ?! ?? год, ?а?а?а
??г. что за ?ремя
?еужели ??? ?о ?рошло,
?еужели ?о ??????
?у?о??ло в наш ей ?а?
в? ??ой
за ??? ?? ?о все, за ???
об?ее, об?ее ... ?
????? ?ил?ое, ?о

————I have not gone to work in the kitchen today. I have not had anything to eat or drink. I have made up my mind not to go, not to idle about in the kitchen. I think it is idleness when two people work where one person could work alone. I think this would be wrong of me. I would like to work in the field. I would like my work to be free. To do something—not the things I have been doing all along. I have always worked. I have always been independent, but I have never been content. The most difficult thing is that one is so utterly lonely here. Good God! If I could have known that it would turn out this way. That it would be such a deception. I came to Palestine for lofty ideals: I had no doubt about whether to come or not. I told myself—this is your idea. Go ahead and do it, but do it in time, not too late. It is terrible when my reality bears no resemblance at all to what I had imagined. Can one think of satisfaction after this? I have looked for purity, I have looked for right and beauty, I have looked for life as it is; there were moments when I imagined—here it is, just look and see! But when I did take a good look, the beauty, the magic, were gone. The hens are cackling, the birds chirping, the dog barking, the sun is warm—a beautiful afternoon in Palestine. The skies are bright, the tall mountains are gently shadowed with different colors. The green fields around have been tilled by our brothers, the farmers; the water on lake Kinneret is still, its surface quivering. I have got all this before me . . .

February 20th, 1913

It is very odd to say this: I cannot tell whether I did right or wrong in coming here. It is five months now since I came to Palestine, and I cannot tell what made me do it, what pushed me along this way . . . Who can tell anything about Palestine from a distance. I am ashamed to say that I do not know and did not know what I wanted. I cannot tell who I am and what I am. I have no answers at all. I have left the life I knew, my own set place, the civilized life. Life is really unfair. I could have lived any way I wanted. I could have lived anywhere, seen the world, met people. I had it all. What was it that pulled me here? To live like a savage, to turn into a savage, without thought, without people, with no family or friends. There is no one close to me here, no relatives, nothing else that could serve in place of my former life, not even in part. When I start thinking about it I feel I should tell myself— here I am leading an honest, pure life, and so on and so forth. But it is only a passing impulse, a wish to withhold things from myself. I do not wish to get to the depth of my soul, of my being. If I do, what state am I going to find myself in? I sometimes think that it is all good, that here is where I can get to know my God.

But when I get to the bottom of my thoughts I must admit that I was not made for this kind of life. I am not what I thought I was . . .

February 21st, 1913

It is now three weeks that I have been working in the field. I feel it is better, purer, pulling me closer to nature. It is frightening, when you look around you cannot believe in what you see. I cannot believe that it is I who sees the infinite beauty around me, a beauty I cannot describe; and when I look on, there is the wild beauty of the mountains round the Valley of Jezreel, and I want to shout—oh God, what power, what demon, has created all this? What for? Perhaps it is all for my soul, my tired, worn-out, tormented soul, so that it should become softer and prettier, infused with light and purity as everything before this great beauty. I wish I were more like this beauty.

February 23rd, 1913

I am living in Palestine—isn't it a dream? I should have been proud of this life; there are hundreds of people who would give so much to be here. I have been here (in Migdal—D.B.), thank God, for 4 months now, I live the life of a farm worker—one should need nothing more to be proud of. I am a worker. And I can also be a housewife, if I wish; but my thoughts are suddenly cut off. I am suddenly not in the mood for writing. Oh God! One could leave work, but then it really becomes hell. Grisha,[9] I am miserable because I cannot tell people the real reason. It is wrong. But one cannot bare one's soul for anybody to see. The nakedness of the soul can be unpleasant like that of the body. Yet I suppose that one might feel better afterwards, perhaps there will be some relief. Grisha, this is very painful for me, but could it be Palestine that has brought me to this state? I do not know what to blame for it anymore.

April 13th, 1913

I am in Migdal, a settlement in the lower Galilee. It was set up four years ago, and only now it's beginning to settle down, very slowly. It is held by a cooperative in Moscow and run by Glikin, a middle-aged man, well educated and active, but extremely egotistical. An egocentric man who dearly loves himself. He often tells of his glorious past, but he does live in the present as well. There are 15 of us here and probably about the same number in Russia. We came here in October 1912. We set out to live together here. But there was no cohesion to begin with. It was not "it." And no one could tell what it was. Bad days came. Disease. There was not a single day without some illness. A great disaster happened

to us in the first month of our communal life: one of the comrades,
perhaps the very best of us, died. After his death it all became
very hard. Work did not go well. Our social life did not develop.
Mundane, everyday things began to wear us down. There were
quarrels over mere trifles. Constant misunderstandings. Six
weeks later, one of the comrades committed suicide.[10] This is the
last letter he left to his friends.

Forgive me friends for having troubled you, but there was no
other way for me. I have found myself in a false position, I had
to get out. Yes, Zalman[11] was right when he said that we were
rude to each other. We never tried to get into each other's spiritual lives, we have not had the sensitivity that would teach us

Figure 9. Young women in Migdal (Labor Archive).

not to offend. There has been a withdrawal from your principles. You refused to understand that even when I did not take part in your discussion, I might have had my own spiritual world. That I was hurt when people were inconsiderate and offensive to me. Your attitude, whenever I spoke, was arrogant and mocking, as if what I had to say did not deserve any attention. Your never-ending reproaches, the comments about my frequent bouts of illness, the orders given offensively—a mere infant would not have been treated this way . . . How should I have presented myself to you? Should I have lied? Motti says that my morality is only theoretical, not practical. That I am cowardly and confused. Ossia[12] says I am lying when I tell you that I used to be a good worker in Poria. Others have not been so outspoken, but people have tried to catch me out. And I have had to pretend that I liked it, that I did not understand. The insults were not intentional. If you knew how much they hurt me, I have no doubt you would not have treated me this way. But it never occurred to you to think of me, to recognize me as an equal. You treated me as you would a naive child with no self esteem, who does not take offense. Enough. Forgive me for the unpleasantness I am about to cause you. May you be successful with your enterprise. May you be better psychologists.

Your comrade,

Moshe.

Please write home that I have died of malaria. It would make it easier for them, anyway.

There is something childish about what he did, but there is a great deal of truth in the letter.

Life in Migdal became troubled. Glikin found it difficult to bear the responsibility. People abandoned the place and neglected their work. Arab workers arrived. There were troubles with the police after the two deaths. The commune of Migdal moved on to Ben-Shemen. Anya left Migdal—it is not known whether she stayed in Ben-Shemen at all—and wandered in the country. The last known document in her handwriting is a letter she wrote to her friend Tzvi (Grisha) Shatz from Kinneret. It was an answer to a letter written by him to her. Both letters were included in her diary.

Dear Anya,[13]

—I just want to tell you that I miss you, that I would very much like to see you or at least to know what is happening to you. We have shared many experiences, Anya, so it hurts me now that you have not written a single line about yourself. Perhaps you did not

get our letter? I do want so much to see you now. I imagine that
you are well and active, since you are a worker. Being a worker in
this country is being at the very center, the true course of life.
Anya, when you left you were so sad, so discontented. It hurts me
that you do not write. I try not to think about you, but it is impossible to forget the beautiful things we shared: the evenings on
lake Kinneret, the yarns. It was you and your presence they were
spun for. But I went aside. No use talking about it now. You
would probably like to know what is happening here with us. We
are all at Ben-Shemen, in one of the Bezalel houses. Tomorrow we
start baking. We are leaving the communal kitchen of the farm.
Rachel will work half day and cook during the other half. She has
been working full time so far, and her hands are all properly
blistered. She planted olive trees, and covered up the holes. We
shall transfer all the agricultural work we need: a hen coop, a sow
shed, vegetable crops, orchards and intensive field crops. I have
recently looked at the letter I wrote to you from Kfar-Uriah, when
you were about to go from Jaffa to Jerusalem. I thought, should I
send it to you? I don't really know a thing about you! Do write to
me Anya dear, and please do not think I have changed my attitude to you, not even a little bit. If that is what you think you do
not know me at all. Good night Anya, dear, sad Anya.

Your Tzvi

Anya's reply

Kinneret.

Dear beloved Tzvi,

I have not deceived myself. I had expected to get a good letter
from you and I did. Thank you dear Tzvi. You have been right
about many things: "we have lived little and suffered much." You
are right. You were also right about my unhappiness when I left
Ben-Shemen. Oh, dear Tzvi! If you were older you could still understand this unhappiness, but to my great distress you are all
younger than me, and so I have to go through such difficulties. If
you could only understand what I went through in Jerusalem and
Ben-Shemen . . . Dear Tzvi, if I could only talk to you at the right
moment, at a moment like this, but it is impossible to write, because the pen does not catch up with the thoughts I had some
time ago, after those difficult experiences, I cannot possibly trace
my own thoughts. There is so much I want to tell you. My letter is
so confused. I will only be able to tell whether you understand
when I read your answer. Tzvi, I was more than unhappy when I
left Ben-Shemen. So much sorrow and fear. As sad as my eyes

looked to you, they could not possibly reflect the pain of my injured soul.

The last we hear about Anya is when she visited Bella Kovner and David Yermanovitz in Beit-Ban.[14] She was with Nahum Kamnitzki who, according to Tsur (ibid.:31) was a rich and spoiled young man who had "snatched" Anya and taken her to Jerusalem to the distress of her friends in the commune. Anya and her friend decided to return to Russia and came to say goodbye to the young couple. Those were the last days before the First World War broke out. Anya left the country less than two years after she arrived.

Excerpts From the Diary of R., 1925–1937.[15]

1925

I have been here in Eretz Israel for eight months now, and it seems to have been a long period in my life. In the very first days after my arrival I already felt as if I had been born here. I have made it my goal to train myself for agricultural work as soon as I came here. This was the be-all and end-all for me. My only thought was of the proper way to get to a healthy economic position, to take roots in the soil. I was not yet sure that I could get used to physical work. But I strongly desired to take part in the process of creation and construction of a new settlement for my people, and felt the need to free myself from the eternal instability and the party politics that were such a heavy burden in the diaspora, such an obstacle to contentment. In my work I found what I had been looking for. I work freely, without tension, and I find my work interesting. Work does not have an abstract value— it is here that I find myself. Here there is room for energy and initiative, especially in a women's collective. This is the beginning of a self-sufficient farm, run by ourselves. If my strength does not fail me, I will not lag behind. There are many thoughts in my mind, and my will is strong, but everything is still formless, still unsettled. I have so far been passive in public and political life. I have watched and followed what happened. The direct contact with the Movement also takes time to establish. But outside our consciousness there is a process of "organic digestion." I have recently begun to feel myself as one of the many members of the great Movement. I feel that I have already earned the right to express an attitude to the various aspects of our life, to have my own opinion. I am beginning to feel that I am deep inside the maelstorm of our problems here in Eretz Israel. But I know that I should first strike roots in my work and hold on to it. Because this task requires much energy. Only when I have accomplished this will I be able to devote myself to public activities.

———I have spent a few days with my friends at the Kibbutz. We have set up a strong familial relationship in the long years of suffering and soul-searching. Our common history has spanned ten years. Even before the February revolution, when we were students, we met in seminars for self-improvement. There were various youths there, Zionist and non-Zionist. In time we divided into Zionists and Socialists, and then into left and right-wing Zionists. The first years of the revolution were the golden age of the Jewish parties. Our party radiated light for Jewish youths and moved every one of us to introspection. Our life was centered on the participation in the general Zionist activity, the pupils' youth federations, the library, evening classes, the hostel. All the rest was incidental, and we did not concern ourselves with it. This was the reason for numerous conflicts with our parents. Our studies, too, were adversely affected. But the idealistic desire, the goal and the means were merged into a single, illuminated essence. Then the civil war broke out in Russia, and along with it came the antisemitic pogroms. These events united us still further. We had already dissociated ourselves from private interest, we were united in the struggle for national rights and we never lost sight of the fundamental goal. We took part in action for self-defence and helped our people who were victims of the pogrom. Later it was Zionism which began to be persecuted. We had to leave Russia not because of personal persecution by the authorities, but because we could see no possibility of Zionist action within this frame of life. We did not escape to Eretz Israel, we were looking for ways to train Jewish youth in the diaspora before they came here. Many of the comrades stayed abroad, myself included. The decision to go to Israel, even after several years, was still not an easy one. As for myself, I knew that my own restless, active soul could only find an outlet in Eretz Israel. I had felt that the special conditions here would help me in the fulfillment of my positive qualities, and I broke out. My friends understood this and tried to help me. My life at the time had a personal dimension which delayed my departure for a while. Already when I was in Russia, my hot blooded woman's temperament was awakened. Yes, I had loved, and it was a great and powerful love! My love was free from pettiness and did not dissociate me from the life of the movement and its enterprise. I was strong and independent, and love illuminated my way. I believed him and respected him. But love did not blind or subdue me. But Z. was gripped by the fear of separation. I could not and would not sacrifice everything for the beloved man. I was thirsty for freedom and desired to go my own way. There was a time when I was weakened, I suffered and broke down, because Z. could not give me completeness. Love only makes one's way easier, but each of us has got to find his own way. I loved him but I could be critical of him. I recognized his shortcomings. He was often weak, helpless and impatient. He was incapable of suffering, but doesn't suffering purify man? A year of internal debate went by before I made up my mind to leave for Eretz Israel. My many friends, and Z. my intimate friend, remained in the diaspora, and I am living alone with myself. I need to share my new impressions and thoughts with him. My personal world is buried deep down, locked behind seven seals. I find it difficult to find the echo of what is happening to me in my letters to my friends. But I am being honest with myself and with Z. I know I have not stopped loving him, and perhaps I love him still more when I am here, because here I am alive, not frozen.

———I am afraid of what fate has in store for me. I fear it may be a cruel blow. All feeling inside me seems to have petrified—only my link to Z., the experience we shared, can restore my private world. My letters to him sound cold, but he should be able to read my love between the lines. He might have doubts, but in spite of the geographical distance I am with him in my thoughts. I still believe in the revival of our feelings.

———The ice has thawed. I am again able to feel. I knew that it was a temporary, superficial freeze. There is nothing in me that would justify that. And I still feel close to Z. Sometimes unhappiness creeps in, but it, too, should pass when he comes here.

———It is now a year since I came here. Eretz Israel has been kind to me. I have met with good working conditions, and grown stronger in body and mind. I have been feeling the ground under my feet, the immediate link with the Workers' Movement. I began my new life under no compulsion, without stress. My love for Eretz Israel is what I imagine the love of a daughter to her mother to be.

———Eretz Israel is very beautiful. There is so much space, and the rocky mountains call for liberty. I feel free, capable of anything. I would like him to see me like this. Everything around me is interesting. I go to scientific lectures and get absorbed in my work. I would like to be conscientious, to acquire knowledge which is the only access to real freedom. I wish to enhance my knowledge of topical, political subjects, as I will one day want to be active in the Worker's Movement. How I would like to share this world of mine with Z.! Would he understand me?

———I have locked myself within again. I am afraid to look inside. The last years in the diaspora must have ruined me, and I am now feeling it acutely. I thought that I would find peace here, but it has not worked out. I have accomplished something in the Women Workers' Group and at work, but my private intimate life is still stormy and restless. I do not do enough with my leisure. I am still waiting for him. I find it hard to concentrate. I am distracted. Sometimes I think that he will never come. That he is growing apart from me, and then I get better. When I struck roots in the land, I believed that Z., too, would find himself here. But I'm tired of suffering and I am often attracted to the warmth I find in other people. Eretz Israel is taking me over. It has penetrated me. I understand it. I have felt it with my instinct and we have come closer, the land and I. No wonder that people don't believe me when I say that this is only my second year here. I have become naturalized at work and in the Movement and recovered in all senses. I live the world of Eretz Israel utterly and wholly, and it is clear to me that my love cannot remain without. If my friend does not enter this life, there will be an abyss between us.

———It has been about two months now since Z. came here. I am disappointed. He is not trying to strike roots, to find a foothold here. He only attends to his own feelings, to his private world, and he does not have enough patience to endure the process of acculturation. He is afraid of being alone with himself, he wants me to be with him entirely, to live for him. And I am looking for something else. I want him to find himself here, to attain spiritual completeness. I want us both to be independent but close in spirit and desire—two people with one way. I am also attracted to other people. It is natural for me. I have always liked a large social framework. I cannot stand the confined environment. The scenes of ordinary domesticity frighten me. My meetings with other friends are not a danger for him, but he does not understand this, and does not try to come nearer to me, to bring his world closer to mine. Instead he gets suspicious, follows me around, puts ultimatums to me. My life has become unbearably difficult.

———I am about to separate from Z. We have always been different and we have responded differently to life. I have involved myself entirely in the life of Eretz Israel. I have chosen my way and followed it indomitably. Here I have obtained the most precious thing—freedom. I have overcome the difficulties and attached myself to the land. I drifted apart from Z. He did not find me in doubt, suffering, tormented and helpless. No, he found a woman who has got faith in her way, who aspires for completeness. And Z. has no credo of his own. Life in this land demands adjustment, the endurance of life and its full burden, a renunciation of one's spiritual and moral property for the movement. Obviously, there is much personal satisfaction in that. But Z. was remote from all this. The crisis in our relationship was therefore inevitable. He needed a sacrifice on my part, a willingness to forsake and forget everything and go with him, to make his own suffering quest easier for him, but I cannot do this, nor do I justify this kind of sacrifice.

———I am going through a very difficult period, in spite of my determination. I am alone with my feelings and thoughts. As long as I loved it was easier for me to bear the suffering, but now I am all alone with it. It is hard for me to forgive him, although I know that all he did was out of love for me. I am pulling myself together, trying to get stronger and recover from my love so that I can start all over again. Can I do it? It is still so difficult for me, although it was I who decided to break up. I feel that only work can heal me. No home of convalescence or resort can remedy my aching soul.

———I have enlisted with my whole heart to the establishment of a new enterprise of the Women Workers' Movement. I have become alive with the Movement and with my friends. I feel the acute situation of the woman worker here, her weakness and her helplessness and the subsequent lack of activity. I would like to help, to have some influence to train the woman, so that she should have an independent economic position in life.

———It has been months and I feel the need to tell of myself again. I am well now, I breathe freely. I have been in several places to help out. I have organized agricultural activity, and felt my creative power. I have also strengthened my character, and I try to find an independent approach to things.

———Again I am happy to be free, to have regained my energy and warmth, and to feel the firm ground under my feet. I believe in Eretz Israel and in the people. I am surrounded by people who have faith. My life is the life of the kibbutz in Israel. I have been associated with the kibbutz movement for several years, but I only now comprehend its depth, and the beauty of going together with other people who believe like me, who strive for a better future. I am not blinded. I can see the negative aspects of our life, I know that there are still many areas which are yet to be infused with the true spirit of communality. We have still got to organize our lives so that what is lacking will not be so sorely missed, and be kinder to each other. I still believe that we can rise over trifles here. Is hatred among people necessary? Don't they depend on each other? Can anyone exist by himself? Why, then, should people be unable to create beautiful relationships? I am happy be-

Figure 10. Collective of women workers—1927.

cause I love the kibbutz and have such faith in its way. I devote
my strength to it. I have been called upon to assist, and I have
always done it with dedication. I would like to help all those who
can understand our truth—who can find a way to us. I would like
to help the women comrades find themselves in work. They, too,
should be autonomous. I do this with all the devotion of a member
in the Movement.

1937

For twelve years I have lived entirely in my work. I was active
everywhere, took the initiative in economic activity and was
aware of everything around me. Now I am restless again. I would
like to nurture my mind, to acquire knowledge and to pool together everything I had once learned. It seems as though all these
years I have been trying to prove to myself and to others that I
could really work. I used to doubt myself in the past, I doubted
whether I could hold on to this way of life I believed in. Now I
know: I have struck roots in life and work. And when I look deep
inside myself I realize that my public awareness has got a deeply
private, intimate dimension. There have been years of personal
oscillation, of alternating weakness and strength, there have been

years of suffering and instability. Have I accomplished my goals? It is hard to give a single answer. In the depth of my soul I have been longing for motherhood for a long time. I have sometimes concealed it from myself. I now know that my child fulfills much in my life. I will give up much in order to preserve his spiritual wholeness. My love is dedicated to my child, to my work and to the Movement.

This is my holy vocation.

Notes

1. Parts of the diary to appear below were first published by Muki Tsur (1984) who received the diary from Musia Lipman who also translated it. The sections chosen by Tsur were published in a biography written by him about Tzvi Shatz, who was part of the "intimate commune" to which Anya initially belonged and towards whom she had a close emotional tie, as we shall later see. Tsur attempted to uncover all he could about her whereabouts and thus we are able to know somewhat more than her diary reveals.

2. Migdal—a village, moshava, near the Sea of Galilee, where a group of workers lived and worked as a collective.

3. Ben Shemen—a farm, owned and managed by the World Zionist Organization.

4. Kinneret—a nationally owned farm which was a center for individual and collectively organized Jewish workers (see Shilo, this volume).

5. We don't know the age of either women. The average age of the young women of the Second Aliyah was very young, 16–17 according to Shilo (this volume). Anya herself might not have been so young as she writes at one point, in a letter to Tzvi Shatz—"to my deep regret you are all younger than me . . ." though there is an adolescent like quality to her writing. R. refers to the fact that she remained in Russia for a few years to help train youngsters for immigration to Palestine, which might very well put her in her early twenties.

6. It was sent to Lilia Bassevitz as a possible contribution to the second volume of the collection *Women of the Kibbutz*, though such a volume never actually appeared.

7. Found in the Labor Archive in the Lavon Institute, Tel Aviv. Translated by Musia Lipman.

8. Hillel Ettin, who died a month after the settlement in Migdal.

9. "Grisha" is Tzvi Shatz who was mentioned in the introduction.

10. Moshe Shapira, a member of the group.

11. Zalman Lifshitz, a member of the group in Migdal.

12. Ossia, is Yoseph Trumpeldor, one of the leading figures of the Second Aliyah, founder of the *Gdud Ha'avoda* (Labor Batalion) of the Third Aliyah, killed in Tel Hai, 1920.

13. The entire letter of Tzvi Shatz was published, in Hebrew, in the book by Muki Tsur (Tsur, 1984:39–41)

14. Bella Kovner was one of the three women members of the commune. She left Migdal when she married David Yermanovitz whom she met when the group stayed in Degania where Yermanovitz was a temporary worker.

15. The collection of Lilia Bassevitz, Container 6, The Archive of the Kibbutz Hameuchad, Yad Tabenkin.

References

Baldwin, C. 1977. *One to One: Self Understanding through Journal Writing*. N.Y.: Evans and Co.

Katznelson-Nesher, Hanna. 1978. *Brother and Sister*. Tel Aviv: Am Oved (Hebrew).

Katznelson-Shazar, Rachel. 1930. *Women Workers Speak*. Tel Aviv: Moetzet Hapoalot (Hebrew).

———. 1975. *The Plough Woman*. New York: Herzel Press.

Malkin, Sara. 1947. "With the Second *Aliyah*—Memories," pp. 488–599 in *The Second Aliyah*, edited by Bracha Habas. Tel Aviv: Am Oved (Hebrew).

Moffat, Mary, and Charlotte Painter. 1975. *Revelations—Diaries of Women*. N.Y.: Vintage.

Nin, Anais. 1951. "Notes on Feminism," *In Favor of the Sensitive Man and other Essays*: Ann Arbor: Edwards Brothers, Inc.

Springer, Marlene and Haskell Springer. 1986. *Plains Woman—The Diary of Martha Farnsworth, 1882–1922*. Bloomington: Indiana Univ. Press.

Tsur, Muki. 1976. *Doing it the Hard Way*. Tel Aviv: Am Oved (Hebrew).

———. 1984. *By Turbulent Waters*. Tel Aviv: Am Oved (Hebrew).

7

A Woman Alone: The Artist Ira Jan as Writer in Eretz Yisrael

—— *Nurit Govrin* ——

Fateful Encounter

Ira Jan was born in Kishinev, Bessarabia, in 1869 and died in Tel Aviv in 1919. Her real name was Esther Slepian but she signed all her paintings and stories with her pen name, Ira Jan. Her father, an advocate by the name of Yoselevitz, was well known in Odessa and his daughter received a general Russian education. He was active in Russian public life and his home was a center for Russian revolutionaries. It was there, according to Tamar Meroz, that Ira Jan met her husband, Dr. Slepian, "a bearded, broad shouldered giant," a fighter for peasant rights and a member of the Revolutionary Socialist Party (S.R.). Not long after their marriage, a daughter Lena was born, "who resembled her father: tall and of sturdy limbs" (Meroz, 1972:18–19,25).

In the summer of 1903, Ira Jan met the national poet Haim Nahman Bialik while he was visiting Kishinev as a member of a delegation sent to inquire into the infamous pogrom perpetrated against the Jews of the city. It was love in the shadow of horror, a friendship that blossomed on the background of the pogrom, a deep affinity between the poet and an admirer, between two artists (Shamir, 1972; Sadeh, 1985). In the course of time, Ira Jan translated a number of Bialik's most important works into Russian and published them in a special edition containing a lengthy introduction on the poet and her own illustration (Shochetman, 1945:3; Govrin, 1989:393–401).

The meeting with Bialik exerted a profound influence on Ira Jan. As a result, she left her assimilated husband and decided, first to settle in Odessa where Bialik was living, and then, after he wrote to her that he planned to go to Eretz Yisrael, to go there as

165

well. At the end of 1907, Ira Jan settled in Eretz Yisrael. Her close friend, Rachel Yanait, quotes her as saying: "I was very happy to have been in contact with our great poet—he who brought me back to my people, he who brought me back to myself" (Yanait Ben-Zvi, 1965).

Behind these words lies the drama of a tormented, perplexed woman, whose life changed completely in the wake of her acquaintance with Bialik. She made all the transitions possible—from assimilationism to an active Jewish identity, from Russian culture to Hebrew culture and Zionism, from the status of married woman and mother to that of divorcee with child, from an orderly and secure existence to an uncertain life of wandering, first in Switzerland and then in Eretz Yisrael of the Second Aliyah.

"The Legend of the Temple"

Ira Jan settled with her daughter in Jerusalem and became associated with members of the "New Jerusalem" circle (as described by Rachel Yanait, 1962 and Gabriel Talpir, 1969:47). These people were the leaders and pacesetters of secular Jewish life in Jerusalem.[1] She was particularly friendly with the families of Yehoshua Eisenstadt-Barzelai, Boris Schatz, Drs. Naftali and Hanna Weitz, Dr. Jacob Thon, Yitzhak Ben-Zvi, Rachel Yanait (later Ben-Zvi), and Hemdah Ben-Yehuda. It was this group which laid the foundations for the Hebrew Gymnasium in Jerusalem at the end of 1908, and at the beginning of the school year 1908–1909, Ira Jan began teaching painting and sketching there (where her daughter was also a student). Under their influence she became connected with the workers' movement and the press in Eretz Yisrael, and began to contribute to the journals of that period.

Rachel Yanait and Ira Jan lived together in a house lent to the group by Boris Schatz and from that period, the letters written in Russian by Ira Jan to Rachel Yanait have been preserved (in the Ben-Zvi Archives). Yanait was in Jaffa, having been sent at doctor's order to bathe in the sea. The letters which have at once elements of lyricism, practicality, poignancy and anger, reveal how involved Ira Jan was in the public affairs of the new Yishuv in general and of Jerusalem in particular. She was a committed woman, determined to fight for what she believed to be just, and against anything which appeared to her to be erroneous, distorted or unjust. Despite the fact that she loved the sea, she loved Jerusalem better and expresses this in one of the letters:

You ask me to come to Jaffa, and Jaffa appeals to me so very little, appeals to me, say, like a kind of Kishinev. I myself don't understand why I have such a prejudice against Jaffa; perhaps my fate will be to live there. In Jerusalem I feel fine and am in no way unhappy. I am not worried [. . .] It is night now, a Jerusalem night. You know what a Jerusalem night is like. One is filled with the desire to live when there are such nights, and when there is a desire to live—everything is wonderful, don't you agree?

Her first piece of writing to appear in the Hebrew press was almost certainly "The Legend of the Temple: Dedicated to an Institution in Jerusalem." It appeared in Hapoel Hatzair in June 1908 (10:1908).[2] It was a sharp criticism of the people living in Jerusalem, their attitude toward the city and the institutions which were to give it new life, their disdain for anything which did not promise financial gain, and their total indifference to aesthetic values and nature.

The legend describes "a city abounding in mounds of graves" and surrounded by a dead sea in which no fish lived. One could not tell if the people of the city were dead or alive.

All their thoughts were given to worldly gold; to them charm was deceitful and beauty vain; they turned a deaf ear to the song of living things around them, and everything was awash with beauty and nobody paid any heed to it; the majesty of nature captivated every stranger, and only the dwellers in the dead city were insensitive to it, because their eyes were fixed on gold.

In this dead place, a temple "sprang up one night" but the people of the city, not hearing the "clink of gold" emanating from it, stood by and spat "their poison saliva on the walls of the temple" yet the temple stood open, waiting.

"From the Diary of a Jerusalemite"

Four months later, Ira Jan began to publish, in three installments, a series of critical sketches called "From the Diary of a Jerusalemite" (1908–9, vol. 2, nos. 2.5.7). The first piece (1908, 2, 2:9–10) was critical of the boredom prevailing at the town meeting hall in Jerusalem (*Beit Ha-Am*) where people would gather "for no particular purpose, largely to meet friends and relax a little." In order to liven things up, there were those who would begin making speeches but boredom continued to dominate the scene. Such criticism of "cultural life" in Jerusalem and the activities at Beit Ha-Am was fairly common then, and a number of stories and articles appeared on the subject in the press during that period.

The second piece (1908, 2, 5:8–9) was written on the background of the introduction of a constitution into the Ottoman Empire. The fictional framework of the story is provided by a malaria-stricken narrator who has lost "her ability to distinguish between imagination and reality." There are certain aspects of this sketch that remind one of the Eretz Yisreal stories of Joseph Chaim Brenner, written at a later period. They also employ a sick narrator and express a pessimistic view of life in the Yishuv, particularly in Jerusalem.

The piece reflects reactions in the Yishuv to the constitution, particularly with regard to such questions as parliamentary representation and army service. Ira Jan was of the opinion that active integration into the life of the Ottoman Empire would open up new possibilities for the Yishuv, an opinion sharply contested by many who believed that such a development would be catastrophic for the Yishuv.

For Ira Jan, the enthusiastic response of "the Sephardic Jews performing exercises as if the heroic splendor in the movements of their courageous ancestors had been preserved in them" represented the dream. The nightmare, on the other hand, was revealed by the response of the narrow-minded Zionist leadership, "who were unable to send even one Hebrew delegate to the first Ottoman parliament." In their view "the worst and most bitter section of the constitution for the seed of the Macabbees was the one dealing with compulsory military service." As a result, Ira Jan writes, "thirty-five young swordsmen, dismayed by the section" ran off to South Africa, with the aid of money collected by their Jewish brethren.

She compares the condition of the Yishuv to that of a sphinx with the body of a dog:

> Skinny, shaggy, and wounded, a dog with broken bones, kicked and beaten by many, sprawled stinking on the ground . . . It would be easy to think of this strange creature as the carcass of a trampled corpse, were it not for the tail which wags now and then, beating against his bent knees like a worn and battered horsewhip, and the resigned smile on his Asiatic European face, which testify to the fact that he is still alive.

In another place, she compares the Yishuv to an ancient tree whose roots are rotting although here and there a few buds plead for life. The gardeners, however, don't cultivate the tree: they are busy watering strange plants in distant lands.

The third piece from the "Diary" (1909, 2, 7:10–11) is also full of bitterness and despair. It deals with the stupor and inactivity in Jerusalem despite the fact that so much is happening (including events and discussions around the constitution), such as the strike of the print workers. It mentions the differences between life in Jerusalem and life in Jaffa, and alludes—in a manner bordering on the absurd—to political attempts to bridge the differences between the various ideologies. In this context she mentions the struggle of the workers for better conditions and the way in which they are fobbed off with false promises.

Once senses that the writer is essentially a socialist thinker, well-versed in practical politics, emotionally involved, an insider, ready to fight for her beliefs. One can assume that Ira Jan brought her views with her from her former life and was reinforced in them by Rachel Yanait and other members of the circle (Yanait, 1962: 79–81). The closing paragraph of the piece is particularly depressing:

> O sink, then, O sun and do not rise again, do not shine again to light up this country, this vale of tears and iniquity, this vale of iniquity and eternal shame for the whole of Israel!

The Path of Truth

Ira Jan published two pieces on two consecutive days in *Ha-Or*, put out by the Ben-Yehuda family. The first was a poetic allegory, "The Anemone" (1910a, 1, 140:2), the second, an article called "Keeping Silent" (1910b, 1, 141:1–3). There can be no doubt that they deal with the same subject. The fact that they were published one right after the other and had, in Hebrew, semantically related titles would point to this, even though they were written in completely different styles. Both allegory and direct commentary reveal a deep love for Jerusalem and a belief in the strength and future of the Yishuv, provided that the people choose the right way, the path of truth. At the same time, both warn against certain negative phenomena in Jerusalem, which were being ignored rather than exposed to the public eye.

They refer to the affair of Yehoshua Eisenstadt-Barzelai, who was fired from his job at the Anglo-Palestine Bank in the summer of 1910 by the imperious and influential Zalman Dov Levontin, director of the bank. What became a minor *cause célèbre* had its roots, apparently, in a personality clash between the two men, followed by Levontin's accusation that Barzelai was either incompetent or careless or, perhaps, both. Barzelai's friends, on the other hand, were thoroughly convinced of his absolute integrity and his professional abilities. Appeals were made by both sides to Ahad Ha-Am to intervene and at first, in a letter to Barzelai, Ahad Ha-Am sided with Levontin (although he changed his position later).

On July 6, 1910, Ira Jan wrote to Ahad Ha-Am (Ahad Ah-Am Archives, National Library, #1283). She was not personally acquainted with him but she considered him an outstanding person whose moral authority was questioned by no one. She felt that if there was anyone who could help, it was he.

The letter, written in Russian, reveals a great sensitivity to what she considered a terrible injustice to a friend. Between the lines, there is, further, a strong sense of personal identification with someone who, like herself, has been the victim of vicious "gossip."

In Ahad Ha-Am's letter to Barzelai, he had asked: "What have your friends done?" and Ira Jan refers to this when she explains her reasons for writing: "A number of accusations were hurled against his friends and because of this, I think, I have the right to write to you. I would not have written if I did not admire you and trust you deeply."

The purpose of her letter was "to restore your shaken faith in him," and so, one by one, she refutes the charges against Barzelai and challenges the reasons for Levontin's right to fire him, as enumerated by Ahad Ha-Am.

> And if you ask what his friends have done, then you must show just what it is that one's friends are obliged to do. After all, the honor of your friend has been trampled on, and you, who have the influence and the ability to stand up to everyone, can do it! But what can we do, we, his friends, who have not even one person of your stature for support? What can I, a powerless woman, do? Wouldn't the filth of gossip be poured over the head of a woman at such a time? It is so easy to bury people under gossip, particularly women. And this is an Asiatic province with Mr. Ahad Ha-Am at its head, and here all manner of noxious weeds grow—here in this distant province. Still, I can say that I have done something: I gave my moral support to a person on the verge of suicide, at the

lowest point in his life . . . Together with their protests, his friends proved to him, who is generous in every way, that not everyone is ungrateful and inhuman!

The Flower of Truth

"The Anemone" is an allegory about grave-laden Jerusalem: "and even before your body dies, your soul can be buried," putting an end to all beautiful ideas and ideals, because "this eternal city is generous with its graves, city of tombs, Jerusalem the Holy." Jerusalem buries friendship, love, truth and heroism: "as the number of your spiritual flowers so are the number of your graves." And further, flowers do not blossom on these graves, only thorns, muck, "swarms of flies and mosquitoes . . . , and all creeping and crawling things will joyfully infest" the mounds of stones which cover these "spiritual flowers."

There is only one flower which survives on these graves, "its visage a blazing fire" and it "will live from generation to generation and the terror of graveyards will not intimidate it no matter how they try to dry it up." This flower is "immortal" and grows everywhere, frightening people in Jerusalem: "Therefore do the children of Jerusalem flinch from it and the elders warn that it is blinding." Nonetheless, the author enjoins "her son": "carry this flower forever, let it blossom within you and fear no man."

It is clear that the legend pertains to the Barzelai affair which stirred up so much public sentiment. At the same time, it points a finger at other public failings in Jerusalem, which she enumerates in detail in the second piece, "Keeping Silent," which appeared the next day.

"Keeping Silent" and the Role of the Press

This is a scathing attack on the existing Zionist leadership to whom she refers ironically as "our wise and understanding leaders, the guardians of Zionism." She accuses them of bureaucracy and refers to the society emerging in Eretz Yisrael as bureaucratic. It deals harshly with the doers and the deeds in the country in general and in Jerusalem in particular. In a series of rhetorical questions the author enumerates a variety of public failings. She takes the gymnasium in Jaffa to task on the grounds that "the Hebrew people cannot support two intermediate schools in Eretz Yisrael."

She mentions the problems of water supply in Jerusalem. The high cost of living; the lack of attention to the provision of fruit and vegetables from the Jewish farms in the vicinity of Jerusalem; the negligence and slovenliness of the outlying areas of the city; the growing number of people leaving the city; the money spent on unnecessary things and the lack of proper supervision of funds; and so on and so forth.

The main thrust of her article is against the policy of "keeping silent" imposed by the leadership on the public because, as they said, regardless of how many negative features one can point to in Zionism, the fact that we are surrounded by so many enemies brings home to us the need "to hold our tongues at this time; it is a time for silence!" Ira Jan denounces this policy, calling for people to insist upon the truth, "because deeds can be fruitful only in the light of the whole truth." Her demand for the truth, and her insistence that silence, suppression and whitewashing must, in principle, be rejected, are vividly expressed in this piece and may, perhaps, reveal something of Ira Jan's underlying psyche:

> "Now one must be silent," say the cooks and bottlewashers of Zionism. Now! but the wounds of a people are not pimples on a bride's nose which can be powdered over, or her bald head which can be hidden under a wig during the interview with the bridegroom. He will see the woman as she really is soon after the wedding.
>
> A national movement is not a match which may end after a few weeks or months. A national movement goes on for years and years. Only a short-sighted person, completely devoid of hope, can believe that a movement, whose very essence is nourished by great ideals, can hold its tongue and tell this to its best people who have chosen to die rather than keep silent and see shame and wretchedness destroying their ideals.

In the course of this appeal to reveal the truth, no matter how painful and bitter, Ira Jan recalls the suicide of a young girl—without mentioning her name (another allusion to the Barzelai affair since he, too, was close to suicide):

> A few months ago, when a blooming young girl threw herself into the deep off the shores of Jaffa because—according to the note left by the girl considered a traitor by the "silencing" gentlemen—it was decreed on the shores of Jaffa, beautiful Jaffa, that she must recognize how impossible and coarse life is although it appeared so beautiful from afar.

It is even clearer from what she told her friends that it was impossible for her to compromise with the suffocating and putrifying atmosphere about which she could not even have dreamed before she came here. And so? It didn't cause our dear teachers and the guardians of Zionism living in Jaffa, or elsewhere in the country, to even raise an eyebrow.

The writer uses this tragedy to assail the veteran Zionist leadership in the name of the young people who have come to Eretz Yisrael from the Diaspora:

You, our public servants, writers and educators, are unable to distinguish between a general matter and a private matter, nor are you afraid of the verdict of your own generation or the verdict of history, you are breathing poison into the air in which the younger generation is growing up and even though they are suffocating in your poisonous vapors, they will take their revenge, in their own time, for the sake of the nation, for the fact that by your silence you are justifying injustice and violence, for the fact that you are silent yourselves and counsel others to be silent too. No! we who are not afraid of the truth will not be silent.

Her conclusion is forthright: better the bitter truth no matter how hard to swallow than ignorance and sweet delusion:

We and all the others who are not afraid of the truth, who are disgusted with those who remain silent, we call upon you, our brethren, wherever you are, who agree with us, who are courageous. We are telling you in advance: you will find a good deal of evil, a good deal of baseness here. But it is better to know it in advance so that despair will not overcome you and you will not hasten—like that young girl who threw herself into the waves of Jaffa—to act desperately.

Ira Jan considers the young girl's suicide an indirect result of trying to obscure "the truth from Eretz Yisrael," the result of the policy of the leadership which causes young people to come to the country unprepared and with unrealistic expectations. As a result they leave en masse or are broken. Only if this policy of silence changes, will people come prepared, and better qualified to deal with the hardships of life in Eretz Yisrael.

Ira Jan assigned the task of eliminating the "conspiracy of silence" to the press. At the end of the list of "sins" which she enumerates, she asks the inevitable question: "what has the press said about all this?" and she answers:

> The press—sometimes it is forthright and then suddenly it shuts up because apparently there is a great danger in angering its opponents, who can abolish it completely . . .

> The press will once have something to say "for" and then something "against," without having to present the whole of possibilities, and so people will keep coming and repeating their questions.

The press, in Ira Jan's opinion, does not fulfill its function as a public watchdog, or it does so in a feeble language and weak voice. It is the servant of the leadership who want to maintain silence and cover up the truth.

The article ends with those on the side of good insisting that the bitter truth be heard as against the wicked, the scoundrels, who wish to hide and suppress it. The former are fighting the war of "the great Israeli people"—"immortal" (son), and Zionism—the "immortal" (daughter):

> And you, you truckers in Zionism, do not kill our faith and hope. You truckers in Zionism, don't throw everything straight into your black abyss. Or do your base work better: deceive us, distort and twist everything, distort your foul lips with your killing laugh whenever you hear something honest. Poison everything you touch with your dirty hands!

> True Zionism contains within itself forces about which you, excellent gentlemen, have not even dreamed. You should know that the worse it is sometimes, the better it is. Zionism is a wonder, just like the wonder of faith. Our hopes have not been dashed by you!

Ira Jan's earlier revolutionary, socialist education, is readily apparent in her choice of terminology, although it is tempered with Zionism and her inherent lyricism.

"Life is Beautiful from a Distance"

Although Ira Jan never mentions the name of the girl who committed suicide there can be little doubt that her readers knew exactly who she was.

Among the young people of the Second and Third Aliyah, suicide was not a rare phenomenon and each time someone took his or her life, public opinion was aghast particularly when the person in question was a young girl. The novel has not yet been written describing a girl like that, who leaves her parents' home in the Diaspora and comes to Eretz Yisrael of those years, only to find life unbearable and put an end to it. Nor has scholarly research provided us with the facts, numbers, motives and details of the suicides. Information of this kind was passed on by word of mouth. Some of the facts can be extricated from the memoirs, letters and diaries of people of that generation, although in part what they wrote was designed to gloss over the bitter truth. Nonetheless, one can find heavy traces in the press of that time (see Tsur, 1976:27–44; Jaffe, 1983).[3]

The name of the girl was Rachel Meisel and a black-framed notice of the suicide appeared in Hapoel Hatzair on March 15, 1910:

> Last Thursday, 29 Adar I, at eight o'clock in the morning, Miss Rachel Meisel (of Grodno, Russia) left her lodgings and did not return. A note in Russian was found on her table which read: "May all my relatives forgive me. Since there is no god, no further steps need be taken. Life is beautiful from a distance. But the distance for me disappeared: from up close, life is coarse and not beautiful. So I am going. I am at peace and happy. Shalom. Rachel." The day was wintry and the sea rough. It is assumed that she met her death in the sea. Her body has not yet been found.
>
> Jaffa, 4 Adar II

A eulogy, "On Losing a Friend," followed the item. It was signed "A Friend," but it was more than a eulogy. It was an attempt to understand the state of mind of such a person and it was, further, a collective admission of guilt: the behavior and actions of the people among whom she had lived had brought her to the point of no return:

> Who can know the secret of a young girl who commits suicide, a secret which she takes with her to her grave! But Rachel Meisel revealed her soul's secret in her eyes, always distracted and searching, and in the smile which so often flitted across her face. Those eyes and that smile seemed to be shouting: I have a rich soul, a soul which needs a great deal of nourishment to satisfy it, and a healthy body, and I am hungry for life and life escapes me!
>
> What Rachel Meisel's soul sought, she hoped to find in Eretz Yisrael, but when she arrived, she lost even that which she had before—her hopes for life. . . .

Like most of the boys and girls her age who came her, Rachel
Meisel was suddenly uprooted from her native soil and found no
other soil on which to stand. Of all the ideals she entertained
before coming here, nothing remained but the necessity of fighting for her existence along with the impossibility of her doing so.
The family and friends among whom she spent her youth, with
whom she both suffered and rejoiced, were suddenly removed from
her by distance and she found none to take their place. The loneliness and hunger—hunger for life in all its aspects, hunger for
work which she didn't find, hunger for ideal—the loneliness and
the hunger were what accompanied her to her eternal rest. Rachel
Meisel while alive, did not find friends and companions who could
stand by her in her hour of sorrow, who could support her failing
spirits and rescue her from hell. Rachel Meisel didn't even want
friends like that because her gentle spirit sensed the vulgarity
and ruthlessness abiding in people, she knew that they were capable only of laughing at her feelings, not of helping her.

My good friend! Before your death you begged forgiveness
from your acquaintances. Poor soul! You were anxious lest your
value decline in the eyes of those you believed in. But they are so
few, and the few that understood, admired and respected you during your lifetime will admire and respect your memory after your
death!

Literature and Life

There can be little doubt that Ira Jan found it easy to identify
with Rachel Meisel and the reasons for her rash act. The note she
left behind vaguely suggests unrequited love. She may have been
used emotionally, perhaps even physically, in addition to the fact
that she was lonely and "hungry for life in all its aspects," as her
friend wrote.

Rachel Meisel was a rather well known figure in her hometown of Grodno and, with her immigration to Eretz Yisrael, became the model for the heroine of A. A. Kabak's novel *Alone*
(1905): Sara, a young Russian-Jewess, struggles with herself over
questions of Jewish nationalism and Zionism. Meisel's suicide
which, in Ira Jan's opinion, was most certainly connected with the
"policy of silence," was bound, then, to have a devastating influence:

There, in the land of her birth, where they knew her, where she
had been portrayed by Kabak in his book *Alone*, there and in
places beyond the borders of her homeland, where her letters were

read during the whole period of her life in Eretz Yisrael, there they were angry, trembling and ill, and our opponents were presented with a new weapon. And what do our dear leaders have to say about it?

"Give Me a Child"

It seems that the last story published by Ira Jan in Hebrew was also the most initimate, the one in which she lays bare her own life. It is almost certain that it bears the imprint of her unsuccessful marriage, of her arguments with her husband and the tensions between them. It was written under the impression of Bialik's visit to Eretz Yisrael in April 1909. If, indeed, she did succeed in meeting him during this visit, then there is some indication that the meeting was a failure and that the hopes and illusions she had nurtured with regard to continued relations between them were dashed. At the same time, it seems that she combined her own personal difficulties with the bitter position of women in general and women in Eretz Yisrael in particular, in the wake of the suicides of Meisel and other women.

Ira Jan protests against mediocrity and resignation, from the angle of a married woman who must resign herself to mediocrity in her own home while she herself is filled with grand aspirations. Her "mediocre" husband lectures her: "The mission of woman was, is, and always will be—the family. One must return to the authentic Hebrew woman. The titles, "wife" and "mother" mean everything to her. Why must you aspire to something else?"

The story, "Dina Dinar," was published in *Hashiloah* (1913:142–152; 239–249). It is the story of a fatal meeting between a married woman—who does not love her husband and three sons—and a poet whom she regards as a superman. The woman suffers from the mediocrity of her daily life and of her times in which no giants—"Herzls" in her language—walk the earth. She wishes to have a child by the poet, a genius who will redeem the Jewish people. At the last moment, when it seems to her that the poet has acquiesced, she changes her mind and commits suicide.

Exile Without Redemption

Ira Jan's last years in Eretz Yisrael were afflicted with hardships which made her earlier years pale by comparison. In the

summer of 1914, her daughter left for a visit to Russia and with
the outbreak of the war remained stranded there. She never returned to Eretz Yisrael and all traces of her disappeared (Tidhar,
1947, 2:836–937).

According to Rachel Yanait (1965) and Nahum Gutman
(1980:86), some months after the outbreak of the First World War,
when Russian citizens were rounded up by Turkish soldiers, Ira
Jan was among them and was deported by ship to Egypt. This was
on Black Thursday, December 17, 1914 (Golan, 1984:65–66). She
just managed to hide all her paintings in the attic of the Brill family. Brill was an important official of the Jewish Colonial Trust
whose daughter was one of Ira Jan's students.

Ira Jan's trials and tribulations in Egypt were reported by
Leah Cohen Weitz, her pupil and the daughter of friends (Testimony of Leah Cohen Weitz, Meroz, 1972):

> We met her again in Egypt where we too had been deported. She
> was living in extreme poverty. She earned her living by giving
> drawing lessons, and we all went to study with her. It was also a
> way in which we could give her material assistance. My father
> was the doctor who looked after her, and it soon became apparent
> that she was suffering from tuberculosis. As everyone was living
> in dire straits at that time, her condition worsened. Finally she
> was unable to work and she was taken to hospital. I went to visit
> her with my father, the doctor, and had an unforgettable experi-
> ence. As we approached her she looked at me and my father. We
> both understood the meaning of that look. She wanted to know if
> the illness was serious and she was dying or if there was a chance
> that she would recuperate. It was clear that if she was dying my
> father would not let me get too close to her. He understood her
> miserable look and made a sudden decision—although he knew
> how ill she was and I was his only child. He said to me: "Go over
> and kiss her." I believe that the relief and joy, which suffused her
> face, gave her the strength to continue living for another few
> months.

Ira Jan's illness prompted her friends, particularly Rachel
Yanait Ben-Zvi to try and insure her early return to Eretz Yisrael
after the war (see Thon to Yanait, Ben-Zvi Archives, 2/1/2/8; Govrin, 1985:98).

Back in Tel Aviv after four years of exile in Alexandria, and
still weak, ill and bedridden, Ira Jan was lodged at the Hotel Spec-
tor. When she was feeling somewhat better, she went over to the
Brill residence to collect her paintings. They had disappeared and

were never found. Brill, an American citizen, had been deported by the Turkish authorities when the United States joined the allies, and his house was taken over, first by the Turks and then by the British. "And we will never know," wrote Nahum Gutman, "what happened to her paintings" (1980:86).

She mourned the loss of her paintings, according to Rachel Yanait, "as one would a kindred soul." Her book on the sculptor, Mark Antokolski, was gone as well. Ira Jan never recovered from these losses and she died in Tel Aviv on April 24, 1919 at the age of fifty.

Before her death, she wrote to her friends Jacob and Florence Mozer (n.d., CZA, quoted in Meroz, 1972):

> I already feel the approach of death. I accept it peacefully. I came from eternity and I return to eternity. That is all. Is human life but a moment of consciousness in eternal life or, as some believe, is it something we understand only after death? I do not regret that I was born, but life is a thing of beauty only for the elect, and I was not among them. I accuse no one, especially since I did have beautiful, wonderful moments.

She was buried in the old cemetery in Tel Aviv, on Trumpeldor Street and her tombstone reads (Kroll and Linman, 1940:250):

The Writer and Artist
Esther daughter of Joseph
Slepian Ira Jan
April 24, 1919

Notes

1. Rachel Yanait also wrote an article, "With Barzelai," in *Davar*, 14.3.33, when his remains were brought to Eretz Yisrael for burial. In the Ben-Zvi Archive (2/1/2/7), there is a note in her handwriting from 6.1.79:

> Ira Jan—(Slepian), an artist and writer—a close friend of Bialik. 1907/8 I lived with her in Ben-Zvi's small commune in a house in Jerusalem in Hahabashim street. The family of Dr. Naftali and Dr. Hanna Weitz lived in the same house. Yehoshua Barzelai was among our close friends. Rachel B.

2. It is hard to know which institution in Jerusalem she was referring to in this legend. There were two possibilities: Bezalel or the Hebrew Gym-

nasium. I would guess that she meant Bezalel, which already existed, and not the gymnasium which was in the process of being established.

3. This is the diary of a student from the Herzliah Gymnasium in Tel Aviv, who committed suicide when he was twenty. He also mentions the fact that a fellow student, Uri Caesari, told him of another ten students who committed suicide.

References

Golan, Arnon. 1984. "Tel Aviv during the First World War." *Idan*, 3:65–66 (Hebrew).

Govrin, Nurit. 1985. "Meeting of the Exiles from *Eretz Yisrael* with Egypt and the Egyptian Jewish Community during the First World War." *Pe'amim*, 25:73–101 (Hebrew).

———. 1989. *Honey from the Rock*. Tel Aviv: Ministry of Defense (Hebrew).

Gutman, Nachum, and Ehud, Ben Ezer. 1980. *Sand Dunes and Blue Sky*. Tel Aviv: Yavneh (Hebrew).

Jaffe, Yitzhak. 1983. *What is Life? A Diary*. Tel Aviv: Yaacov Sharett (Hebrew).

Jan, Ira. 1908a. "The Legend of the Temple (dedicated to an Institution in Jerusalem)." *Hapoel Hatzair* 1, 10:10 (Hebrew).

———. 1908b. "From the Diary of a Jerusalemite. A Short Feuilleton." *Hapoel Hatzair* 2, 2:9–10 (Hebrew).

———. 1908c. "From the Diary of a Jerusalemite. A Short Feuilleton." *Hapoel Hatzair* 2, 5:8–9 (Hebrew).

———. 1909. "From the Diary of a Jerusalemite. A Short Feuilleton." *Hapoel Hatzair* 2, 7:10–11 (Hebrew).

———. 1910a. "The Anemone (Dedicated to Mrs. Mozer). Translation." *Ha'or* 1, 140:2 (Hebrew).

———. 1910b. "Feuilleton. Keeping Silent. (Translation)." *Ha'or* 1, 141:1–3 (Hebrew).

———. 1913. "Dina Dinar. (Illustration)." *Hashiloah* 28, Shvat Sivan: 142–152; 239–249 (Hebrew).

Kabak, A. A. 1905. *Alone, A Novel*. Toshiah: Warsaw (Hebrew).

Kroll, Zvi and Zaddok Linman (eds.). 1940. *The Old Cemetery in Tel Aviv*. Tel Aviv (Hebrew).

Meroz, Tamar. 1972. "Love Story." *Ha'aretz*. 15/12/75 (Hebrew).

Sadeh, Pinchas. 1985. "She Wrote Me a Brief Letter," pp. 198–213 in *Selected Poems of Chaim Nahman Bialik*, edited by Pinchas Sadeh. Tel Aviv: Dvir and Schocken (Hebrew).

Shamir, Moshe. 1972. "Bialik's Love." *Moznaim* 36, 1:11–19 (Hebrew).

Shochetman, Baruch. 1945. "Bialik in Translation." *Ha'olam* 33, 3:39 (Hebrew).

Talpir, Gavriel. 1969. "Artists in Israel Who Have Passed Away: Ira Jan (Esther Slepian): 1868–1919." *Gazit* 26, (April-November):47 (Hebrew).

Tidhar, David. 1947. *Encyclopedia of the Pioneers and Builders of the Yishuv*. Vol. 2. Tel Aviv: Sifriat Rishonim (Hebrew).

Tsur, Muki. 1976. *Without a Coat of Many Colors*. Tel Aviv: Am Oved (Hebrew).

Yanait, Ben-Zvi, Rachel. 1965. *Ira Jan* Photo Album with Introduction and Biography. Jerusalem: Neumann (Hebrew).

———. 1962. *Ascending to Eretz Yisrael*. Tel Aviv: Am Oved (Hebrew).

8

The Women Workers' Movement: First Wave Feminism in Pre-State Israel

—— *Dafna N. Izraeli* ——

The Women Workers' Movement in pre-state Israel developed within the Labor Zionist movement as a reaction to the disappointment of a small group of women with the limited role they were assigned in the emerging society. From its beginnings in 1911, the movement aimed to expand the boundaries of the Jewish woman's role in pre-state Israel and to secure her full and equal participation in the process of Jewish national reconstruction. Members of the movement were nationalists and idealists who had come as pioneers from eastern Europe during the years 1904–14, and they were joined by women who arrived in Palestine after the First World War, from 1919 through 1923. These periods, known in the history of Zionism as the Second and Third Aliyah, are considered the formative periods of Israeli society. Because they were marked by social creativity, readiness for experimentation, and remodeling of institutional forms, these periods were also crucial for the status of women in the new society.

The pioneers of the Second Aliyah emigrated from Russia following the pogroms that took place in 1903 and after the October revolution in 1905. Many pioneers were infused with radical and socialist ideas prevalent in Russia at the time, but they had been disappointed by the social reform movement there and by its failure to solve the problems of the Jewish people. The immigrants consisted primarily of middle-class young, single people or young couples, who came without parents. In a new country the usual restraints and obligations that bind women to domestic roles and traditional definitions of their domain were reduced, which allowed women freedom to experiment with alternative roles. Furthermore, there are indications that these women composed a self-selected group that had liberated itself from the effects of traditional social-

ization. The move to Palestine required determination and idealism from all the immigrants, but even more so from the women. It
is thus not surprising that women were only a small proportion of
the immigrant pioneers, five to ten percent in the early years and
rising to close to twenty percent in 1913.

Women came to Palestine ready to participate more fully in
social life than they had been permitted to do in Jewish bourgeois
circles in Russia. They did not expect to struggle for women's place;
they thought equality would be an accompanying feature of their
move to the new homeland.

While this account is a study of a specific place, time, and circumstance, it highlights dilemmas that commonly confront women
in socialist movements generally, especially during periods of economic and political upheaval. At such time the commitment of a
movement's participants tends to be heavily taxed, and the demand for undivided loyalties is great. Identification with a larger
movement creates a set of constraints on the development of feminist ideology and on the creation of separate feminist organization,
particularly when feminist dissatisfaction is directed toward the
position of women within the movement itself (Slaughter, 1977).
These constraints, and their consequences for the career of the feminist movement in Palestine, are the major themes of this chapter.

Years of Incubation, 1904–11

Ideas and ideology played an important role in shaping the
character of the pioneering society. A basic tenet of the ideology
was the value attributed to the collective. The individual was expected to sacrifice personal interests to the welfare of the new Jewish society whose members included not only those who had already immigrated but also the multitudes of Jews who would
"return home" in the future. Among the two most important cultural creations of the Second Aliyah were the image of the ideal
pioneer—the *halutz*—and the ideal form of social organization—
the *kvutza*—(forerunner of the kibbutz) (Eisenstadt, 1967:17). Halutz literally means a member of the vanguard, one who goes before the camp and fulfills its highest purposes. During the Second
Aliyah physical work was idealized and elevated to a religious
value (Bein, 1954:31; Preuss, 1965:119; Gordon, 1959:373). The key
elements of the halutz ideal had an essentially masculine character, which heightened the relevance of biological differences between the sexes.

The most urgent problem facing the new immigrants upon their arrival in Palestine was employment. In vain they knocked on the doors of the established farmers of the First Aliyah (1882–1903), who were unwilling to substitute Jewish labor for the cheaper, more experienced, and amenable Arab labor. Women faced greater obstacles than men. The First Aliyah farmers considered their insistence on having "men's jobs" as "unnatural". Faced with unemployment and filled with a desire to establish a new type of Jewish society, the Second Aliyah workers moved north to the lower Galilee, and established a new type of communal life—the kvutza—a small collective settlement in which everyone labored. This form of living very quickly became a normative ideal.

In the kvutza the conscious rebellion against the traditional occupational structure of Jewish society did not extend to women's work. The women were automatically assigned to the kitchen and the laundry (Katznelson, 1948, 4:179). It seems that among the men and many of the women it remained part of the "world taken for granted" that domestic work was the woman's responsibility. Domestic chores, although physical work, had low status among the pioneers who established a hierarchy of value according to both the conditions under which work was performed and the type of work engaged in. A member of a collective had higher status than someone who was an employee; "productive work", work that produced marketable goods, was deemed more valuable than "non-productive work", such as services provided for the members of the collective. Thus, cooking, laundering, and mending were not considered productive work, and they ranked low among pioneering values. Cooking for a collective held greater prestige than cooking in a private household, but it was less "worthy" than tilling the soil. Within productive work, agriculture, specifically field crops (*falcha*), became the embodiment of the halutz endeavor, symbolizing economic self sufficiency as well as rejection of the pattern set by the farmers of the First Aliyah with their dependence on Arab labor and foreign markets.

One of the unintended consequences of this pioneering ideology as well as of the new forms of social organization was that they relegated women to secondary roles in the new society. The *halutza* (female form of halutz) had virtually no opportunity to become a bearer of the effective symbols of the halutz ideology. In the kvutza, the women's dissatisfaction and growing sense of deprivation came to focus on three issues: women's formal status as second-class members, the limitations on their participation, and degrading attitudes of the male members.

Despite their disappointments, however, the women pioneers in the communes of the Galilee found new hope in occasional incidents. For example, in the fall of 1907 at Sejera, a small group of farm laborers decided to form an independent agricultural collective. Among the members was Manya Shohat, a radical labor leader and known activist prior to her immigration, as well as the first to promote the idea of collective settlement in Palestine. The one year experience at Sejera, in which women proved themselves capable of plowing, provided a sense of efficacy and justified the claim for participation in physical work, while an experiment in vegetable gardening supplied a suitable model. Women could become farmers by creating new agricultural branches compatible with their physical abilities.

A women's training farm at Kinneret (on the Sea of Galilee) was founded in 1911 after Hanna Meisel, a trained agronomist who had developed vegetable gardening in Sejera, had obtained funds from a women's Zionist group in Germany. For the time being, at least, these women gave up the idea that their equality could be achieved in the mixed group.

Beginnings of the Movement

The transformation of dissatisfied people into a social movement requires their awareness that they share a situation which is in some important aspects unjust (Smelser, 1963). This process of change first manifested itself in 1911 in Kinneret at a meeting initiated by Hanna Meisel for the purpose of explaining her plans for the women's training farm. Although only seventeen women attended, this meeting—providing as it did the first opportunity for the halutzot (female plural of halutz) to exchange experiences, share their individual grievances, and give each other moral support—laid the foundation for the emergence of a women's movement within the Labor Zionist camp in Palestine (Even-Shoshan, 1963, 1:215). First, "the problem of the woman worker" emerged as a social reality and legitimized the establishment of a separate organization. Once socially identified and labeled, the issue could become the basis for social action. Second, the meeting defined the goals of the movement's future, outlined the strategy for change and identified a group of leaders among the second wave of pioneers. The ideological orientation first formulated at Kinneret, and reiterated at every subsequent conference of women workers, emphasized the need for self-transformation. To achieve their goal, namely, equal participation, women had to change themselves. As they proclaimed: "We, the women laborers, like the men, aspire first and foremost to rehabilitate our spirit and bodies through work . . . in the field and in nature, and in this way we can rid ourselves of the habits, the way of life and even the way of thinking that we brought with us from the diaspora" (Group of women workers, 1913:12–13).

Turner and Killian list three conditions as essential for a movement to follow the route of self-transformation rather than that of institutional change: a belief that widespread improvement is possible, a belief that the state of the social order will reflect "the integrity and character of individual man", and an acceptance by the people of responsibility "for their present unsatisfactory conditions" (Turner and Killian, 1972: 275). Belief in the possibility for transforming the Jewish Luftmensch of the diaspora into a manual worker and tiller of the soil, as we have seen, was fundamental to Labor Zionism. In defining self-alteration as their major goal, the halutzot adopted a stance that fit well with the dominant ideology and was, therefore, attractive. The women believed that they had the same potential as men, though for historical reasons it had remained dormant. Through training as manual workers they would overcome their passive, dependent character. Once the halutza proved her skill, not only would she be accepted as a full member in the kvutza, but men would seek her out. "At the dawn of the movement we thought that we had only to overcome the barrier of occupational training, and as for equality, it would all follow automatically", wrote Ada Maimon, one of the leading figures in the struggle for women's equal participation (Maimon, 1972:121).

Men were not to be blamed for women's unhappy predicament since they, too, were conditioned by habitual ways of thinking and behaving. However, since they seemed unable to understand the problem of women workers, they could not be relied upon to bring about the necessary changes. Women would have to transform themselves (WWC, 1914:12–13). An ideology oriented toward self transformation, rather than toward changing men and social institutions, helped to legitimate the creation of a separate women's movement within Labor Zionism in that it avoided direct conflict with the male-dominated ideology and with the male pioneers. The network of social ties that linked the feminists of the Second Aliyah with the male leadership of the labor movement discouraged the development of a "we-they" dichotomy. A number of highly influential male comrades had encouraged the halutzot. Some of the women's leaders and these men were members of the same political party and the same kvutza, they came from the same town in Europe, or they shared friends, and relatives. These allegiances put pressure on the women who feared that their desire for separate institutional arrangements would lead to accusations of lack of trust and even of the betrayal of their male comrades. The ideology of self-transformation mitigated this danger by emphasizing the common goals of men and women pioneers: women must be helped to change so that they could contribute more effectively toward the realization of shared values and goals.

The Kinneret meeting defined the operational goals of the women's movement. The strategy was to push for the development of new agricultural branches, such as vegetable gardening, poultry, and dairy farming, that were considered "suitable for women". The women also demanded a monopoly over these areas of work, since, they argued, men had many other jobs to do. Two main tactics were adopted. First, the farm at Kinneret was to serve as a training center where women could learn technical skills and begin personal transformation within a supportive environment, unhampered by the presence of men. Second, in the future women would join only those kvutzot willing to accept at least ten of them, so that rotation between household and agriculture would be feasible (Maimon-Fishman, 1929:23). The former tactic aimed at achieving the goal of self transformation, the latter that of participation.

The women's desire for a separate organization resulted from their growing awareness that their goals could not be realized through the existing structures of the Labor Zionist movement in Palestine. These consisted of two competing political parties, which were the most important organizations of the labor movement prior to the First World War, the agriculturally oriented, leftist Hapoel Hatzair and the radical socialist Poalei Zion, as well as two unions of agricultural workers, one in the Galilee and one in Judea. The parties sent representatives to the unions, which negotiated with the Palestine Office of the World Zionist Organization on behalf of the agricultural communes and mobilized resources for new settlements. Because very few women were influential or active in the labor parties, they hesitated to raise their particular problems. In addition, there were always "more important" problems of survival that took priority. Nevertheless, the disregard for women's problems struck even a male observer, who found it necessary to comment on the point in a labor newspaper: "I have been in the country five years and have taken part in many workers' meetings where every conceivable subject was discussed. To my complete surprise there was one subject that was never discussed, not even in passing; the situation of our women workers" (Mamshi, 1911:5). The failure to permit women to participate in the various decision-making forums of the labor movement organizations had a cumulative effect. When the agricultural union of the Galilee neglected to invite a woman representative to its fifth conference in 1914, the halutzot barged into their meeting and vociferously protested, (Maimon-Fishman, 1929:52; Shapira, 1961:140) but a more important result was the women's decision to convene their own conference of women agricultural workers only three months later. Thirty delegates met representing 209 women workers (WWC, 1914). Thus, the organizational arm of the women's movement was established. In the war years the women's movement created two organizational structures: an annual conference, five of which were held between 1914 and 1918, and the women workers' committee to organize and coordinate the activities of the movement between the conferences. The leaders were not anonymous women but women linked to the inner circles of Palestine's emerging elite. Some had political experience, and according to the evidence none received monetary remuneration for her work in the women's movement.

The issues on the agenda of the various conferences were similar to those which had been raised at Kinneret in 1911, though there were additions. When the halutzot gave birth to their first children, the problem of how to combine child care with public activities became urgent. If each woman had to care for her own children, she would have to give up many tasks outside the home, and the gains made would be lost. The solution adopted was collective child care with women in the collective rotating the responsibility (Porat, 1977). Women's participation in the labor movement was another issue at consecutive conferences, as women came increasingly to realize that doing agricultural work did not automatically lead to participation in the decision-making bodies either of the labor movement as a whole or even of the commune (Harari, 1959: 492).

The most pressing general issue for all the pioneers of the time related to employment. During the war years, the movement achieved some important successes in providing work. Women were trained on the Kinneret farm and then integrated into the kvutzot. The shift in economic policy within the agricultural communes between 1914 and 1918 from total reliance on grain crops toward greater diversification opened new branches and thus new opportunities for women. In 1919, a drop in the price of grain and a drought accelerated the process toward diversification and self reliance (Bein, 1954:55, 164). Women joined grain-growing collectives which successfully sold their produce in the markets (Ettinger, 1919:5–6). They managed vegetable gardens which were usually situated next to the workers' public kitchens where the women were employed as cooks. Most of the projects received modest financial assistance from the agricultural union and, through the intervention of the women workers' committee, from Zionist women's groups abroad.

The change in women's self-image and in their status within the labor movement is reflected in the differences noticeable between the first meeting at Kinneret in 1911 and later conferences. At Kinneret the doors were closed to men. Those who showed up were accused of having come to ridicule or out of curiosity, and they were thought to be indifferent to the problems of the halutzot. At the opening session of the fifth conference held in Tel Aviv, apart from the seventy women delegates, there were a large number of invited guests, including several official male representatives of the parties and the agricultural union (Maimon-Fishman, 1929; Harari, 1959:492). This change of policy manifests the increased self-confidence of the movement and its recognition by the pioneering community.

Although the women's movement brough about important cultural change in the norms regarding woman's role, it did not institutionalize a social structure to serve as a power center in relation to other organizations in the Yishuv or the World Zionist Organization (the major source of funds for the pioneers in Palestine). The women gave relatively little attention to organizational activity, partly because they were so few and partly because they accepted as their major structural framework the agricultural unions, where they had gained official recognition. An important additional factor was that the women preferred "doing" to "organizing others". A characteristic of the Second Aliyah as a whole was that it was oriented more toward the implementation of ideals through direct participation in grass-roots activities associated with Zionist fulfillment than toward political activity.[1] No organizational bodies were developed between the years 1914 and 1918 apart from the conferences and the elected committee. Whatever funds were obtained whether from the agricultural union or from women's organizations abroad, were ear-marked for specific employment and agricultural training projects. But these financial contributions were not institutionalized in a structural commitment of continuous support.

The Career of the Women's Movement, 1918–27

The end of the First World War ushered in a period of developments in the Yishuv, where new dilemmas for the women's movement emerged. Comparing the Yishuv before and after the First World War, Eisenstadt observes that "if the period of the Second *Aliyah* was the period of ideological emphasis, the [British] mandate ushered in a period of stress on the formulation and practical implementation of the major goals of the Yishuv . . ." (Eisenstadt, 1967:24). The ability of the Women Workers' Movement to implement its goals was affected by two major developments: first, the arrival of the Third Aliyah (1919–23); second, the establishment of the Histadrut—the General Federation of Jewish Labor.

The Third Aliyah, arriving after the First World War, was encouraged by the Balfour Declaration, which affirmed the British government's support for the establishment of a Jewish homeland in Palestine. In many of its social and ideological characteristics the Third Aliyah was a continuation of the Second: a sizable portion of the immigrants were young socialist pioneers from eastern Europe; and they too had been influenced by ideas prevalent at the time of the Russian revolution. From the perspective of the women's movement, however, the Third Aliyah differed from the Second in three aspects. First, the proportion of women among all immigrants during the Third Aliyah was larger, 36.8 percent. Among the single immigrants the proportion was 17 percent in 1920, increasing to 30 percent in 1922. Among the pioneers affiliated with the socialist movement women comprised some 17–18 percent, compared with approximately 10 percent during the Second Aliyah (Even-Shoshan, 1963, 1:400; Erez, 1948:43). Second, the pioneers arrived as members of different pioneering groups and social movements, most notably *Gdud Ha'avoda* (Work Battalion) and *Hashomer Hatzair* (The Young Watchman). These were created in the diaspora and organized in communes committed to the principle of equality in production and consumption. Third, larger numbers of pioneers gravitated to the towns, where they formed part of the new urban proletariat. There, unemployment was particularly acute for women.

The period began ominously for the women's movement. The women's vegetable-growing collectives collapsed due to competition from British imports. The farm at Kinneret was closed for lack of financial means. The settlement department of the Zionist Organization discontinued its support of women's farming collectives, believing that women would find their place in kibbutzim[2] (Bein, 1954:157–8; Hahistadrut Hahakla'it, 1951:549). The women's committee had failed to gain the recognition granted to other institutions of the labor movement, particularly the political parties, by the World Zionist Organization. In other words, in 1918 on the eve of the arrival of the Third Aliyah, the Women Workers' Movement lacked its own mechanisms for coping with the new problems of unemployment and for pursuing its goals.

The new sources of employment that developed after the establishment of the mandate, namely, rail and road construction and then building in the towns, did not welcome women. Nevertheless, women pressed for entry, and in 1922 they composed 16 percent of the total membership in construction collectives, although half of them supplied the domestic services such as cooking. The Construction Workers' Union in 1924 resolved to increase the number of women accepted into the work groups; train women in building crafts; establish work groups in the crafts suitable for women such as floor tiling, plastering, and painting; and put women in line for suitable jobs. These resolutions, however, were never translated into a program of action.

Working in construction became the epic expression of the halutz ideal and a challenge to the women's movement seeking to conquer new fields, as agriculture had been for the halutzot of the Second Aliyah. Again, however, women faced strong opposition. Jobs were scarce. They were mainly allocated through the labor exchange of the respective political parties and, after 1920, through the Histadrut (General Federation of Jewish Labor). Since work contracts were assigned to groups, getting a job depended on being accepted to a work group, which was problematic for women. As Tehiya Liberson, a member of the Construction Workers' Union reported: "The men had quite a number of reasons for keeping us out. Some said the work was too strenuous for women. Others argued that if women were admitted to the building trade communes, which contracted for work as a group, the output would decrease and the pay with it" (Liberson, 1975:176).

Faced with resistance to their acceptance by male groups, and indignant at being accused of causing financial deficits, women formed their own work communes and even competed with men for job contracts. In the mid-1920s there were two women's construction groups, several floor tiling communes, as well as tobacco and laundry collectives. The women's organization established half a dozen training farms modelled on the Kinneret experiment. Women also formed *havurot*—small collectives based on a combination of vegetable gardening and outside employment (Hanoh, 1926:7–8; Maimon-Fishman, 1926:4). Organizing, encouraging, and financing these projects were the major acitvities of the executive committee of the Women Workers' Council, the organizational arm of the Women Workers' Movement within the newly established Histadrut.

After the First World War there had been a trend toward unification among the labor groups in the *Yishuv* which in 1920 led to the establishment of an umbrella organization, the Histadrut. The trade unions, the sick fund, the consumers' union, labor exchanges, immigration office, public works, a building office, schools, and workers' public kitchens, which had been created by the political parties, were transferred to the Histadrut. The consolidation of these structures within a single organization, which controlled virtually all the resource-generating institutions of the labor movement, meant that the women's movement became dependent on the Histadrut.

Election of delegates to the founding convention of the Histadrut held in December 1920, was by proportional representation of political parties. As the women's movement did not consider itself a political faction but viewed its goals as cutting across the ideological differences that segmented the labor movement, it did not submit a separate list of candidates and was not officially represented. Among eighty-seven delegates to the founding convention of the Histadrut, only four were women, all sent by the *Ahdut Ha'avoda* party (an extension of the Poalei Zion party). The more committed feminists, such as Ada Fishman (later to become Maimon) and Yael Gordon, leading members of the Hapoel Hatzair party, were among the thirty or so women who had been invited to attend the proceedings as guests. Restricted to passive participation these guests objected strongly to the poor representation of women by the political factions and to the failure of the convention to deal with the special problems of the woman worker. In the last hours of the closing session, Ada Maimon, leader in the struggle for women's electoral rights in all institutions of Jewish self-government, declared that the female delegates, having been chosen by the parties and not by the women workers, did not and could not represent them. She announced that the women planned to form their own association within the Histadrut, and if refused representation on the Histadrut Council they "would feel forced to submit a separate electoral list to compete for representation on the Histadrut Council in the next election"[3] (Histadrut, 1970). Maimon's proposal won the support of leading figures in the major parties and was accepted by the convention. Two places were reserved for representatives to be elected directly by the women workers.

The admission of the women's movement into the Histadrut stimulated a new wave of organizational activity among the women. The leadership set out to mobilize support among the new immigrants particularly those pioneers who had arrived as part of organized ideological movements. They were potentially most cooptable. First, they were physically concentrated and thus more accessible than the mass of individual women employed primarily as seamstresses and domestics in private homes. Second, more than other women, their immigration had been motivated by aspirations similar to those of the feminists of the Second Aliyah; namely, realization of the pioneering goals of Socialist Zionism. Third, they were the most predisposed to egalitarian ideals.

The meeting between the Second and Third Aliyah pioneers may be analyzed in terms of an encounter between "sociological generations". The halutzot of the Second Aliyah had been excluded from full participation in the kvutzot, and their aspirations had been ridiculed. After a decade of struggle, they found that women were still discriminated against in all areas of public life. The halutzot of the Third Aliyah belonged to sexually mixed and strongly ideological socialist groups which provided work for their women members. They did not feel as deprived as did their forerunners. Although dissatisfaction with the gender division of labor and status existed even within such aggresively egalitarian groups as the Gdud Ha'avoda, it was expressed, if at all, within the organization through its internal media (Drori, 1975:14–17), and did not spark collective action across factional boundaries. Loyalty to the group and its goals took priority over the issues that had united the women a decade earlier. Nonetheless, out of reverence for the women of the Second Aliyah, they attended the founding conference of the Women Workers' Council (WWC) held in 1921. The 1921 conference, with forty-three delegates representing 485 workers, officially established the Women Workers' Council as the or-

Figure 11. Delegates of the second convention of the WWM, 1922 (Labor Archive).

ganizational arm of the Women Workers' Movement within the Histadrut. The council elected an executive committee and representatives to each of the major departments within the Histadrut (Maimon-Fishman, 1929:91–2).

By the time of the second conference in 1922, at which thirty-seven delegates represented six hundred women members, the underlying tensions within the women's movement had surfaced. Two major opposing factions emerged. I refer to them as the "radicals" and the "loyalists". The difference between them may be analyzed in terms of degrees of commitment to feminism and of trust put in the male leadership. The old leaders, joined by the disenchanted among the Third Aliyah, were the more radical. They put little trust in a male-dominated Histadrut to look after women's interests and advocated a strong, separate organization—free of party control and in contact with grass-roots members—that would initiate and monitor women's training and employment opportunities. The newly arrived Third Aliyah pioneers held the loyalist position which recognized that women had special problems but believed there was no need for a separate women's organization to solve them. They argued that the newly constituted Histadrut should look after all workers alike. The Women Workers' Council should concentrate on re-educating and activating women for participation in public life. In relation to the Histadrut it should limit itself to an advisory role and certainly not duplicate the services of the labor exchange and other bodies that generated and allocated resources. Organizational segregation was objectionable also because it implied lack of faith in the men which, the loyalists felt, was not deserved (Maimon-Fishman, 1929:182–83).

The dispute over the Women Workers' Council's (WWC) role was not merely an internal matter. The positions defended and the relative influence of the respective protagonists were ultimately determined by the interests of the male leaders of the Histadrut, whose response to the WWC was a reflection of its general policy toward particular interest groups. Analysis of the events in the 1920s therefore requires some understanding of the wider sociopolitical context.

At that time, the leadership of the Histadrut faced two major organizational problems. The first was how to safeguard the stability of the new, unifying institution, which had been forged from a variety of divergent ideological streams within Labor Zionism and incorporated a number of conflicting power groups. The second problem concerned the relationship of the political parties to the Histadrut. Although elements within Ahdut Ha'avoda argued that after the establishment of the Histadrut, political parties were no longer necessary and should be dissolved, those in favor of their perpetuation prevailed. The latter faction, furthermore opposed a pluralistic structure and pressed for centralization of the party organization and for party control over the Histadrut (Shapiro, 1976). Clearly, women's organization independent of party control conflicted with the interests of Ahdut Ha'avoda, which argued that separatist tendencies among particular interest groups would waste resources and weaken the Histadrut. At the same time the leadership was generally sympathetic toward the special problems and goals of the women pioneers. The decision to include the WWC in the Histadrut may be viewed as a form of co-optation, a mechanism of social control first defined by Selznick as "the process of absorbing new elements into the leadership of the policy determining structure of an organization as a means of averting threats to its stability or existence" (Selznick, 1949:13).

As noted, in 1920 the Histadrut's control over the worker community was still precarious. The leaders of the Ahdut Ha'avoda party feared the separate organization of various factions among both the Second and Third Aliya. For Histadrut leaders at the 1920 convention, Maimon's threat that the women workers would submit an independent electoral list made it expedient to absorb the leadership into the council, especially since events outside the labor management gave the threat greater credibility. The conflict over women's voting rights in the newly forming National Assembly, the Jewish parliament of the Yishuv, had made feminism a salient issue and a legitimate basis for organizational differentiation. By 1920, the Association of Hebrew Women for Equal Rights in Eretz Yisrael (Palestine) had been established and was mobilizing support outside the labor sector. The association was an umbrella organization of women's groups which formed after the First World War in the urban centers and larger agricultural villages (moshavot). The members were mainly from the educated middle-class and secular elements of the Jewish community.

In the elections to the National Assembly, some eight months before the founding convention of the Histadrut, the Association had submitted a separate women's list that won seven mandates—the same number as there were women elected by the two labor parties to the Assembly. These developments influenced the response to the demand of the women workers for representatives and their incorporation in the Histadrut Council.

The Transformation of the Feminist Movement, 1921–27

From the perspective of the Histadrut and particularly that of the Ahdut Ha'avoda party, which was struggling for dominance within the newly established political structure, the women's movement posed a problem of social control. Its accusations of discrimination undermined the legitimacy of the Histadrut's claim to represent all workers. To offset the potential costs of such allegations, the Women Workers' Council was defined as an embarrassment to the labor movement. This perspective emerges in the report presented by Ben Gurion, then leader of Ahdut Ha'avoda to the second convention of the Histadrut in 1923 in which he explained that the "very existence and need for the existence of a special institution in the form of the WWC to protect the interests of the women workers does not add to our honor" (Histadrut, 1923:26). This stance was shared by those women in the WWC who were closely identified with the male leaders of Ahdut Ha'avoda and committed to them; one such woman was Golda Meir who at the same convention declared: ". . . It is a sad and shameful fact that we are forced to create a special organization to deal with matters of the woman worker" (ibid.:49).

The tactical aspect of this admission about the WWC is two-fold. First, when viewed as a concession to an unfortunate and embarrassing reality, the organization became a vestige of some unresolved past rather than a positive creative force projected into the future and devoted to the creation of a better society. Second, presented as a kind of "bastard" child of the labor movement (unwanted and unplanned for by the father), the women's movement was discredited for exposing the labor movement's failure to live up to its own ideals. Another tactic employed to confine the amount of resources the Histadrut would be required to divert to satisfy the demands of the Women Workers' Council was to understate the magnitude of the change aspired to. The women's goals were translated into specific objectives and defined in negative rather than positive terms. For example, describing women's aspirations for equality as the need to eliminate discrimination at work made fewer demands on the system than a definition that called for affirmative action in all walks of life. In the same address in 1923, Ben Gurion went on to explain that:

> there is no special Histadrut for women workers nor is there a need for such a Histadrut, but we cannot ignore the bitter truth that the matter of equality for women, which we accept as a first principle, is only formal . . . there is still a need for a special institution for the women workers which will stand guard and concern itself with the social and economic position of the female worker so that she not be discriminated against within the community of workers (ibid.:26).

Ben Gurion's interpretation of the role of the Women Workers' Council discounts the importance of the movement in the ideology and activity of national rebirth. Instead of being depicted as a creator of a new cultural image for women in the emerging socialist society, it was ascribed the role of watchdog guarding the interests of a "minority" group. Its members are thus denied the right to pride in a mission whose importance for the labor movement is discounted. According to Ben Gurion, implementation of the women's movement's goals, such as creating employment opportunities, was to be left to the Histadrut. His statement that no special union for women existed as it did, for example, for agricultural workers, was intended as a warning that separation would not be tolerated and that women would have to solve their problems through the existing structures of the Histadrut.

The need for women workers to prove that they were indeed not "creating a separate platform" for women (the phrase used to accuse them of separatism) put the movement on the defensive. On all public occasions, such as the Histadrut and Women Workers' Council conventions, WWC leaders repeatedly declared their loyalty to the Histadrut and denied that, in demanding greater opportunities, women were seeking a "separate platform" for themselves (e.g., Histadrut, 1923:17,99; Katznelson, 1927;15–20).

The electoral system, based on proportional representation, gave the political parties and particularly the dominant Ahdut Ha'avoda considerable control over the Histadrut in general and over the WWC in particular. Each political faction constructed its list of candidates so that the voter elected a party rather than an individual. Representation was indirect, since the party members elected delegates to the national convention, the convention to the council, and the council to the central committee of the Histadrut. The party bosses constructed the lists of candidates to the convention, which meant that they virtually controlled the access to all important and paid positions within the Histadrut and secured control of the top leadership over the organization. Women candidates usually made up no more than twenty percent of the list.

What weakened women's bargaining position was first, that so few were politically active and second, that many, particularly the "loyalists", experienced ambivalence regarding the definition of women as a special interest group. Sex as a basis for interest aggregation was unacceptable to those who wished to participate as equals and not as members of a category which, by implication, was in some way inferior. Willingly or not, however, women on a party list were almost inevitably perceived as representing women.

In the Histadrut, the political "logic" of party list construction was aimed at selecting people who could claim to represent the respective interest groups but whose loyalty to the party was not in question. Selective sponsorship of leaders by the dominant coalition, according to Gamson, is a strategy of social control similar to co-optation (Gamson, 1968:135). Because only the loyal are sponsored, the strategy reduces the need for direct intervention and continuous monitoring by the establishment. The sponsorship strategy is evident in the Histadrut's intervention through the selection of the leadership of the WWC and in its control over the organization's election system.

The Histadrut leadership strengthened the position of some women and weakened that of others through its appointments to policy-making and resource-allocating committees of its various agencies. Although formally the executive committee of the

Women Workers' Council had the right to recommend representatives to these bodies, they required the approval of the Central Committee, which used its prerogative to appoint and depose committee members in accord with its political interests. For example, in 1925 Maimon, a member of Hapoel Hatzair, was removed from the important immigration committee because she fought for fifty percent representation for women among those allocated immigration permits to Palestine. While the male leadership opposed her on this issue, they objected even more strongly to her independent behavior (Maimon, 1972: 252). She was replaced by a male member of Ahdut Ha'avoda.

There is also evidence that the Histadrut intervened and affected leadership recruitment within the Women Workers' Council. Golda Meir records that in 1927 David Remez, an influential member of the Ahdut Ha'avoda faction in the Central Committee of the Histadrut, invited her to become secretary (equivalent to chairperson) of the WWC (Meir, 1975:85). In 1921 Golda Meir had immigrated from the United States, where she had been an active member of the Poalei Zion party, forerunner of the Ahdut Ha'avoda party. The following year she was elected to the executive committee of the WWC, and in 1923 she and Maimon were elected to the Histadrut council (WWC, 1923:8, Histadrut, 1923:10).

The process of centralization within the Histadrut was combined with the creation of a network of labor councils to implement Histadrut policy at the local level. Under the initiative of the WWC, committees of women workers were established within the councils in the cities and agricultural villages. The WWC defined their role as "activating" women workers and representing them in the various departments of the local labor council, such as the Offices of Public Works and Immigration, as well as in trade unions. Antagonism developed between the party functionaries of the local labor councils who controlled employment opportunities and other resources and the members of the women's committees whose direct election by the local female constituency weakened the former's control over them. Work was scarce, and the functionaries rejected the women's claim to special consideration, refusing to grant them "privileges" (WWC, 1922:12).

The issue came to a head in a debate concerning the system to be employed for electing members of the women's committees. There were two camps in the WWC: the radical feminists who favored direct elections by a general meeting of women workers at the local level without regard to women's party affiliation and free

from party intervention, and the loyalists who advocated that candidates be appointed by the party functionaries of the local labor
council in cooperation with the WWC. The two views came to be
known as "elected committees" and "appointed committees". The
radical feminists, headed by Ada Maimon-Fishman, Tova Yaffe,
and other members of Hapoel Hatzair, argued that direct elections
were essential to arouse women to active involvement in public
life. The major concern of the radicals was that with appointed
committees there would be no meaningful ties between the delegates and the women workers. Members would be selected on the
basis of criteria such as compliance and party allegiance, and not
on the basis of their ability and readiness to represent women's
issues. Direct election of candidates, therefore, was essential to
promote women's confidence in the representatives and to assure
that the latter would be loyal first and foremost to the female constituency.

The loyalists argued that such low trust of the local labor functionaries would result in conflicts, which would make the women's
committee ineffective. It was, therefore, in the women's interest
that the committees be appointed, with the advice of the WWC, by
the local functionaries who would consequently feel more responsible for them (Minutes of the Second Meeting of the Executive Committee of the WWC, June 1926, Labor Archive, Haikin, in Histadrut, 1927:225).

The issue was hotly debated during the meeting of the WWC
in June 1926, at which Ben Gurion, representing the central committee of the Histadrut, commented: "There is no need to create a
negative attitude toward the women's committees among the local
labor councils from the start. A committee elected from among the
community of women workers will create a negative attitude on
the part of the local labor councils." (Minutes of the Second Meeting of the WWC, Labor Archive). The implication that withdrawal
of Histadrut support would be the price the WWC would have to
pay for its independence and that by raising such demands they
were intensifying interparty conflict within the Histadrut, was intended to intimidate those who opposed appointed committees.
These statements, however, do not reveal what appears to have
been the deep concern of the male leadership.

Ahdut Ha'avoda feared that separate elections for women
would set a dangerous precedent for other interest groups, such as
Orthodox and Yemenite communities, which could result in a
weakening of the control of the center over the periphery (Sharet,

Figure 12. Ada Maimon, leader of the Women Workers Movement.

in Histadrut, 1927:126). Despite pressure from the male leadership, however, the executive council of the WWC decided twelve to eight in favor of elected committees at its November 1926 meeting. Women members of Hapoel Hatzair and other parties voted for them and those of Ahdut Ha'avoda against them, and it is apparent that the division between the radicals and the loyalists more and more paralleled that between the two labor parties (WWC, 1926:13). Because the struggle among political factions for control within the Histadrut had intensified the demand for party loyalty, party rivalries were penetrating the WWC. The Histadrut leadership, which by the mid-twenties was mainly in the hands of the centralist Ahdut Ha'avoda, encouraged the loyalists. The leaders of the ideologically pluralist Hapoel Hatzair party, fearful of the growing control of its rival party, favored independently elected committees. At the third Histadrut convention in 1927, the majority of whose delegates came from the Ahdut Ha'avoda party, the vote was ninety-seven to seventy-nine in favor of appointed women's committees. Thus, by the end of the 1920s, the struggle between the "radicals" and the "loyalists" had been determined in favor of the latter. At the following Histadrut conference, held in 1932, all candidates were sponsored by the respective political factions and proportional representation was officially implemented (Even-Shoshan, 1963;3:165ff").

The Histadrut, while extending its control over the women's movement through selective sponsorship of leaders, was also under pressure to make concessions to the WWC. In terms of its original goals, however, the WWC was able to exact a small price from the Histadrut for its active support. It developed six agricultural training farms as well as a number of vocational training courses for women; however, these were financed almost entirely by Zionist women's organizations abroad. By 1926, the Histadrut had not yet assigned a budget to the WWC or determined salaries for its representatives on the major Histadrut committees (Minutes of the Second Meeting of the Executive of the WWC, 1926, Labor Archive). The WWC conference of that year reports a list of abortive attempts to gain concessions from the local labor councils in the field of employment. The economic crisis that hit Palestine, and especially the cities, in the years 1926–29 resulted in large-scale unemployment for both women and men and intensified the competition between the sexes for scarce jobs. By 1930 the proportion of women in non-traditional jobs had dropped considerably. Only 0.4 percent of the employed urban female labor force was then employed in construction and public works, while 46.1 percent were employed in private homes (Even-Shoshan; 1963,3:165). In addition, the Histadrut made only insignificant concessions to the WWC's demands for power. A few token women were assigned to various Histadrut committees in the early-twenties, but their numbers dwindled as the decade progressed. Apart from Fishman-Maimon, who was a member of the economic council of *Hevrat Haovdim* (economic enterprises of the Histadrut), women were not found in any of the policy-making bodies of the economic organizations created by the Histadrut in the 1920s. No woman was represented on the fifteen member committee which in 1925 negotiated the first collective agreement between the Histadrut and employers in the Yishuv. In this agreement, unskilled women workers employed in factories were officially discriminated against in wages—a situation that continued until the 1970s. A review of the minutes of the Histadrut Executive Council meetings held between 1921 and 1927 reveals that the problem of women was raised only four times, invariably by a woman and without recorded response from other members.

The problem of the woman worker, which was an item on the agenda of the second Histadrut convention in 1923, was dropped from that of the third in 1927. It was argued that with the creation of the WWC the problem had been solved. Although the subject was returned to the agenda in later conventions and even became a permanent item, it was an issue to which only women gave their attention. The position of women within the new worker community was and remained the responsibility and concern of the WWC. Once the organization ceased to make unacceptable demands and its energies were harnessed to advance the interests of the Histadrut establishment, the sex division of labor and a large women's organization proved highly convenient. Looking after women's issues functioned as an outlet for the political energies of women while it freed the men for dealing with the "more important" issues of the day. Every woman who joined the Histadrut was automatically registered as a member of the WWC—a bureaucratic procedure that enabled the WWC in later years to boast of being the largest women's organization in the country.

The year 1927 marks the eclipse of radical feminism within the women workers' movement. Two events that year reflect the transformation that took place in the WWC and that led to the displacement of its original goals. The first was the decision in favor of appointed committees, which has already been discussed in some detail. The grass-roots organization was co-opted by the local councils. This discouraged sustained feminist pressure to give priority to women's emancipation since there were always "more pressing" problems that required attention. "Pressing problems" were usually those for which pressure could not be eliminated, and the silencing of the radical elements was as much a consequence of the WWC's weakness as a cause of it.

The second event was the replacement of Ada Maimon as general secretary of the WWC by Golda Meir. In view of their very different conceptions of the role of the WWC, this change represents the culmination of the struggle for power between the old guard and the new generation.[4] Although Maimon was re-elected to the WWC executive committee after 1927, she and the old guard had lost ground. Power had shifted to the loyalist faction.

Meir's entrance into office symbolizes the succession of generations and marks the beginning of the transformation of the WWC into a social service organization. The generation that had put women's self-transformation above party politics gave way to a cadre whose priorities were determined by the interests of the overall party organization. Meir, who was selected by the male leadership of Ahdut Ha'avoda, was, according to her own report, attracted to the WWC not so much because it was concerned with the issue of women as such, but because she was "very interested in the work it was doing, particularly in the agricultural training farms they set up for immigrant girls" (Meir, 1975:88). For her, the WWC was a brief interlude in a long career within the male establishment of the Labor Party. With the election of Beba Idelson as general secretary of the WWC in 1930, a position she held for forty years, the WWC changed its name to The Organization of Working Mothers and was finally transformed into a social service organization meeting the needs of women in their traditional roles of wives and mothers, albeit working mothers. It sponsored child day-care centers to enable women to enter the labor market. Its occupational training prepared girls primarily for traditionally feminine roles as hairdressers, dressmakers, nursemaids and the like. It turned its attention more and more to looking after welfare needs of mothers and children in the urban centers, leaving the political decisions, the trade union activities, and economic policy in the hands of the male establishment. In addition it served ancillary political functions, the most important of which was mobilizing female support for the party at elections.

Conclusion

From its inception, the Zionist women workers' movement avoided defining itself as engaged in a struggle against male oppression. Nonetheless, during the period between 1911 and 1927 the commitment of the women's movement to self-transformation and equal participation in the building of the new society united its members across the competing political factions within the labor movement. As a united front it pressed for greater equality in the allocation of scarce resources such as immigration certificates, job opportunities, and participation in decision-making bodies of the various organizations of the labor movement.

The structural integration of the WWC within the Histadrut as a separate, but not autonomous part of the socialist movement, brought it under the control of the emerging power centers. From the late 1920s two forces diverted the women's movement from a sustained struggle for sexual equality: first, the demands of the political parties within the Histadrut and particularly of the dominant Ahdut Ha'avoda for the women's undivided commitment to the wider interests of the labor movement as these were defined by the party; and second, the party's failure to develop a real commitment to women's emancipation in the construction of the new economic, political, and social institutions of the Yishuv. These forces also shaped the course of the WWC for decades to come. The feminist movement, which had emerged in response to the wish of women pioneers to be equal partners in conquering new fields of work and building the nation, became the largest voluntary social service and later, welfare organization in the Yishuv. In addition, the movement institutionalized and thus reenforced the categorical treatment of women; at the same time it monitored their public careers. Women in the labor party (which dominated the country until 1977) were "expected" to rise through the ranks of the WWC, while its leadership acted as gatekeepers between the female enclave and the male establishment, allowing only a selected few, sponsored by them, to pass. Those who succeeded were rewarded with a seat in the Knesset (Israeli parliament) and other central bodies, and they provided the few tokens that bolstered public belief in the notion that "capable" women do "make it". The lack of institutionalized rotation in the leadership, however, set stringent limits on the number who ever did.

Despite the WWC's shift in activities, the organization remained officially committed to the full participation of women in public life. Consequently, the existence of this powerful women's organization which claimed to be the vanguard of women's interests, helped to perpetuate the myth of equality and to discourage the emergence of alternative definitions around which women could organize.

Notes

1. Gorni (1975) found that prior to immigration, 51 percent of the immigrants belonged to a political party; after immigration that figure de-

clined to 33 percent. Shapiro (1976:19) suggests that the preference of the Second Aliyah for activities directly related to self-actualization explains these findings. This preference was probably stronger among women than among men.

2. Kibbutzim developed during the Third Aliyah. They were larger social units with one hundred or more members and differed from the kvutzot which were restricted to twenty to thirty members and where social relations were modeled on the intimacy characteristic of family.

3. Maimon reports that it was Rachel Yanait, one of the official delegates of Ahdut Ha'avoda at the conference, who had asked her to speak on behalf of the women. Yanait was a party leader and "it seemed she felt it not appropriate nor in good taste for her to do the task; to demand elected representatives for the *poalot* (women workers), and therefore she turned to me" (1972:105).

4. In 1926, three months prior to the third WWC convention, a crisis arose within the executive committee of the WWC when Maimon was sharply criticized for ruling the organization with her "favorites" and neglecting others. Maimon resigned, the council disbanded, and the executive committee of the Histadrut appointed an interim committee to prepare the third WWC convention.

References

Bein, Alex. 1954. *The History of Jewish Agricultural Settlement in Palestine*, 3d ed. Tel Aviv: Massada Press (Hebrew).

Bluwstein, Shoshana. 1947. "Life in the Kinneret Commune," pp. 814–821 in *Memoirs of Eretz Yisrael*, Vol. 2, edited by A. Ya'ari. Jerusalem: Zionist Organization Youth Department (Hebrew).

Drori, Chasia. 1975. "From Soviet Russia to the Conference in Haifa," pp. 14–17 in *The Plough Woman*, edited by Rachel Katznelson-Shazar.

Eisenstadt, S. N. 1967. *Israeli Society*. London: Weidenfeld and Nicolson.

Erez, Yehuda. 1948. *The Third Aliyah*. Jerusalem: Zionist Organization Youth Department (Hebrew).

Ettinger, Akiva. 1919. "Cooperative Groups in the Year 1919." *Kŏntres*, 12:5–6 (Hebrew).

Even-Shoshan, Zvi. 1963. *The History of the Workers' Movement in Eretz Israel*. Tel Aviv: Am Oved (Hebrew).

Gamson, William, A. 1968. *Power and Discontent*. Homewood, Ill: Dorsey Press.

Gordon, Aharon, D. 1959. "People and Labor." In *The Zionist Idea*, edited by Arthur Herzberg. New York: Meridan Books.

Gorni, Yoseph. 1975. "Changes in the Social and Political Structure of the Second Aliya between 1904–1940," pp. 49–101 in *Zionism: Studies in the History of the Zionist Movement and the Jewish Community in Palestine*, edited by D. Carpi. Ramat Gan: Massada Press (Hebrew).

Group of Women Workers. 1913. "In Answer to Mrs. Thon." *Hapoel Hatzair* 6, 26:12–13 (Hebrew).

Hanoh, G. 1926. "With Regard to the Women Workers' Conference." *Hapoel Hatzair* 19, 22–23:7–8 (Hebrew).

Harari, Yehudit. 1959. *Woman and Mother in Israel*. Tel Aviv: Massada Press (Hebrew).

Hahistadrut Hahakla'it. 1951. *The Union of Agricultural Workers in its Thirtieth Year*. Tel Aviv: Hava'ad Hapoel (Hebrew).

Histadrut. 1923. "The Second Histadrut Convention." *Pinkas Hahistadrut*, 2:18–54 (Hebrew).

Histadrut. 1923. "Decisions of the Second Convention." *Pinkas Hahistadrut*, 2:3–10 (Hebrew).

Histadrut. 1927. "Protocol of the Third Histadrut Convention". *Pinkas Hahistadrut* (Hebrew).

Histadrut. 1970. "Protocol of the First Convention of the Histadrut, December 1920." *Asufot* 1, 14:5–80 (Hebrew).

Katznelson, Berl. 1948. *Writings*. Tel Aviv: *Mapai* Publication (Hebrew).

Katznelson. Rachel. 1927. "The Participation of the Female Workers." *Kŏntres*, 14:15–20 (Hebrew).

Katznelson-Shazar Rachel. 1975. *The Plough Woman*. New York: Herzl Press.

Liberson, Tehiya. 1975. "Women Build Houses," pp. 176–79 in *The Plough Woman*, edited by Rachel Katznelson-Shazar.

Maimon-Fishman, Ada. 1922. "Report of the Second Conference of the Women Workers' Council." *Hapoel Hatzair* 14, 23:11–13 (Hebrew).

Maimon-Fishman, Ada. 1926. "The Condition of the Woman Worker." *Hapoel Hatzair* 19, 24:4–7 (Hebrew).

Maimon-Fishman, Ada. 1929. *Women Workers' Movement in Eretz Israel*. Tel Aviv: *Hapoel Hatzair* (Hebrew).

Maimon, Ada. 1972. *Along the Way*. Tel Aviv: Am Oved (Hebrew).

Malkin, Sarah. 1912. "The Woman Worker in Kinneret." *Hapoel Hatzair* 5, 11–13:14 (Hebrew).

Mamshi. 1911. "On the Question of the Women Workers in the Galilee." *Hapoel Hatzair* 4, 4: 4–6 (Hebrew).

Meir, Golda. 1975. *My Life.* London: Futura Publication.

Porat, Reuben. 1977. *Education in the Collectives and Kibbutzim.* Tel Aviv: Hakibbutz Hameuchad (Hebrew).

Preuss, Walter. 1965. *The Labor Movement in Israel.* Jerusalem: Rubin Mass.

Selznick. P. 1949. *TVA and the Grassroots.* Berkeley: University of California Press.

Shapiro, Yonathan. 1976. *Ahdut Ha'avoda Party: The Power of Political Organization.* Tel Aviv: Am Oved (Hebrew).

Shohat, Manya. 1975. "The Collective," pp. 19–25 in *The Plough Woman,* edited by Rachel Katznelson-Shazar.

Slaughter, J. M. 1977. "Women and Socialism: The Case of Angelica Balanbanoff." *Social Science Journal* 14, 2:57–65.

Shapiro, Yosef. 1961. *Work and Land—Fifty Years of the Histadrut of Agricultural Workers.* Tel Aviv: Am Oved (Hebrew).

Smelser, J. Neil. 1965. *Theory of Collective Behavior.* New York: Free Press of Glencoe.

Turner R. I. and L. M. Killian. 1972. *Collective Behavior,* 2d ed. Englewood Cliffs, N. J.: Prentice-Hall Inc.

WWC. 1914. "The First Women Workers' Convention." *Hapoel Hatzair* 7, 37:12–13 (Hebrew).

WWC. 1922. "The Second Conference of the Women Workers' Council." *Pinkas Hahistadrut* (Hebrew).

WWC. 1923. "The Decisions of the Women Workers' Conference in Haifa." *Pinkas Hahistadrut* 1, Appendix 5:6–8 (Hebrew).

WWC. 1926. "The Women Workers' Council." *Hapoel Hatzair* 20, 9:13 (Hebrew).

9

From Revolution to Motherhood: The Case of Women in the Kibbutz, 1910–1948

—— *Sylvie Fogiel-Bijaoui* ——

The kibbutz, as an egalitarian, democratic and lay co-operative, constitutes an exceptional social phenomenon. It is therefore not surprising that it has been the object of interest for several decades now for sociologists. One of the most studied fields within the kibbutz, especially during the past twenty years, has been that of sexual equality (Talmon, 1974; Tiger and Shepher, 1976; Spiro, 1980; Rosner, 1972; Palgi and Rosner, 1983; Blumberg, 1983; Ben-Rafael and Weitman, 1986). It is however surprising to note that sociologists, who differ in their theoretical approaches,[1] share a number of common assumptions concerning gender equality. They agree that the kibbutz, as early as its foundation in 1910, was structured so as to achieve sexual equality, and with the exception of Blumberg they also stress that with the establishment of the State of Israel, in 1948, the women of the kibbutz had the same rights and duties as men. The purpose of this article is to examine the common argument concerning the initial sexual equality in the Kibbutz. The approach adopted is the feminist materialist one, whose philosophical foundation was laid down by Simone de Beauvoir in *The Second Sex* (De Beauvoir, 1975). Since then, an abundant sociological literature has developed along these lines (e.g., Eisenstein, 1978; Kuhn and Wolpe, 1978; Sayers, 1982:173–203. See also the interesting update on Marxism and Feminism in MacKinnon, 1982). We shall examine the basic axiom of sexual equality in the kibbutz during the pioneer era (1910–1948) by studying the integration of women in the production process in parallel with the institutionalization of parental roles.

Within the feminist materialist approach maternity will be defined at both a social and an individual level. Referring to Engels (1972), maternity will be seen as a social institution which, while of biological origin, differs in content according to time and space. Maternity is defined, by those who hold authority within the society, as a function of the organization of production on the one hand and of the requirements of reproduction on the other. At the individual level, though, a woman does not experience her maternity only as a function of the institutionalized definition. She also experiences it as a function of her own existential conditions, of her personality and of her social framework (e.g., Aries, 1973; Shorter, 1977; Badinter, 1986).

Gender equality will be defined as a set of rights and duties allowing both sexes equal access to "fundamental social gratifications" as defined by Weber: wealth, power and prestige.

The interplay between production and maternity will be analyzed, dividing the period into three—

A. The first decade: In the name of equality, or "What do young girls dream of?" (1910–1920).

B. The second decade: Maternity or the limits of the revolution.

C. The years 1930–1948: Equality, Maternity and War.

These will be followed by a brief concluding discussion.

A. The First Decade: in the Name of Equality, or "What Do Young Girls Dream of?" (1910–1920).

The first women pioneers (halutzot) who came to Palestine to build a new society, a society of workers according to the Zionist socialist conception, met on their arrival with almost total incomprehension. The farmers in the agricultural villages, the moshavot, refused to employ them, considering them both inefficient as workers and immoral as women, living on their own among men (Habas, 1947; Maimon, 1955:7–12; Shilo, 1981.) In the new communal settlements—small groups of ten to thirty living and working communally—the kvutza, the situation was not much better. The men invited only a small number of women to join the kvutza as "housekeepers" rather than as equal members and workers. The pioneer women, however, were far from resigning themselves to this situation. On numerous occasions they had raised the problem of their scarcely enviable status within the kvutza, which was considered the most revolutionary creation of the Jewish Workers'

Movement in Palestine. However, they soon realized that it was useless, and that a real change in their status required collective action on their apart.

Sociological literature teaches us that collective action is determined first and foremost by two chief elements (Gamson, 1968; Smelser, 1963; Piven and Cloward, 1977):

A. Anger and frustration when confronted with a given situation. These were indeed the feelings of the halutzot when facing the lack of understanding and the contempt they encountered at every turn.[2]

B. The conviction that it is possible to change things. Several factors reinforced the halutzot's conviction: First, their "sociological profile", that of very young women, single, intellectual and politically minded (Fogiel-Bijaoui, 1981:141–145), which gave them faith in their ability to change their destiny. Second, their Zionist Dream, in its Socialist version, which entailed the transformation and improvement of the individual and of society. Third, their very concept of equality which set equality of duties as a precondition to equality of rights and implied self-emancipation of women by women. Thus, they began organizing because they were driven by their anger and their frustrations on the one hand, and their hopes on the other.

As early as 1911 the first organized meeting of halutzot took place in Kinneret, on the shore of the Sea of Galilee, to discuss the place of women in the Zionist revolution, in the (Jewish) Workers' Movement and within the kvutza. In this encounter, the seeds of the Women Workers' Movement were sown (Maimon, 1955:16–17; Izraeli, 1981.)

By 1918, at the end of the Second Aliyah, the status of women within the kvutza in no way resemble the traditional status of women in general, and of Jewish women in particular:

a. Women belonged to the kvutza not through their families but rather as individuals, free and independent, having got rid of all male tutelage, whether of father, brother or husband.

b. The rigid and traditional distribution of roles according to sex, a feature of the beginning of the kvutza, had loosened up with time. Men had indeed agreed to participate *from time to time* in performing the "dirty work" hitherto reserved for women: dishwashing, lighting the stoves, carrying heavy pots, chopping wood, cleaning the floors, etc. (Blum, 1980:63).

c. In Palestine, Jewish women had become agriculturalists. They had even developed new branches of agriculture, especially that of

market gardening which was then integrated into pioneer agriculture and remained for a long time a predominantly female activity.
d. The most radical change for women within the kvutza, however, was the creation of a new type of woman at the crossroads of Jewish history: that of the halutza who refused to be the "eternal number two" and fought to share with men the same duties and the same rights. Although she never won this prize within the kvutza, far from it, it is certain that in 1918, unlike 1910, it was ideologically accepted that the halutza was to be considered as the equal of the halutz (Shilo, 1981).

Between this positive development and sexual equality, however, there remained a long way to go and in fact, *within the kvutza, women were never the equals of their male companions.*
a. Women never entered agricultural production on an equal footing with men. While the latter agreed to perform, from time to time, some of the "dirty work", the principle whereby household work was women's work was never abolished (Maimon, 1955:39). Women did work in agriculture at that time, but they did so on an "internal rotation" basis, some of the few women of the group taking care of the "household chores" while the others enjoyed the "privilege" of agricultural work, without the men being required to participate in such rotation (ibid.).
b. During this period women were not defined as full fledged members of the kvutza. They were employed by the male members as wage labor, and their monthly income was less than that of men, even if they also worked in agriculture. Moreover, the hours spent by a mother in taking care of her child were deducted from her salary—the work day of a mother was specified in the register of work as being equivalent to three quarters of a normal work day (Maimon, 1955:58).
c. Women were not always invited to take part in the internal decisions of the kvutza. For according to Tehiya Liberson, one of the first women agricultural workers—"the pioneers were unable to get used to considering them as full fledged members; neither were they ready to accept the fact that halutzot should express themselves freely, nor would they countenance the firmness with which they stuck to their opinions" (Liberson, 1913:21).[3]

It is clear that in spite of the real gains women made on the road to sexual equality within the kvutza, their goal was never achieved. The question is: Why?

Three factors will help answer this question:

1. Exaltation of masculinity.
2. De facto organization of production according to the traditional definition of sexual roles.
3. The conception of maternity.

1. Exaltation of Masculinity

The liberation of women, as far as the halutzot were concerned, meant, primarily, ascending to the level of men. Emulating the male model, they wanted to make the functions, qualities and goals of men their own, without demanding a similar change on the part of the men, without demanding that they "feminize". Deference to masculinity was further reinforced by the more than difficult conditions then prevalent in Palestine, since permanent insecurity and primitive technology only served to increase the importance of "masculine" qualities in the daily life of the communal settlement. *Inter alia*, physical strength became one of the first criteria for the distribution of social roles within the *kvutza*, and for their evaluation.

2. Organization of Production According to the Principles of Productivity and Profitability

Due to the importance of physical strength women were defined, from the beginning, as *less productive* than men, and were steered primarily toward work "suitable" for them, i.e., cooking, cleaning. Such an approach seemed all the more logical since the kvutza was fighting for the recognition of its economic viability. Under these conditions it seemed that women ("less productive") entering agriculture *instead of men* would put the entire group in danger. It is therefore not surprising that, from the beginning, the kvutza economy was made up of two quite distinct branches: one with a clear male majority, considered the "productive branch", was the branch of grain cultivation; the other, the female one, included "collective household chores" as well as the henhouse, the barn, the vegetable garden and the beehive. Following the development of two spheres of economic activity, distinctly defined along sexual lines, women were never afforded full access to the same prestigious kinds of work as men. Nor did they win the prestige enjoyed by men as full time farmers, the true pioneer ideal.

3. The Concept of Maternity

Within the framework of the kvutza which valued masculinity and profitability, and which interwove the two in a causal relationship, *motherhood* could only undermine the status of women—all the more since women pioneers had no more developed an adequate ideology and pattern of organization on this matter than had their male counterparts.

When the first children were born the care of the newborn was immediately entrusted to the mother. And even though demands were made here and there that fathers participate in the care of children, such a solution was never seriously considered.

Indeed it seemed totally dysfunctional and illogical within the realm of agriculture to exchange a man, a "productive worker", for a woman, a "less productive worker" and all that in order to steer the male comrade toward child care while the mother, or any female comrade, *"by her very nature"* could do that job, and far better too.

Torn between their maternal duty and their desire to remain full-fledged members of the kvutza, women tried to solve "their problem" individually. Thus they were able to see Miriam Baratz, the first mother of Degania,[4] taking her child everywhere with her, even to her work in the barn or in the vegetable garden, thereby facing the hostility of her companions who accused her of putting her child in danger:

> The comrades of the Kvutza were of the opinion that I should dedicate all my time to my child. With all my might I opposed this way of thinking for I knew that if I were to accept it I would have to give up the group and everything happening therein (Baratz, in Katznelson-Shazar, 1964:7).

However, after the birth of the fourth child, given the fact that mothers positively refused to give up their work within the kvutza, it was suggested to secure the services of a professional nurse (Baratz, 1960:68). Joseph Bussel, one of the founders of Degania and one of the most eminent personalities of the group, stoutly opposed it at the time. Instead he proposed another solution, whereby *it was up to the community to assume the burden of part of the traditional maternal functions*:

> The child belongs to his parents, but responbility for his support and his upbringing is that of the entire community. *All women*

whether married or not, will participate in the care of the newborn, in turn, so that mothers may continue to work. The communal settlement as a whole will take care of expenses entailed by upbringing (Baratz, 1960:68–9) (emphasis added—S.F.B.).

It is in such a spirit that the basis of "collective care" of the children of the *kvutza* was established; later on it developed into "collective education" in the kibbutz.

It is important to stress that though the "collective care" was considered most revolutionary, it included neither night hours nor a common dormitory; it included "only" the care given the child during the daytime. After the day's work the child rejoined his parents, played with them and slept in their room.

Nevertheless, such a day nursery system did not lead to enthusiasm on the part of the "founding mothers", quite the contrary. It became necessary to convince most of them that they could give up taking care of their baby in the daytime without the child suffering thereby. In 1918, in Sharona, at the Conference of Women Workers, this subject even set off a stormy debate among several mother-delegates. It was then that Joseph Bussel, who had also been invited to this encounter, explained that the day nursery system was the *sine qua non* condition for the survival of the kvutza: without it the group could not survive over an extended period as a socialist communal settlement (Maimon, 1955:39–40). From that time onward the day nursery system became part and parcel of the kvutza. Of course this was a revolutionary system whereby the traditional maternal functions of the "Jewish mother" were shifted during the day to collective services, equal for all, and supported by the community. Nevertheless, no matter how revolutionary it might have been, such a system was not a "revolutionary-egalitarian" system as regards gender roles; indeed, from the very beginning, only the women comrades operated the services allocated to the newborn, without the men ever entering the scene. In other words the sucklings and small children were fed, bathed, changed, dressed, taken out for walks, lulled to sleep and cared for by the women of the kvutza (by their mothers and the other women acting as "second mothers" to them) while the role of the father consisted generally only of playing with his child.

At any rate, at the end of the Second Aliyah, after the birth of the first children of the kvutza, the unequal division of gender roles created from the very beginning by the principle of economic profitability, was legitimated by the definition of parental roles instituted within the communal settlement. From that time on the economic logic of profitability and the social definition of parental roles were to reinforce each other.

B. The Second Decade: Maternity, or the Limits of Revolution (1920–1930)

Jewish immigration to Palestine resumed after the end of the First World War and the establishment of British rule, with the arrival of the first immigrants of the Third Aliyah in 1919. Most of these immigrants were members of the Halutz, a socialist-Zionist youth movement directed to communal agricultural settlement. The main source of employment at the time was road construction, initiated by the British. Many of the Jewish workers were organized in collectives. The young women of the Third Aliyah faced many of the same difficulties of their forerunners. There was resistance to employing them in road construction. The collectives often refused women who wanted to join them fearing they might cause deficits in piece work. Eventually some of the women determined not to give up, formed their own collectives and managed to keep pace with the others (Erez, 1964). All in all, three hundred women worked on the roads, half of them in construction and half in the workers' co-operative kitchens (Maimon, 1955:57). Once road construction ceased, most pioneering immigrants moved to the towns where the main source of employment was house construction. Once again women found it very difficult to obtain employment as individuals or to be accepted into male collectives. A small number managed to overcome these obstacles, to learn construction skills and form women's collectives, but most faced severe difficulties, high levels of unemployment and domestic service as a major source of employment for women, in total contradiction to their pioneering aspirations (Bernstein, 1987).

Compared to this situation the state of women in agricultural communities was better by far.[5] Women had succeeded in becoming, *at least partially*, agricultural workers. What is more, a decisive change took place, starting with the Third Aliyah, aimed at encouraging real and equal integration of women into collective life. Collective services were established, not only common services such as meals, the kitchen, the refectory, the laundry (even clothing and showers were collectivized for a time), but also the

Figure 13. Women working in gravel preparation for road construction (Labor Archive).

"children's house", where children slept together outside of their parents' dwelling (Tsur et al. 1978:173–213).

As a result, not only did the kibbutz family no longer function as a production unit, its function as a consumer unit was reduced to a minimum, while its educative function was largely restricted, as education and child care were mostly the task of the community (Shepher and Fogiel-Bijaoui, in press).

The kibbutz family cell, at that time, constituted first of all an "emotional shelter" for its members; a parent-child relationship did of course exist but it was placed under the vigilant eye of the community. And so, once out of the hospital, the newborn were housed in the "children's house" and spent only a few hours daily with their parents, in the afternoon (between two and four hours, depending on their age). Modalities of education were determined by the Committee on Education of the kibbutz. As for the "great fundamental decisions" they were made by the General Assembly of the kibbutz (ibid.).

It is surprising that within such a revolutionary framework, which openly stressed sexual equality, sexual inequality persisted. In 1926, for instance, in the work archives of kibbutz Tel Yossef,[6] agriculture (the prestigious branch) was almost totally occupied by men while services (the "non-productive" branch) were almost entirely composed of women (Rozen, 1984:77). Such a traditional division of labor according to sex was also to be found at that time among the key positions of the kibbutzim, at Ein-Harod[7] among others. Yokheved Bat-Rachel, one of the leading figures of the kibbutz, writes on that score: "I noticed that even in the kibbutz it is the men who decide everything, just as in patriarchal society" (Bat-Rachel, 1981: 94).

And further:

> I realized that at Ein-Harod, the secretariate of the kibbutz was all-male, even though the women work in the barn, the henhouse, the garden and do all kinds of hard work and though, in addition, they carry the burden of the upbringing of the children after working hours (ibid.).

In order to deal with this situation and insure a minimal representation of women, a group of Ein-Harod women, among them Bat-Rachel, demanded a quota of one third for women delegates within the institutions of the Kibbutz Movement and of the Workers' Movement in general (Bat-Rachel, 1981:96). This proposal having been accepted, became the "Law of the Third", and remained for years a legislative principle within the Workers' Movement, even though it was not always applied (ibid.).

We have yet to explain the fact that during the twenties, *the most revolutionary era of the kibbutz*, sexual inequalities nevertheless persisted. Two complementary factors are of central importance:
1. The priority of economic profitability.
2. The social definition of parental roles.

1. The Priority of Economic Profitability

From the very beginning the kibbutz saw itself as an egalitarian and modern co-operative, able to compete in the outside market. By reducing consumption to a minimum, it was able to channel the greatest number of people into production, thus reducing investment in non-productive fields. Such collectivization of services had allowed women to become integrated into production, but "with reservation", without breaking the laws of profitability. Deference to masculinity[8] (which was further expressed at that time by the external appearance of the women—the way they dressed, did their hair, etc.), as well as the importance of physical strength, given the quite low level of technology at the time, had made the male members of the kibbutz the most "adequate" and "profitable" ones for agriculture.

The result was that, even during the twenties, pioneer women continued to work according to the principle of "internal rotation", dividing their activity between certain agricultural branches (the henhouse, the barn, the vegetable garden, the beehive), auxiliary services (cooking, linen, cleaning) and child care. As for men pioneers, they participated once in a while in auxiliary services (if assigned the duty or during labor shortages) but they were never to be seen in the kitchen and never took care of small children. Such work was definitely too female. Moreover, since men still made up between 70 and 75 percent of the membership of the kibbutz (Maimon, 1955:238–239; Rozen, 1984:10–13), there was relatively no shortage of men and no urgent need to call upon women in the agricultural branches.

The question remains how could the pioneer women, who denied the legitimacy of the profitability principle as a basis for the distribution of sexual roles in society, resign themselves to such a situation in the kibbutz. In our opinion, the answer lies in the definition of the maternal role as instituted in the kibbutz.

2. The Social Definition of Parental Roles

Collectivization of services and of child rearing during the period under investigation, as radical as it might have been, in no way meant the end of the family and the negation of parental roles. Rather, it meant the end of the patriarchal family and the creation of a new nuclear family, whose existential basis was no longer private property but the affective bonds between its members (Shepher and Fogiel-Bijaoui, in press). Within this context the place reserved for the child in Jewish tradition remained intact. In the kibbutz, just as within the framework of traditional Judaism, the child remained synonymous with love and happiness (Tsur, 1981:182). Motherhood was perceived as the very essence of the feminine nature, allowing any woman, whether or not a mother, to take care, in the best possible way, of that invaluable treasure, the child. That was the reason why, given deplorable living conditions and a high child mortality, breast feeding was unanimously adopted as the only means to insure the survival of the suckling as well as its physical and psychological development.[9]

The mother was therefore the one who, of the two parents, not only fed her child, but also took care of all its needs when the child was in his parents' room. Moreover, according to the concept of the maternal instinct, which construes every woman as a "mother by nature", all women were first steered toward tasks involved in the care of children. The result was that women, obligated above all to provide services, had an even harder time than in the past in entering the "productive branches".

In other words, the concept of the maternal role, as introduced into the kibbutz, was to finally legitimate the organization of production according to "criteria of profitability", and this not only in the eyes of the men pioneers, but above all in the eyes of their women counterparts.

Although crucial traditional elements in the rearing of children (responsibility and love of parents for their children) were preserved, not everybody, far from it, was ready to accept the principles of collective upbringing, an educative system unmistakably implying a minimalization of family functions and redefinition of parental functions. That is why those who, at that time, left the agricultural communal settlements were numerous.

As for kibbutz members, even among them there was no consensus on the education system to be established, and the price paid for its constitution was one of doubts, failures and anguish. The most affected were the women, especially those who wanted to be totally integrated into kibbutz life without jeopardizing their motherhood (Bassevitz and Bat-Rachel, 1944:57; Bat-Rachel, 1981: 49).

To be both mother and pioneer was, it seemed, the maximum equality women could aspire to. Economic and social independence of women, the collective system of education and the community of services were the very symbols of the Socialist sexual revolution. Their implementation in the kibbutz, at that time, constituted one of the boldest human experiments, even when compared with the "Big Sister", Russia (Hall, 1938; Kollontai, 1975; Rowbotham, 1974:134–169; Stites, 1978:317–421). Hence a feeling of impasse set in among women, one constantly voiced during the twenties . . . The issue of sexual inequality did not leave the scene, appearing however as "the problem of women", the "problem of the woman worker or pioneer", i.e. as the problem of a specific and marginal group and not as the problem of kibbutz society as a whole (Rozen, 1984:114–148).

To sum up this period, once again the fact that equality of parental functions was not institutionalized in the kibbutz, and that production was organized as a function of a profit-related sexual division of labor, both explain why sexual inequality existed in the kibbutz during the twenties—the most critical formative years of the Kibbutz. It is therefore not surprising that sexual inequality should have remained, since that time, as a constant feature of the kibbutz.

C. The Years 1930–1948: Equality, Maternity and War

During the 1930s the leaders of the kibbutz movement themselves acknowledged the failure in achieving equality between men and women. For example, in 1935 Meir Yaari, one of the leaders of left wing Kibbutz *Artzi*,[10] speaking during a meeting of his movement, asked: "Why have we failed so miserably in this field?" (Yaari, in Shur, 1976:132).

Data referring to the late 1940s, compiled by Lionel Tiger and Joseph Shepher (1976) on the sexual distribution of functions in the kibbutz, confirm such a remark. According to their research, sexual equality did not exist either in the domain of work or in the area of politics. Tiger and Shepher report that in 1948, in eight kibbutzim of the *Ihud* kibbutz movement, 78.3 percent of the women worked in services (services for adults, child care, education) as against 16.7 percent of the men. That same year 15.2 percent of the women worked in production as opposed to 58.2 percent of the men (see Table 1).

Table 1

Division of Labor Between the Sexes
in Eight Kibbutzim of the Ihud in 1948 (in %)

Area/Sex	Men	Women
Agriculture	27.6	11.1
Non-agricultural production	3.9	2.8
Services	26.7	1.3
Services to adults	11.3	38.3
Childcare and Education	5.4	40.0
Administration	25.7	6.6
Total	100.00	100.00

(According to Tiger and Shepher, 1976:86).

Table 2

Political Participation Among 3400 Members of
24 Kibbutzim of Kibbutz Artzi Federation
1943–1944, According to Sex*

Sex/Function	*Men (no.)*	*Women (no.)*	*Percentage (women)*
In committees, executive duties	944	385	29%
Branch management in agriculature industry and services	292	176	37%
In external activity and positions within the movement	437	105	19.4%

(According to Tiger and Shepher, 1976:124).

*This represents about 50% of the total number of kibbutzim belonging to Kibbutz Artzi in 1943–44.

The situation was not fundamentally different in political life. At any rate, that is what emerges from Table 2, which summarizes data dealing with Kibbutz Artzi, the kibbutz movement most firmly committed to the implementation of sexual equality.

1. Growth and Modernization

A partial explanation of this sexual inequality is linked with the growth of services that was characteristic of the kibbutz during the years 1930–1940, following the rise in the standard of living and the increase in the birth rate.

During that period, the modernization of agriculture (extensive use of tractors, introduction of electified systems in the hen-houses, the switch to intensive agriculture, etc.), with its increase in yields, allowed a gradual but constant rise in the standard of living in the kibbutz (Shur, 1976:196–199).

On the demographic side, a significant change occurred during that same period. Between 1931 and 1948, the population of the kibbutz movement as a whole grew from 4,391 to 47,408 persons while its percentage with respect to the total Jewish population of Palestine went up from 2.5 percent in 1931 to 7.5 percent in 1948, a record figure never reached either before or after (Shur, 1976:197–198). This demographic surge was due in great part to the Fifth Aliyah, of the mid-30s. However, no less significant was the increase in the birth rate. Already at that time many of the kibbutzim were composed of families, with a far more equal ratio of women to men, especially in the old kvutzot and the old kibbutzim where women sometimes made up as much as 50 percent of the population (Haikin, 1964:74). By 1946, the birth rate was 1.30 to 1.76 children per family on the average, depending on the age of the kibbutz, while during the years 1910–1920 there was, on the average, barely one child for each two couples in the kibbutz (Shatil, 1955:191–192).

Thus the rise in the standard of living and the increase in the birth rate allowed and entailed the extension of services. However, such an evolution in itself does not explain why the work force steered toward the services was a distinctly female one. In order to understand this we must, here as above, consider the social definition given to parental roles in the kibbutz, as well as the economic organization supporting these roles.

2. The Definition of Maternity

As in the 1910s and 1920s, this period was also marked by the considerable importance given to the child by the members of the kibbutz. This attitude was expressed by permanent and "massive" recourse to education professionals (pediatricians, psychologists, teachers) in order to construct an optimal educational system. For their part, the parents, having been freed of the economic burden, became the "main suppliers" of their children's needs for tenderness and security, always under the watchful eye of the community and of the house-mother—the *metapelet.*

This revolutionary system of upbringing did not please everybody and quite often one saw waves of departures, generally on the initiative of women refusing such modes of child rearing (Maimon, 1955:152–153).

But even those, and especially the women, who remained in the kibbutz were asking themselves many questions regarding collective child rearing, as they were torn between their traditional Jewish conception of parenthood and the new definition they themselves were working out. This anguish would burst out in almost cyclic fashion during heated discussions, every time the question of "our kids" was raised (Tsur, 1981:286–296). Such dilemmas and anguish, stemming from a desire to give the best to the children, only served to stress the importance of the mother in relation to the father, in the eyes of men as much as in those of women. And indeed it seems that at that time the values of Judaism (the "Jew-

Figure 14. Mothers in a Kibbutz, the 1930s (Labor Archive).

ish mother") coincided with the most modern theories in the fields of education, of psychology, of medicine, by affirming the predominance of the mother over the father in order to insure the optimal development, both physical and mental, of the child (Bassevitz, 1981:98).

As a result of this approach of "innate motherhood", the sexual division of roles within the family grew more and more traditional. At the collective level it caused women to gradually leave production and to concentrate on children-linked services.

3. The Organization of Production

This distribution of work according to sex was also based, during these years 1930–1948, on the economic rationality of the preceding years. And indeed, bringing men into services, men who were technically prepared for production, and their replacement by women who had acquired non-vocational training, was rightly viewed a plain waste. But, as pointed out by Bat-Sheva Haikin, this was not the crux of the real problem; it was rather the vicious circle which had been created as a function of sexual stereotypes: since women were (most of them) steered in advance toward services, they did not work in "productive sectors", as a result they had no access to vocational training the way men did, which in turn, kept them even further from the productive sectors (Haikin, 1964: 72). It is to be noted, as stressed by R. L. Blumberg, that this happened at a time when kibbutzim were growing thanks to a steady inflow of persons. The majority of these new members still being males, there was no need to call on women in the "productive sectors" (Blumberg, 1983:133).

However, in order to better understand this sexual inequality in the kibbutz in the years 1930–1948, we must take into account other factors directly interwoven with contemporary events. At that time, particularly in the mid-1930s, the Yishuv was fighting for its security and its future, and the role of the kibbutz was that of a vanguard, of an "elite in the service of the nation".

Women participated in the struggle for a national home and eventual independence, but this in no way changed the sexual distribution of roles in the kibbutz. One of the reasons, we would argue is that, in spite of their feelings of frustration and anger, the war restrained women from struggling for equality of rights, and caused them to fight for equality of duties. This came about for three main reasons:

a. In war-time, the rights of the individual and of the citizen become secondary, not only as far as the government is concerned but also in the eyes of the individuals themselves (Bar-Yosef and Eisenstark-Padan, 1975). Thus, at times when issues of life and death were critical for the Yishuv, and for the entire Jewish people, the problem of sexual equality became even more secondary than before in the eyes of the kibbutz and of its women members.

b. The concept of equality, adopted from the start by the women of the kibbutz, was one which made equality of rights subject to equality of duties. Thus the more militant women mobilized for "the right to do their duty" for the Yishuv and the Jewish people (Maimon, 1955:195–205, 251–256), rather than to fight against growing sexual inequality within the kibbutz.

c. Despite women's participation from the very beginning in military organizations affiliated with the Labor Movement (*Hashomer, Haganah*[11]) their position was in question, and no system had ever been worked out regarding their rights and duties (Brenner, 1980; Slutzki, 1972, 3:1223).

This hardly comfortable situation reached its apex in the eyes of the women of the kibbutz during the "events of 1929",[12] during which not one of them was allowed to stand guard, while in the cities women had taken part in civil defense and had thus been allowed to carry weapons. In 1929, there had been no organized action by women.

In 1936, however, with the outburst of the Arab Revolt,[13] when men once again refused their female comrades the possibility to stand guard around the kibbutzim, a rebellion took place. Under the leadership of a handful of women from Ein-Harod, the women of the kibbutzim demanded to be included in the defense of the communes. The "Women's Rebellion", as it was called, was both swift and strong and quickly won its goal. As early as the summer of 1936, in the majority of kibbutzim, women were able to stand guard. This was the last collective action by women to protest their position in the kibbutz of the pre-1948 era (Bassevitz, 1981:112–114; Bassevitz and Bat-Rachel, 1944:89; Slutzki, 1972, 3:1224).

In spite of this, each time the Haganah assumed new tasks, the debate on the role and contribution of women within its ranks began again with increasing vigor. Such debates also took place within the elite commando of the Haganah, the *Palmach*, of which one third of the members in 1948 were women, mostly from the kibbutz (Slutzki, 1972, 3:1225).

The role of kibbutz women in the national struggle in no way changed the distribution of sexual roles in the kibbutz; these were economically structured and reinforced by a non-egalitarian definition of parental functions. Thus, it was precisely during this period that sexual inequality increased, especially in the economic sphere.

In Conclusion

Our analysis allows us to refute the accepted postulate of sexual equality in the kibbutz in the pioneer era; it also enables us to conclude that the sexual inequality, characteristic of today's kibbutz (Shepher and Tiger, 1976; Ben-Raphael and Weitman, 1986; Fogiel-Bijaoui, in press), is no innovation due to the "normalization" of the kibbutz. It is indeed the outcome of a long continuous historical process during which, in spite of their struggles and their attainments, women have never been the equals of men.

Our analysis of the kibbutz during the "pioneer years" confirms at the micro-social level what revolutions in Russia and China have taught us at the macro-social one. Change in female status takes place, and not without fierce struggle, up to the exact point which allows women to enter production in accordance with the demographic needs of the society, as these are defined by those holding the power, i.e., by men.

The kibbutz experience reveals the limits of all sexual revolution, including the one that swept western countries during the years 1960–1970. It teaches us that along the lengthy road toward equality of the sexes in rights and duties, a change in the traditional role of women implies one in that of men. In such a process, the most radical change is that of a resructuring of the apparatus of production as a function of an egalitarian social definition of parental roles.

Notes

1. We considered here the "classical" sociological research on the subject. In the last decade a number of works have been published which come to opposite conclusions, mainly—Safir, 1983; Shilo, 1981 and Izraeli, 1981, both reprinted in this volume and Fogiel-Bijaoui (in print).

2. Testimonies of women pioneers of the period can be found in numerous sources, among them: Maimon, 1955; Bassevitz and Bat-Rachel, 1944; Katznelson-Shazar, 1930; Habas, 1947.

3. See also Katznelson-Shazar, 1930, Katznelson-Shazar, 1964; Habas, 1947; Bassevitz and Bat-Rachel, 1944; Yanait-Ben-Zvi, 1976.

4. The first child of the kvutza was born in Degania in 1913.

5. During the twenties the membership of the kvutzot and kibbutzim grew to 3,900 persons in 1927 from 500 persons in 1918, representing 2.6 percent of the Palestine Jewish population at that time (Shapiro, 1975:187; Shur, 1976:196). In 1930, the average kibbutz had 67 members while in 1922 it had only 18 (Shur, 1976:195). The term kvutza refers to a smaller, more intimate agricultural collective, while kibbutz refers to a larger collective, aimed at a mixed economy.

6. One of the first kibbutzim, founded in 1923, by some of the members of Gdud Ha'avoda (The Labor Batalion), the most radical communal movement in Jewish Palestine.

7. One of the early kibbutzim, founded in 1921, by members of Gdud Ha'avoda.

8. Here used with the meaning of sexual stereotype.

9. On the child and maternity, and on the problems of child mortality and breastfeeding, cf.: Katznelson-Shazar, 1930:130–167; Tsur et al., 1981:

182–194; Rozen, 1984; as well as the testimony of A. Sturman, K. Giladi and others, in Bassevitz and Bat-Rachel, 1944.

10. In the late 1920s kvutzot and kibbutzim organized into three federations:

a. *Hever Hakvutzot* (later called *Ihud Hakvutzot Ve-Hakibbutzim*) was founded in 1925, composed mainly of small, agricultural, collective settlements. It has always been "pragmatically socialist".

b. *Hakibbutz Hameuchad*, founded in 1927, stood for large agricultural as well as industrial collective settlements, open to all.

c. *Hakibbutz Ha-Artzi*, also founded in 1927, has always been the most radical in its socialist orientation. In 1980 the *Ihud Hakvutzot Ve-Hakibbutzim* united with the *Kibbutz Hameuchad* to form the *Takam*, the Unified Kibbutz Movement.

11. Hashomer, (meaning, in Hebrew, The Guard) was the first military organization, established in 1907 to guard early Jewish settlements who had been guarded, till then, by Arab guards. The Haganah (meaning, in Hebrew, the Defense Organization) was established in 1920, as a paramilitary organization, recognized by the British. The latter was originally under the auspices of the Histadrut and eventually under the auspices of the elected National Council.

12. Outburst of riots of Palestinian Arabs opposed to Zionist settlement, against Jews, after eight years of relative quiet.

13. 1936–1939, prolonged Palestinian Arab uprising against the British and the Zionist settlement.

References

Aries, Philippe. 1973. *The Child and the Family in the Ancient Regime.* Points Histoire, Paris: Seuil (French).

Badinter, Elisabeth. 1986. *The One is the Other—Relations Between Men and Women.* Paris: Editions Odile Jacob (French).

Bar-Yosef, Rivka, and Dorit, Eisenstark-Padan. 1975. "Women and Men at War—Role Change in Times of Stress." *Megamot* 18, 1:36–50 (Hebrew).

Baratz, Yoseph. 1960. *A Village on the Banks of the Jordan.* Tel Aviv: Ministry of Defense (Hebrew).

Bassevitz, Lilia and Yocheved Bat-Rachel (editors). 1944. *Women in the Kibbutz.* Ein Harod: Hakkibutz Hameuchad (Hebrew).

Bassevitz, Lilia. 1981. *Only an Echo.* Tel Aviv: Hakkibutz Hameuchad (Hebrew).

Bat-Rachel, Yocheved. 1981. *The Path in Which I Went*. Tel Aviv: Hakkibutz Hameuchad (Hebrew).

Beauvoir (de) Simone. 1975. *The Second Sex*. N.Y.: Penguin Books.

Ben-Rafael, Eliezer, Weitman, Sacha. 1986. "The Reconstruction of the Family in the Kibbutz." *Pardes*, 4:15–34 (French).

Bernstein, Deborah. 1987. *The Struggle for Equality, Urban Women Workers in Prestate Israeli Society*. New York: Praeger.

Blum, Shlomit. 1980. *The Woman in the Labor Movement During the Second Aliyah*. M. A. Thesis, Tel Aviv University, Tel Aviv (Hebrew).

Blumberg, L. Rae. 1983. "Kibbutz Women—From the Fields of Revolution to the Laundries of Discontent," pp. 130–150, in *Sexual Equality— The Israeli Kibbutz Tests the Theories*, edited by Palgi Michal et al. Norwood, PA.: Norwood Editions.

Brenner, Uri. 1980. "Women's Role in the *Shomer*." *Shorashim* Vol. 2 (Hebrew).

Eisenstein, Zillah (editor). 1978. *Capitalist Patriarchy and the Case for Socialist Feminism*. New York: Monthly Review Press.

Engels, F. 1972. *The Origins of the Family, Private Property and the State*. New York: International Publishers.

Erez, Yehuda. 1964. *The Third Aliyah Book*. Tel Aviv: Am Oved (Hebrew).

Fogiel-Bijaoui, Sylvie. 1981. *The Rib of Eve—The Jewish Women of Palestine, 1881–1948*. Ph.D. Dissertation. University of Paris-X, Nanterre (French).

Fogiel-Bijaoui, Sylvie. (in press). *Revolution and Maternity. A sociological history of the condition of women in the kibbutz, 1910–1986*. Tel Aviv: Everyman University (Hebrew).

Gamson, William, 1968. *Power and Discontent*. Homewood, Ill, Dorsey Press.

Habas, Bracha. 1947. *The Second Aliyah Book*. Tel Aviv: Am Oved (Hebrew).

Hall, Faninna. 1938. *Women in the Soviet East*. London: Martin Secher-Warburg Ltd.

Haikin, Bat-Sheva. 1964. *By and About Bat-Sheva Haikin*. Tel Aviv: Hakkibutz Hameuchad (Hebrew).

Izraeli, N. Dafna. 1981. "The Zionist Women's Movement in Palestine, 1911–1927: A Sociological Analysis." *Signs*, 7:87–114.

Katznelson-Shazar, Rachel. 1930. *Women Workers Speak*. Tel Aviv: Moetzet Hapoalot (Hebrew).

Katznelson-Shazar, Rachel. 1964. *The Rhythm of Our Generation.* Tel Aviv (Hebrew).

Kollontai, Alexandra. 1975. *Marxism and the Sexual Revolution.* Texts chosen and presented by J. Stara-Sandor, Paris (French).

Kuhn, Annette, Ann-Marie, Wolpe (editors). 1978. *Feminism and Materialism.* London: Routledge and Kegan Paul.

Liberson, Tehiya. 1913. "The Question of the Woman Worker." Reprinted in *Pirkei Hapoel Hatzair* Vol. C, pp. 212–214. Tel Aviv: Twersky (Hebrew).

MacKinnon, Catharine, A. 1982. "Feminism, Marxism, Method and the State—An Agenda for Theory." *Signs* 7, 3:515–544.

Maimon, Ada. 1955. *Fifty Years of the Women Workers' Movement.* Tel Aviv: Ayanot (Hebrew).

Palgi, Michal, J. R. Blasi, Menahem Rosner, and Marylin Safir. 1983. *Sexual Equality—The Israeli Kibbutz Tests the Theories.* Norwood, PA.: Norwood Edition.

Palgi, Michal, and M. Rosner. 1983. "Equality between Sexes in the Kibbutz, Regression or Changed Meaning?" pp. 255–296 in *Sexual Equality,* edited by Palgi, M. et al.

Piven, Frances Fox, Cloward, Richard, A. 1977. *Poor People Movements Why they Succeed, How they Fail.* New York: Vintage Books.

Rozen, Ora. 1984. *Changes in the Status of Women in the Agricultural Settlements, 1919–1929.* M. A. Thesis. Tel Aviv (Hebrew).

Rosner, Menahem. 1972. "Women in the Kibbutz," pp. 235–242 in *Readings in the Psychology of Women,* edited by J. Bardwick. New York: Harper and Row.

Rowbotham, Sheila. 1974. *Women, Resistance and Revolution—A History of Women and Revolution in the Modern World.* New York: Vintage Books.

Safir, P. Marylin. 1983. "An Historical Perspective: the Kibbutz as an Experiment in Social and Sexual Equality," pp. 100–129 in *Sexual Equality,* edited by Palgi, M. et al.

Sayers, Janet. 1982. *Biological Politics—Feminist and Anti-Feminist Perspectives.* London and New York: Tavistock Publications.

Shapiro, Yonathan. 1975. *The Organization of Power.* Tel Aviv: Am Oved (Hebrew).

Shatil, Yoseph. 1955. *The Economy of the Kibbutz in Israel: History and Principles.* Tel Aviv: Sifriat Hapoalim (Hebrew).

Shepher, Joseph, and Sylvie Fogiel-Bigaoui. (in press). *A Sociological History of the Family in the Kibbutz from its Beginning to the Present.* Tel Aviv: Everyman University (Hebrew).

Shilo, Margalit. 1981. "Women's Farm at Kinneret, 1911–1917: A Solution of the Problem of the Working Woman in the Second *Aliyah.*" *The Jerusalem Cathedra,* 2:246–283.

Shorter, E. 1977. *The Making of the Modern Family—Points.* Histoire, Paris, Seuil (French).

Shur, Shimon. 1976. "The Kibbutz and the Israeli Nation Building: The Problem of Periodization." *Hakkibutz,* 3–4:186–201 (Hebrew).

Slutzki, Yehuda. 1972. *The History of the Hagana.* Tel Aviv: Am Oved (Hebrew).

Smelser, J. Neil. 1963. *Theory of Collective Behavior.* London: Routledge and Kegan Paul.

Spiro, E. Melford. 1980. *Gender and Culture—Kibbutz Women Revisited.* New York: Schocken Books.

Stites, Richard. 1978. *The Women's Liberation Movement in Russia. 1860–1930.* Princeton: Princeton University Press.

Talmon, Yonina. 1974. *Family and Community in the Kibbutz.* Cambridge, Mass.: Harvard University Press.

Tiger, Lionel and Joseph Shepher, 1976. *Women in the Kibbutz.* New York, London: A Harvest Book.

Tsur, Muki, Zevoulun, T. and H. Porat. 1982. *Here on the Face of the Earth.* Tel Aviv: Hakkibutz Hameuchad and Sifriat Hapoalim (Hebrew).

Yanait, Ben-Zvi, Rachel. 1976. *Manya Shohat.* Jerusalem: Yad Ben-Zvi (Hebrew).

10

Human Being or Housewife: The Status of Women in the Jewish Working Class Family in Palestine of the 1920s and 1930s

—— *Deborah S. Bernstein* ——

Introduction

Critique of the traditional Jewish society as it existed in Eastern Europe at the turn of the century was an essential component of Socialist Zionism. To what extent was this critique aimed at traditional patriarchal values? Did alternatives proposed by Socialist Zionism offer a change in family structure and in women's status? What type of family was developed in Jewish Palestine? As the social structure of the Yishuv evolved, how did the family organization change? What impact did social, political and economic processes within the Yishuv have on the formation of the "private" sphere of family structure and its significance for women? Answers to these questions are the focus of this study of the organization and values of the urban, working-class Jewish family in the 1920s and 1930s.

The Family—in Search of an Alternative

The family was the cornerstone of traditional Jewish community, a patriarchal society in which power and prestige were vested in men. Religious studies, the highest source of value in this community, were intended for men only. The many religious functionaries were men. Men also held the wealth, the second source of respect and standing in the community.

People lived their entire lives within the family context, passing with no interval from the family of origin to married status, and few indeed existed as individuals without any family framework. The family gave a person social standing and determined one's chances for a secure economic position and for education. In the patriarchal family, the father's authority was recognized and respected. The mother's role was to bear the yoke of the family's existence: to bring many children into the world, to see to their education, to take care of the family's daily needs, and frequently, to work to contribute to the family's sustenance. At times, when men were absent for long periods of time, mothers functioned in effect as a single parent. In spite of these encompassing responsibilities the status of the women in this society was secondary. Although many women did win esteem, there were many who suffered neglect and oppression both in their families and within the community. The pain, humiliation and suffering of the woman whose husband had tired of her, of the childless woman, and of the poor, unfortunate widow are well documented in works of literature (for striking examples in literature, see the stories of Deborah Baron, 1973; and of I. L. Peretz, as discussed by Adler, 1980).

Jewish families were units of both production and consumption. The minor trade and the small workshops, which were the "basic industries" of the Jewish *shtetl* economy were in most cases family businesses. Married women played a role in this economic activity, at times as sole breadwinners, the helpmates of husbands, who spent their days in religious studies or on the road; at other times working alongside their husbands in the workshop, bakery, or stall on market day. Generally a woman's economic activity granted her neither authority nor prestige, nor did it change the basic ideal norm that a Jewish woman's honor was to be expressed within the confines of her home.

Socialist Zionists rejected many of the qualities embodied by the Jewish family as it existed at the turn of the century. In particular Socialist Zionism reacted against inequality, against the precarious Jewish economy and against class exploitation. Inequality was manifested in the dependence of the wives on husbands, the unstable economy was based on small, shaky family businesses which could barely maintain the impoverished Jewish petite-bourgeoisie; class exploitation was rife in family workshops which employed hired help.

Despite this rejection, the family was almost never mentioned in Socialist Zionist publications on social criticism, or in the social alternatives explicitly spelled out by the movement. Nevertheless, papers and notes left by the pioneering immigrants provide evidence of their attitude to the family, their experiences and their aspirations for the future. There were those who saw in the family a threat to the new collective, egalitarian "Workers' Society" which they hoped to establish. They viewed the family as a competing structure which reflected the foundations of bourgeois-capitalist society: private enterprise, private ownership, and the values of competition and individualism. Their solution was to restrict the family domain, to limit its role, and to transfer many activities from the hearth to the new collective (Talmon, 1972).

Such a plan meant a more substantive change than merely restricting family functions and transferring them to collective authority. Critique of the family and proposals for an alternative were not intended to create a more limited model of the existing family pattern. The intention was to create a type of family that would embody the principles and relationships according to which the new society was to function. The resultant tension between the revolutionary collective and the family would be dispelled not simply by narrowing the centrality of the family, but also by compatibility between the new family and the new society. Far reaching change in this spirit was suggested by Menahem Elkind, leader of the Gdud Ha'avoda (literally the Labor Brigade), the most radical of the communal movements of the 1920s. In 1926, Elkind demanded:

> The destruction of the bourgeois experience and of the economic and psychological foundations of capitalist culture, the abrogation of the economic basis of the family, the release of the woman from childcare and from serving her husband, the introduction of the woman into productive work, the destruction of the family as the basic unit of society, the emancipation of the woman, a lessening of the place of the family and its limitation in erotic domains (quoted in Margalit, 1980:161).

Ten years later Yitzhak Tabenkin, leader of the Kibbutz Hameuchad movement, called for a similar change. He condemned the urban family format which had developed in Jewish Palestine, in which the woman was economically dependent on her husband, arguing that thus she attained neither economic nor personal autonomy. He went on to add:

> We must renew the family in such a way that the woman is not educated solely for family life, in which the content of her life is to be a "man's wife". When that alone is the content of a woman's education and of her social position, she is not independent. Being

Figure 15. Young men and women, Gdud ha'avoda (Labor Archive).

a "man's wife" means that the measure of this person's, this woman's, life is not her independence, rather it is her dependence.

Tabenkin concluded by reiterating that "economic independence is the basis for the equality between man and woman. We must return to economic independence in order to regain a way of life that is grounded in equality" (Yad Tabenkin Archive, Tabenkin—private collection).

Pioneering immigrant women themselves spoke and wrote little in public about the "destruction of the bourgeois experience", or about the socialist revolution and the abolition of private property. However in letters, notes, and diaries, they described the relations of both partnership and autonomy which they wanted to maintain with men. They strove for intimate relations between two persons who shared the same way of life and the same goals. Their attachment would be enriching and meaningful, they thought, because of shared involvement in activities beyond intimate relations of the couple and the family. The couple had to construct the relationships between them as two independent whole human beings, and to continue in this manner throughout their life together. Partnership and autonomy were perceived as strengthening and enriching both man and woman, implying neither contradiction nor mutual threat (Pekelman, 1938; Katznelson-Shazar, 1930:219–229).

This outlook is clear in the personal notes of women of the Third Aliyah at the beginning of the 1920s. Thus Henia Pekelman, who came to Palestine in 1922, wrote of her thoughts as a girl in Eastern Europe, where every girl's hope, and every mother's dream, was to find a successful bridegroom: "It was difficult for me to explain (to my mother—D. B.) that though I don't think of remaining an old maid, it's not my aim to sit around and wait for a husband, just as the man has other goals than just marriage. The man and the woman, both of them, need to aspire to a life of equality" (Pekelman, 1938:37). Another young woman, from a *Shomer Hatzair* group (left wing of the Labor-Zionist movement), wrote to her mother in 1927:

Do you remember the time when I burst into the room, my cheeks flushed from the strong winds outside and the stormy discussions in a secret meeting? Well, I don't know how it happened, but the wall of misunderstanding between us broke down, our hearts opened up to each other. Because of me, you agreed to remarry, to someone you didn't love, in order to assure me, the daughter of the love of your youth, in order to provide me with a home, a family, light, warmth. You took upon yourself this subjugation because you did not trust your own powers, the powers of a woman: how would she withstand the winds of life with no vocation to support herself and no shield for her soul? Well, mother, I understood your silent bravery, whose roots lie in the weakness of your female experience. That same rainy night, I revealed to you my secret dreams: a renewed land, a commune for all, and within it a creative, productive woman, working hand in hand with the man (in Katznelson-Shazar, 1930:221).

The outlook of women pioneers with regard to male-female relations was intertwined with their attitudes towards the status of women in general. Women's confrontation with the inequality that prevailed in Palestine, their special difficulties in obtaining work, the inequality in wages between men and women, and the lack of support for their aspirations even among their own comrades, put the "woman's question" on the agenda. These women desired complete involvement in goals shared by men and women alike. Concrete demands were raised principally in the domain of work, centering on the possibility of doing manual work, which was considered productive and creative labor; on the chance to acquire new skills and to join in jobs that were manned by men only; and on equal compensation. These demands, however, expressed a more general aspiration toward the full expression of woman's personality in all areas of life—in work, the labor movement, as well as in friendship and love.

The Urban Family and its Function

The majority of the pioneering immigrants at the beginning of the 1920s were single, but permanent attachments were formed quickly and families established, with the overwhelming majority of liaisons ending in marriage. According to data based on the census of 1931, only 1.5 percent of all Jewish women in Palestine reached the 45–50 age group without having been married (Baki, 1945: Tb.66). In the cities, where some 75–80 percent of the Jewish population lived (Gertz, 1947:38), the nuclear family fulfilled a wide variety of roles. The narrowing of family functions which was part of the radical social outlook of Elkind and Tabenkin, did not actually occur. The function of social and biological reproduction remained in the family: sexuality, the bearing of children, socialization, and consumption.

Sexuality

Very little is known about pioneering women's attitude towards sexuality, and towards intimate relations between the sexes. The few testimonies that do exist show conflicting tendencies and ambivalent attitudes. As mentioned above an ideology of "free love" prevailed in narrow circles. In wider circles, too, there were misgivings over accepted norms regarding the exclusiveness of the relationship between husband and wife. There were those who expressed the desire to extend one's close intimate relations beyond those with the chosen permanent partner. In her notes S. (identifying herself only by her initial) related to this matter:

> It happens that a person has serious relationships with other close people before deciding on the one person. And after they start family life, the former relations slowly come to an end and new ones do not take their place. Is this natural, is it necessary? Contact with people enriches one's inner life more than any other source. And especially during late adolescence and the expansion of one's circle of interest—it is customary to confine oneself within the life of two. Can this bring satisfaction? One should not hope, nor should one wish, that everything that is close and of interest to one person will also be close to the other. As long as the two, they alone take in life's impressions together, their lives are inevitably poorer than they could have been (in Katznelson-Shazar, 1930:227).

However, S. makes clear that the desire for variety and enrichment was not intended as a substitute for the one special relationship, which is more intimate than all others. "I consider the relationships in the life of the family", she added, "the relations of the spirit and the body, to be so special that no other relations are like them. None replaces them nor contradicts them" (ibid).

From these and similar expressions, one may conclude that along with the search for more enriching, egalitarian family norms, the family based on the fixed stable couple, remained the focus of sexual—erotic—intimate relations.

The Bearing of Children

The vast majority of children were born within the framework of a family, to couples having a fixed and binding relationship. An ideology of "free love" was common apparently only within very narrow circles. The attitude to giving birth outside the family context was ambivalent, as minifested in *Dvar Hapoelet* in 1934, the year the journal of the Women Workers' Movement (WWM) first appeared. The possibility of giving birth out of wedlock or outside of any permanent relationship, was known and did exist. Dr. M. Aharonova, who wrote about women who came to her in this matter, encouraged them to continue with their pregnancy if she judged that they wished to do so. On the other hand, various reservations were also raised, foremost among them being the fear of economic difficulty, the need to work and to care for a child at the same time. Other opinions expressed apprehension regarding the welfare of a child in need of a father and fear of hostile public opinion, as may be seen in letters to Dvar Hapoelet, such as " . . . they also tell of cases of suicide out of despondency and the fear of appearing in public with the baby" (Vol. 1, 2:249; also Pekelman, 1938).

Socialization

There was no attempt to remove child care and socialization from the family, especially at younger ages. Other socialization agents, such as school and youth movements, were not meant to replace the family; and especially not the mother. Ancillary services available to the family for baby and small-child care were very few; responsibility for young children lay almost exclusively with the mother.

Consumption

The need for shelter, clothing and food were overwhelmingly supplied in the family context. People lived in a family household. There were attempts in the 1920s to establish urban communes and collectives (kibbutzim). Very little is known of these experiments. Apparently they did not last very long. The workers' neighborhoods that were set up in the 1930s were based on family households, each individual household supplying the daily needs of its members. Family consumption served not only household members but also supplied, at a price, the needs of people who lived outside of a family framework. Although there were many restaurants, among them workers' kitchens, there were also people who regularly ate at some family's house or who lived with families as boarders. Thus, even persons who did not establish family households of their own, were dependent on private family units for their daily needs.

To sum up, the functions of the working-class urban family unit were not reduced and limited. It is difficult to point out any function transferred from the family to public agency in particular those created along egalitarian—co-operative lines.

Division of Labor in the Family

Within the family there was a fixed, agreed division of labor. The man was the provider, and the woman was, first and foremost, a homemaker. Husband and wife were defined as "the two heads of household". Their partnership, to the degree that it was actualized, was manifested in the wife's involvement in the man's world of work, trade union, political party, etc. There is no hint of the men's involvement in women's roles and burdens.

Among married women, many worked for wages outside their homes. Some did not want to give up a job they had obtained with great effort before their marriage. Some wanted to realize skills acquired prior to, or after, immigrating to Palestine. The wide-spread norm among women, and among some of the men, was in favor of married women working outside the household. Moreover there was frequently an economic need to supplement the family income, especially during recession or crisis.

Married women who continued to work for wages bore a dual burden. Many employed maids to fill their tasks and their place during the day (Bernstein, 1987:86–87). Many did so with mixed feelings, aware of relationships based on control that inevitably developed between the lady of the house and her hired help, who in many cases may herself have been a pioneer who aspired to pro-ductive, creative work. The full trap of the double burden was ex-pressed in H.'s protest: "And everything rebels in me against this oppressive burden (of housework—D. B.). Can it be that a maid will be our salvation? Can it be that in order for me to do produc-tive and creative work my comrade will have to work in my place, doing the service work that I loathe?" (quoted in Katznelson—Shazar, 1930:137).

There were women who, although they continued to work out-side the home, gave clear priority to everything connected with the home; tending to the children and playing the roles of supportive wife. It is possible that this step was taken by many without any inner conflict, but that was not always the case. Tension was also a likely outcome when expectations of partnership gave way to the subordination of women's aspirations to those of their husbands. R. writes about one of her friends:

> N. visited me yesterday. She told me about her work and about her close friends. I thought to myself: N. is a talented person who

desires a life of her own. Why, then, does her husband carry on his life out in the open, while she does so surreptitiously, with many interruptions, and only after she has taken care of the needs of the house, her husband and the children? Why is her life but a narrow stream running parallel to the main flow of life—his? In what way is he better than she? (in Katznelson, 1930:226).

Most women were unskilled workers and acted differently for lack of choice. In the absence of childcare services, on the one hand, and of meaningful labor options on the other, most married women left the labor force and devoted themselves to their difficult household work. There were those among the homemakers who felt part of the community of workers, and accepted the title, "worker's wife" or "comrade's wife", awarded them by the Labor Federation (Histadrut), as reflecting a status of actual membership. Undoubtedly, though, for many women the transition from independent worker to "homemaker" was fraught with personal, social, and economic difficulties.

In the 1926 conference of the Women Workers' Movement, one of the delegates asked, "Does family life have to deprive us of our true face?" (*Davar*, 28 April 1926). And Rachel Keren-Zvi of Petah Tikva described the difficulties facing the new mother:

Difficult material conditions demand of the mother no end of concessions. Only yesterday she was an equal member of the Histadrut, was aware of all its activities, had her own membership card and paid her dues. And now, with the appearance of the child, the family must economize. It is necessary to give up one of the membership cards. It is difficult for the mother to understand, at first, why she has to be the one to give up her card. And she is told that that is the accepted rule, the rule of the Histadrut. And even if her whole consciousness rebels against this deprivation of her rights she must surrender and enter the Histadrut, with the special appellation, "worker's wife". This is her first concession, to be followed by many others—books, lectures, even the newspaper that she had waited for anxiously day after day. And all this is done involuntarily, with inner bitterness. She is loaded down with both worries and work, troubled, all on her own, within the confines of her four walls. With the birth of her child, society seems to close down before the worker-mother, because such is demanded by the difficult conditions of her life (in Katznelson-Shazar, 1930:165).

Bracha Habas, a labor activist and leader, stated the case forcefully and sharply:

The mother, whether in the city or in the moshava, becomes by necessity—in spite of her doubts and struggles—a man's woman", "helpmate" or "housewife", with everything that these terms imply. The birth of a child represents a frontier, a very difficult social and spiritual passage. She is cut off from her work—which she was able to hold on to only with great effort—even when that work represented not just a spiritual need, but a grave economic need as well. She withdraws, perforce, into her own house, disconnecting herself from social and public life. She does not give up easily. The conflict between the woman as human being and the woman as housewife is severe, filled with bitterness and unresolved struggles (in Katznelson-Shazar, 1930:167).

In summary, the traditional division of labor re-emerged within the nuclear urban working-class family. This involved a hierarchy between spouses, with the man as provider and the woman necessarily dependent on him economically. Women focused on housework and the family, and lost sight of activities that went on outside the household and its immediate environment. As a result, those social spheres that possessed the highest esteem—work and public activity—were the domain of men.

Equality Eludes the Family

A wide range of social, political, economic and ideological factors help explain the hierarchy that developed within the new nuclear family, despite aspirations to the contrary.

The Urban Capitalist Structure

The inability of the family to develop along new, egalitarian lines stemmed mainly from the absence of a significant alternative to the urban private economy. The aim of the pioneering immigration was to create a socialist society, a "workers' society", in the language of the period. However, there was little actual change in the urban social structure. Most of the workers remained wage earners, whether in the private sector or in Histadrut enterprises. Labor relations were not much different in the two sectors. Social conditions may have been better in the Histadrut sector, but there too differences in wage grades existed not only between managers and laborers but also between skilled and unskilled workers (Sussman, 1973), as well as between men and women (Bernstein, 1983). Collectivity in the area of consumption was even more limited. Urban kibbutzim were few and temporary, and in the workers' neighborhoods no collective consumption of any form took place. There was a sense of working-class hegemony at the work place and in certain neighborhoods, but there was no reorganization of the whole social system nor any attempt to develop new ways of satisfying basic human needs. In the absence of such changes the family inevitably continued to fill all its previous roles.

The Histadrut and the Labor Market

The labor movement was active largely in the sphere of work. The Histadrut was a strong, active factor in organizing both male and female workers, in the consolidation of trade unions, and in organizing cultural and educational events. Histadrut activities went far beyond the usual scope of activities of a trade union. It ran a sick fund, published a daily newspaper, set up schools and sponsored youth groups, and even opened a marketing network for local Jewish products. Yet, despite the fact that women constituted fifty percent of Histadrut membership, both as hired labor and as "workers' wives", the labor federation hardly ever related to their *special* needs. It is true that an organization of women homemakers was set up (called "the Organization of Working Mothers" or, in full, "the Organization of Mothers who Work in Their Own Household"), but this organization never operated as a trade union to advance the interests of its members. Homemakers were in need of services other than those required by all other groups of workers. They needed services which would fill some of the family tasks allotted to women, particularly adequate child care services. But such services were barely supplied. Zippora Bar-Droma of Tel Aviv addressed this need:

> Even in the city the burden carried by the "workers' wives" can be lightened by the organization of a chain of high-quality baby care centers, of a mutual-help sick fund, of co-operative kitchens, of playgrounds that would be opened for several hours even during holidays and on Saturdays. Though the workers in the city do not live next to each other, and though they are not as cohesive as people in the co-operative agricultural communities, mutual help among working women in the city is entirely possible (in Katznelson-Shazar, 1930:133).

Rachel Keren-Zvi of Petah Tikva voiced similar needs:

> The mother's work lasts from early morning to late at night. There's no question of the number of working hours. Even when

she falls dead tired on her bed, her work is still not finished. Caring for a child demands of the inexperienced mother all her time—and the question remains: Is it up to the mother alone to bear sole responsibility? Hasn't the time come for someone to see to the establishment of a children's home in the moshava? (in Katznelson-Shazar, 1930:164).

And as a matter of principle Pnina Yagel-Avatihi (apparently of Tel Aviv) wrote: "Our demand is that homemaking be recognized as one of the industries of the labor market, and women who work in this field [be recognized] as workers and as productive members". She then added:

> I am far from believing that by recognition on the part of Histadrut institutions [of the homemaker-mother being a member in her own right—D. B.] our problem will be solved. A necessary condition for this is the collective basis of life, mutual aid, the joint caring for and educating of the children. These will expand the awareness of the urban woman worker and will increase her public activity (in Katznelson-Shazar, 1930:136).

Thus, although there were women in the Histadrut who called for collective services in the city, the Histadrut concentrated its efforts on the familiar workplaces, and mothers were left to bear their burden alone.

Women in the Labor Market

The marginal status of women in the labor force was also responsible for causing women to give up employment after marriage, especially after the birth of their first child. Women suffered more from unemployment than did men, and were hurt more by the recessionary periods frequent in Palestine during this period. Many women did not have an occupation which could assure them higher income and more permanent employment (for a more detailed discussion of the employment situation of women, see Bernstein, 1983, 1987a, 1987b).

The urban economy was based primarily on construction, an area in which very few women were employed. Women were pushed, therefore, to more marginal sectors. In 1930, after a severe crisis that had begun in 1926, some 47 percent of working-women were employed in service work—housecleaners, cooks, waitresses, and laundresses. By 1937, following prosperity brought on by the Fifth Aliyah (1932–35), some 33 percent of the women continued to work in these vocations. The salary for service jobs was very low, and turnover high. During this period, another 23 percent worked in light industry, mainly textiles, clothing, food, and cardboard work. In these sectors, too, women remained principally in unskilled jobs and were subjected to seasonal fluctuations as well as low salaries. Domestic workers earned, in most cases, up to four Palestine pounds (PP), the lowest wage category in the workers' census of 1937. Light industry workers were paid on a daily basis, their wage also remaining at the lowest level of 15–25 Palestine piasters (*grush*) per day.[1] Clerical work and trade employed another 11 percent of the women in 1930, and 18 percent in 1937. Their wages were higher although there were large variations, with women earning anywhere from four to eight Palestine pounds per month. Lastly, 14 percent of women worked in the health professions (mainly as nurses), and in education, and their salaries there were higher, some eight PP per month. The remaining 10–15 percent of urban women workers were divided among various work spheres—agriculture, construction, the professions, and others.

Women's wages were concentrated, for the most part, in the lowest wage grades. Men's wages were in intermediate and high wage ranges. Among day workers, 60 percent of the women were in low salary grades, 35 percent in the middle range, and only 5 percent in high wage grades. Among men, by contrast, only 15 percent were concentrated in the low salary grades, 48 percent in the middle ranks, and 37 percent in the high wage grades (Histadrut, 1937: Tb.35,39). Similar differentials may be found between monthly male and female workers (ibid.: Tb.36,40).

It is reasonable to assume that the absence of skills, the high rate of part-time work, and low wages, all led married women to leave the labor market. Indirect proof of this assumption lies in the fact that among those women who did obtain skilled jobs and reasonable salaries, the percentage of married women was much higher than among the low skilled, low paying jobs. About a third of all women workers in health and education were married, compared to 20 percent of light industry and restaurant work, and 11 percent in household service (data relate only to Tel Aviv; see Tel Aviv Worker's Council, 1939).

Image and Identity

A great deal of evidence exists showing that men in the labor movement continued to view women—their comrades in the movement, in the collective, and in the party—as being different from themselves. Men found it difficult to change firmly rooted outlooks on sexual identity. It was with mixed feelings that they accepted working women in general, and in particular they opposed any breakthrough into the existing domain of men's work. They assumed, as a matter of fact, that the man would be the provider while the woman would do the house work. The man would constitute the "main flow of life", in the words of Rachel Katznelson-Shazar, while the woman, was "the narrow stream running alongside".

Women's perception of themselves was far more complex. There were images and attitudes that were rooted in childhood experience, to which two new and somewhat contradictory elements of the new female identity were now added. One element was the "woman-as-person" who, like the man, was a partner in all social activity by virtue of common humanity. The other element was "the woman-as-mother", who enjoyed an experience unique to her which expressed her distinct physical and psychological character, the experience of motherhood. On the basis of this self-image motherhood was not woman's only role but it was hers alone. The father is mentioned from time to time, when women wrote about motherhood, as a kind of appendage only doubtfully integrated into the unique mother-child relationship. The poet Fania Bergstein gave special expression to this complex relationship to motherhood when she wrote in 1934:

> When I see you standing by our small son's bed, your eyes anxious and bewildered, your hands trembling from the touch of his small finger—my smile goes out to you as in pity. Now, for the first time, I feel so much richer, so much stronger than you. Everything have I shared with you. My bread, my fate. But this, my sweet pain, my agonizing happiness, my silent laugh mixed with tears—when first I heard my son, his crying—this I cannot share with you. The whole force of this richness, which I hoarded in my soul during those hours of affliction—how can I tell you, how would you understand? I was at the threshold, at the edge of an aweful mystery. And I returned stronger and richer than I was before. Forgive me, but these riches I will not share with you, my friend. They are for me, walled up within me in my soul, screaming from my eyes. And when your lips touched the hand of our little son—my pitying smile went out to you. Just as one who has a secret pities those who do not know its meaning (in Bassevitz and Bat-Rachel, 1944:352).

It is difficult to identify all the reasons for this paean to motherhood,[2] but it is also difficult not to feel the tension between the desire for full partnership in the human experience of creative labor and public action and the glorification of the role of motherhood as a unique female role.

The Private Domain—Attitudes of the Histadrut and the WWM

In this phase of national and social struggle, the collective stood at the center of things, and the individual's needs and feelings were pushed aside. The conflict of women, who aspired to live a full life and not be shut-in within the four walls of their home, remained a personal and private one. As Bracha Habas said, it had not yet become a general question impinging on the mind of the public.

> The problem has not yet received public attention. It is still a private problem, the problem of this or that family, falling under the burden, lacking clear traditions, not knowing how to cope; it is the problem of this or that woman who in her corner, room or shack struggles with her fate, bitter, unsatisfied and entirely alone (in Katznelson-Shazar, 1930:168).

Nearly ten years later Rachel Katznelson returned to the same subject, now as the leading spokeswoman for the problems of the woman as homemaker and mother:

> The common conception is that the needs, desires, and struggles of the Histadrut end at the threshold of the worker's home, where private life begins. Laws and obligations are valid for the group, the moshav, the neighborhood, the union. They are the subject of public discussion, of criticism and of demands, but the movement has no interest in what happens inside the comrade's home; does the woman also have leisure time and is there a just division of the burden between father and mother; does anyone concern himself with the mother's affinity to the Hebrew book; is the woman, who makes all the family purchases, encouraged to spend the wages in a way appropriate to the needs of workers; and who counsels the mother—the caretaker and educator? (Dvar Hapoelet, 1943:179).

How does one explain the fact that the workers' movement remained outside the threshold of the home, while the women workers' movement, though it peeped through the opening, also never crossed the threshold? The two movements were caught in a web of contradictions that prevented, or at least limited, their actions.

The Histadrut reinforced inequality within the family both directly and indirectly. Its leadership benefitted from having the needs of the (male) worker satisfied within the family, by the unacknowledged labor of his wife. The Histadrut thus exempted itself from having to provide such needs as housing, food, clothing, and child care. However, the preference for this way of fulfilling mundane needs gave rise to unavoidable tension between the Histadrut and the family. The plethora of family tasks became a focus of activity that competed with that of the movement. The woman who had been excluded from the labor force in order to fill family members' needs was being blamed for the family's focal attraction for its members. She was even blamed for the fact that the privacy of the family became an end in itself, distancing the worker and his children from the movement and its goals. An expression of these accusations may be found in the words of Aba Khoushi, then secretary of the Haifa Labor Council, in a "public trial" in which the "worker's wife" was put on trial. Khoushi, later mayor of Haifa, was the prosecutor and his words were stinging:

> The great mass of married women devote themselves to the life of the family—which is important in itself—but the family and family life are only part of the life of the society and the Movement. And the isolation in family life has negative by-products which endanger the future of the Movement, like: the weaving of threads of petty bourgeois life, later anti-social—the woman is concerned with having a nice home, attractive furniture—the rooms turn into furniture warehouses—in workers' neighborhoods we begin to have competition between one woman and another—one decorates a bedroom for 20–30 pounds, and the other tries to outdo her. The laborer's family is over its head in debt— the worker is affected and pulled into the stream of petty bourgeois life, the child—the future of the Movement—is brought up in this atmosphere of the desire to have "a modern bedroom" (quoted in Bernstein, 1987:193).[3]

The Histadrut wanted to have its cake and eat it. It was interested in a family system which would supply male workers' needs without becoming an alternative focus of attraction. The status of "member's wife" was supposed to resolve the contradiction between family and movement. The woman would continue to fulfill the needs of her husband, wage earning member of the Histadrut, and by virtue of filling this task would herself gain membership. Her membership in the Histadrut would prevent her dissociation from the movement and reduce any harmful effects. Not surprisingly, the concept of "worker's wife" or "member's wife" did not create any direct or meaningful tie between the woman homemaker and the Histadrut. Rather it angered those women who seriously sought a way of being part of the movement with which they identified.

The Histadrut did not resolve the contradiction that lay at the basis of its relationship to the family. Despite the problems presented by Abba Khoushy (above), the contradictions implicit in family life could remain unresolved without undermining Histadrut activity. The situation, however, was different with regard to the Women Workers' Movement (WWM). The contradictions in the organization's relationship to the family and to the woman homemaker lay at the heart of this movement.

The Women Workers' Movement accepted the Histadrut's basic outlook. The WWM also set the collective goal of "building the land", establishing a "national home" above all else. It saw in the domain of labor the essence of the self-actualization of individuals and the consolidation of the movement. Despite paying lip service to the unpaid work of women in the home, the WWM saw in the female wage worker, the *po'elet*, the only true laborer. Nevertheless, the movement could not regard the homemaker's role as meaningless. First, the movement's leaders were more sensitive to the difficulties faced by this woman, who alone had to shoulder all household work. Second, criticism was aired from the "workers' wives" against the leadership of the movement, from whom they expected some real action. A movement that aspired to activate all women could not disregard this criticism.

The WWM tried to operate among the "workers' wives". In 1930, the Organization of Working Mothers (OWM) was established and soon became the most active arm of the WWM. This organization called mothers to take upon themselves assignments that were of importance to the Histadrut. Among them were welfare work with Histadrut members in cases of sickness and unemployment, collecting clothing for needy families, arranging hospitalization and recuperation services for Histadrut members, freeing parents from school fees, including kindergarten in case of need, nursery school fees, and supervising domestic service so that only Jewish labor, i.e., Jewish maids, were employed. All in all, they were called upon to cultivate, in their home, the atmosphere

Figure 16. Children's day care, Tel Aviv, run by the Organization of Working Mothers (Labor Archive).

and cultural milieu deemed appropriate for the organized working-class. Considerable activity was devoted to setting up children's clubs, summer day camps and to a much lesser extent to maintaining day care centers and nursery schools (Katznelson, *Dvar Hapoelet*, 1934:221–228).

The question of how all these activities would affect the homemakers' marginal and dependent status was never asked, let alone answered. The Organization of Working Mothers started to fill, at the movement level, the role of concern and care for the needs of others that the worker's wife filled in her home, without any remuneration and therefore, without independence and status. Despite the fact that the WWM valued woman's work in the home, it attributed much more importance to working outside the home. Thus, the clear message was that women had to contend, at one and the same time, with both motherhood and salaried employment. In the words of Rachel Katznelson, "Just as we say to the worker in general: 'This is your destiny here in Palestine', so we should turn to the young woman worker and say: 'You have your sublime destiny; you must find harmony between your two roles, that of a working mother and that of a worker'." Rachel Katznelson was unique in highlighting thé deep conflict between these roles. In a seminar for women workers, held by the Women Workers' Council in Tel Aviv, 1937, she said as follows:

> This expression may perhaps be somewhat too sharp and cruel, but it is true to say that in some respects those two elements: work and family, are dire enemies in the life of the woman worker. This is not so in the life of the male worker. For him there is no chasm between family life and work life. He can be dedicated to his vocation, to public activity, and with all this still be a good father. By contrast, in the life of the woman worker, especially the wage earner, the element of work destroys the family element and vice versa. Our movement must recognize this tremendous conflict, which is the crux of the difference between the position of the woman worker and that of the man. If the woman worker wants to devote herself to her work, to master a profession, to be included in the trade union, and generally to be active in the labor movement and we expect all that of her—she may well say: "Enough, I have sufficient strength for this only." But here in this hall about 60 percent of the women are mothers. If we ask ourselves, "What is it to be a mother?" and if we remember that it is the wife of the worker who has to educate the children, keep house, decorate and design it, come into contact with doctors and teachers, then once again we may say: "This is enough for one person. We have no more strength." (Lilia Bassevitz Collection, Hakibbutz Hameuchad Archive Unit 15, Container 6, Yad Tabenkin).

She sees no way out of this double bind nor does she seek one. The two-fold contradictory burden is, according to Rachel Katznelson, a given situation. The challenge is to recognize the latent blessing embedded in it: "Frequently we forget that work and motherhood are the sources of life in general. And of course the origins of life create difficulties. There is no discrimination here. No evil hand is plotting against the woman. The woman must be educated to understand that this is also a source of happiness, of fulfillment" (ibid).

All of the factors discussed above, taken together, indicate that in the absence of a need for women's work in the economy, in the absence of supportive political institutions, in the absence of a social movement that offered an alternative to the existing relations among women, family, and society, women continued in their homekeeping work to ensure societal continuity and, as a result, to ensure the continuity of their own subordinate status.

Conclusion

The nature of the family is determined by the social functions it fulfills and by the division of labor and authority within it. A change in the character of the family is a difficult, multidimensional process. It requires a radical change in the identity of individuals and in the definition of sexual identity. It requires examination of the relationship between motherhood and parenthood in general. It requires changes in the social and economic structure, which will lead to changes in patterns of consumption, of socialization and of companionship. Finally, a radical change in formal structure requires a change in the words and symbols which reflect and shape thinking and behavior.

During the period discussed in this chapter important steps were taken. An alternative concept of the family was advanced by socialist Zionists, based on a partnership of spouses through shared involvement and commitments. Marriage as legal and symbolic status became secondary to the quality of relations between husband and wife, the two "heads of the household". Attempts to realize this new outlook, however, met with deep contradictions that remained unresolved. No economic, political, and social system was created to make possible such family organization. No changes in image and identity vital for a full partnership between man and woman took place. The tension between the woman-as-human being and the woman-as-housewife was not dispelled.

Notes

1. The monetary system in Palestine was linked to the British sterling pound. The basic unit was the Palestine pound (equal in value to the sterling pound), which was composed of one hundred piasters, or "*grushim*". Thus daily wages were measured in piasters and monthly wages in Palestine pounds.

2. This perspective is very different from that which is widespread today among women who aspire to equality, who tend to emphasize the partnership of the father in parenting.

3. The defense was conducted by Ada Maimon. It is interesting to note that Aba Khoushi repeated, among his charges, many of the points previously raised by various women. The latter raised the points as an accusation to society while, in Khoushi's view, the blame lay with the women themselves.

References

Adler, Ruth. 1980. *Women of the Shtetl, Through the Eyes of Y. L. Peretz.* London: Associated University Presses.

Baron, Deborah. 1973. *A Selection of Stories.* Tel Aviv: Yahdav (Hebrew).

Bassevitz, Lilia, and Yokheved Bat-Rachel (eds.). 1944. *Women in the Kibbutz.* Ein Harod: Hakibbutz Hameuchad (Hebrew).

Baki, Roberto. 1945. "The Custom of Marriage and Birth among Different Segments of the Settlement and Its Influence on Our Future," pp. 105–248 in *Immigration, Settlement and Natural Mobility among the Population in Palestine,* edited by Roberto Baki. Jerusalem: Department of Statistics of the Jewish Agency (Hebrew).

Bernstein, Deborah. 1983. "The Plough Woman who Cried into the Pots—The Position of Women in the Labor Force in Pre-state Israeli Society." *Jewish Social Studies* 45, 1:43–56.

———. 1987(a). *The Struggle for Equality, Urban Women Workers in Pre-state Israeli Society.* N. Y.: Praeger.

———. 1987(b). "The Women Workers' Movement in Pre-State Israel, 1919–1939." *Signs* 12, 3:454–470.

Gertz, A. 1947. *Statistical Handbook of Jewish Palestine, 1947.* Jerusalem: Department of Statistics of the Jewish Agency for Palestine.

Histadrut Haóvdim Be'Eretz Israel. 1938. "The Working Public in *Eretz-Israel* in the towns, *moshavot* and collective villages—the summary of the March 1937 census." *Pinkas,* Vol. 1936–38.

Katznelson-Shazar, Rachel (ed.) 1930. *Women Workers Speak.* Tel Aviv: Moetzet Ha-Poalot (Hebrew).

Pekelman, Henia. 1938. *The Life of a Woman Worker in Palestine.* Tel Aviv: Private publication (Hebrew).

Talmon, Yonina. 1972. *Family and Community in the Kibbutz.* Cambridge: Harvard University Press.

Sussman, Zvi. 1973. "The Determination of Wages for Unskilled Labor in the Advanced Sector of the Dual Economy of Mandatory Palestine." *Economic Development and Social Change* 22, 2:95–113.

Part III

Women's Rights, Women's Spheres

Just as the women of the labor movement attempted to transform their socialist Zionist goals into feminist goals, so did the women of the middle-class. The middle-class of the Yishuv was composed of various social groups known at the time as the *Hugim Ezrahi'm*—the civic sector. These were a somewhat mixed assortment of groups without a clear-cut common denominator. The civic sector included all those elements which were not identified as belonging to either the right wing, the left wing, ethnic groups or religious groups. This would include groups such as the private farmers of the moshavot, industrialists, merchants, intellectuals with a general liberal orientation, the political center organized in the General Zionist party and so forth. This assortment of groups, which never developed one overall representative organization, was matched by a variety of women's organizations from among the women of the same constituency. They developed their Zionist aspirations for a liberal, modern, secular Jewish society into liberal feminism. They aimed at a society in which women would enjoy equal rights without challenging or transforming women's conventional roles. They organized to enhance women's contribution to the new society by advancing women's spheres rather than by challenging the distinction between the spheres.

If the historiography of the Yishuv created a myth around the women pioneers (the halutzot), it ignored the women of the civic sector. Their achievements were either taken for granted or deemed unimportant. Both chapters in this section aim to redress this bias caused by an interplay of male dominance and labor movement dominance in the conventional historiography.

Sylvie Fogiel-Bijaoui, deals (in her contribution to this section) with the strength and success of the women of the civic sector. Hanna Herzog deals with their marginality and weakness. The difference between them is primarily one of focus. Fogiel-Bijaoui studies the one major success of the women's movement, led by the

257

Association of Hebrew Women for Equal Rights, in the struggle for suffrage. Herzog discusses a wide range of additional initiatives and achievements, but focuses on the marginalization of that success and of the many other successful initiatives in the accepted historiography.

The struggle for women's suffrage took place during the formation of representative institutions of the Jewish community in Palestine. These would provide leadership to the developing community and represent it before the governing authorities—the British mandatory government. The deep splits within the Jewish community, especially those between the Old Yishuv, the ultra-orthodox, highly conservative non-Zionist and anti-Zionist sector and the New Yishuv, which was nationalist, modern and non-religious, came to bear on all decisions concerning the formation of its representative institutions. Thus the issue of women's right to vote took on added significance as a touchstone to the nature of the new Jewish society. For the ultra-orthodox the introduction of women into the public sphere of political participation was seen as a basic deviation from religious law and norms. For the women and their socialist and liberal allies the right to vote and to be elected was, as Fogiel-Bijaoui claims, "an inseparable part of their Zionist revolution which aspired to create a new society, based on liberty and human equality in the Liberal or the Socialist sense of these terms."

In her analysis of women's success in obtaining the vote Fogiel-Bijaoui focuses on the broad women's movement which emerged, bringing together women of different sectors of the New Yishuv, under the leadership of the liberal center, the women of the civic sector. She identifies ideological, political and organizational factors which combine to explain the women's special achievement, not only in gaining the vote, but in increasing women's representation far beyond that achieved by women in other societies at the time. Given the inability of women to achieve many of their other goals, as can be seen in the chapters of this book, the analysis of this successful venture is of special importance.

Hanna Herzog does not deny this success. On the contrary, she presents a detailed discussion of a wide range of additional achievements—the establishment of legal bureaus (by the Association of Hebrew Women for Equal Rights in Eretz Israel), the establishment of mother and child clinics and the beginning of social work in Palestine (the Federation of Hebrew Women) and the advancement of agricultural education for girls (WIZO). Herzog then goes on to ask why the women's organizations which were in fact successful in many of their initiatives, remained on the margins of the historical discussion. Thus, she sees the weakness of the women's organizations of the civic sector not in their inability to achieve their goals, but rather in the lack of acknowledgement and recognition of their pioneering role. This weakness, she claims, was due both to the political weakness of the civic sector and to the "feminine" areas of activity in which the women's organizations engaged. The achievements were obtained, the credit was not given.

11

On the Way to Equality? The Struggle for Women's Suffrage in the Jewish Yishuv, 1917–1926

——— *Sylvie Fogiel-Bijaoui* ———

The issue of Women's Suffrage in the Jewish settlement of Palestine, the Yishuv, has not been considered in the literature dealing with the history of the community (Horowitz and Lissak, 1977; Shapiro, 1978; Eisenstadt, 1967).[1] It is no wonder, therefore, that the prevalent view is that "women did not have to put up any form of struggle in order to obtain suffrage" in the Yishuv, or that the proponents of women's suffrage (men and women alike) only had to contend with the ultra-orthodox religious sectors (the *Haredim*), which they did successfully and with no particular difficulties (Goldberg, 1982:29–30).[2]

But when one studies the history of the Yishuv more closely, it becomes clear that the "controversy over women's suffrage" was one of the main political concerns of the community for eight years, from 1918 to 1926. "The controversy illuminates most of all the opposition between the Old and the New Yishuv, between a society rooted in Jewish tradition and a society wishing to model its life on modern Western ideas, on social justice, on democracy and on equality of the sexes" (Friedman, 1977:146).

It was in the context of this controversy that a women's movement was formed under the leadership of the roof organization, "The Association of Hebrew Women for Equal Rights in Eretz Israel", and scored one of the most notable victories of women in the history of the Yishuv: they obtained the right to vote and to be elected. The women's movement was composed of women from all sectors of the highly bifurcated Jewish society. There were women from the center and right wing sectors, known as the civic sectors (or in Hebrew, the Hugim Ezrahi'im), and there were the women workers. The former were organized in the Association of Women for Equal Rights and in additional organizations such as the Federation of Hebrew Women, while the women workers were organized in the Women Workers' Movement. As will be shown, the women's organizations of the civic sectors were the dominant and leading force in this struggle.

The central question of the present article relates to the factors which made the achievement of the vote possible within a relatively short time. How can one account for the fact that after having been categorically denied suffrage in the Assembly at Zikhron Yaakov (1903), Jewish women in Palestine did vote and were elected in 1920? How did it happen that the second Elected Assembly promulgated full civil, legal and political equality for women in its first session in January 1926?

In order to answer this question we will focus on the actions and struggles of the women's movement organized at that time. Like every other social movement, it was a general framework for various protest groups, pressure groups, voluntary organizations and political parties. It aspired to take part in the process of social transformation, to help in shaping the new social order established by the Zionist enterprise, and to obtain suffrage for women (on the subject of social movements see Freeman, 1983; Touraine, 1971; Zald and McCarthy, 1987).

The present study is divided into three sections:

1. In the first part, "Between Democracy and Theocracy", we will present the historical developments from the viewpoint of the women's movement.

2. In the second part, "The Power of Women: The Politization of the Status of the Woman", we will examine the source of women's power and discuss the predominant wing of the women's movement, the organizations affiliated with the center and right civic sectors, in relation to the weaker left wing, the Women Workers' Movement (WWM).

3. In the third part, "A Limited Victory", we will draw conclusions and examine the significance of the achievement for women in the Yishuv in Palestine.

Between Democracy and Theocracy:
The Struggle for Women's Suffrage

The struggle for women's suffrage in the Yishuv can be divided into three phases according to the development of the women's movement until its final victory: 1. 1917–1919; 2. 1919–1920; 3. 1920–1926.

1. 1917–1919

One of the necessary, (but not sufficient), conditions for the formation of a social movement is a "constructive crisis" which affects a group of people who have hitherto not translated their common views and attitudes into practical work, and motivates them into action (Freeman, 1983:9–10).

This "constructive crisis" was triggered for the women of the Yishuv who wanted to take an active part in the building of a new society, by the Balfour Declaration (2 November 1917), and the organizational and institutional activity which followed it. The Declaration, which promised the Jewish community political autonomy, presented the women with the question of their own status as citizens of the future national homeland.

In spite of the fact that the World Zionist Organization recognized women's suffrage as a fundamental principle since the Third Congress in 1899 (Fogiel-Bijaoui, 1981:131), the recurring experience of the women in Palestine bode ill for this prospect: at the end of the First Aliyah, the Assembly at Zikhron Yaakov (August 28, 1903), which was the first attempt to unite the institutions of the Yishuv, denied women's right to suffrage, and the Assembly held in Petah-Tikva immediately after the Balfour Declaration (November 18, 1917), followed suit, notwithstanding the presence of Rachel Yanait Ben-Zvi, a woman representative of the workers' sector, who was a member of the Temporary Council of the Jews of Eretz Israel (Azaryahu, 1947:6–7; Atias, 1963:10; Kahana, 1984: 37).

The denial of women's right to suffrage was reiterated in the first Constitutive Assembly, convened after numerous delays in January 1918 at Jaffa-Tel Aviv. The purpose of the Constitutive Assembly was to agree upon the guiding principles for the election of a national assembly which would decide on matters of the community and represent the Yishuv before the British Mandatory authorities. In view of the fact that in this Constitutive Assembly there was no representation of the religious sectors and the Old Yishuv, it looked like a significant failure for the women. It was then that the full extent of the opposition to women's suffrage, even outside the religious circles, became apparent.

The Second Constitutive Assembly (June 1918), where Jerusalem, the stronghold of the Old Yishuv, was represented, was not an improvement on the first. The issue of women's suffrage was at the heart of the controversy between delegates of the workers' sector and the civic sectors who supported the women's claim on the one hand, and the representatives of the religious orthodoxy and those delegates of the civic sectors who opposed it, on the other. Given the stalemate between the contending parties, the Zionist religious party (the *Mizrachi*) suggested a compromise, as they would try and do on numerous occasions. At this point they suggested that women be allowed to vote but not to be elected. The workers' parties, the women's allies, accepted the suggested compromise, at least for the time being (Atias, 1963:10; Rubinstein, 1979:152–153; Azaryahu, 1947:14; Maimon, 1955:211–212).

The women did not remain passive during that time. The first ominous signs at the Assembly in Petah Tikva (November 1917) marked the beginning of the first phase in the development of the women's movement. They began to organize themselves locally in "Women's Associations" in the towns and in the moshavot (rural settlements). This was the first time that women from the center and right wing organized for social and political objectives rather than charity work (Azaryahu, 1947:8–12; Maimon, 1955: 209–210).

But the turning point in the formation of the women's movement was the third Constitutive Assembly (December 1918) which was called the Council of Eretz Israel, as the entire Yishuv was represented in it. The representatives of the women, in an advisory capacity, were Ada Maimon (of the workers' sector) and Sarah Thon (of the civic sectors.) The discussion in the Assembly revolved mainly on the principles which were to guide the elections to the national assembly, to be called the Founding Assembly. As in previous discussions, the moot point was women's suffrage: the workers' representatives insisted that it should be definitely established in the constitution of the election, whereas the representatives of the Old Yishuv of Jerusalem were entirely opposed to it (Friedman, 1977:154–155). Since the Old Yishuv was not represented according to its demographic weight, the proponents of women's suffrage were a majority. A temporary committee of thirty-two members, including one woman (S. Thon), was set up at the end of the Assembly. It was charged with the task of preparing for the election to the Founding Assembly in which every adult in Eretz Israel would have the right to vote and to be elected (Maimon, 1955:212).

The response of the *Haredi* (ultra-orthodox) sector was not immediate, but under the pressure of their constituency in Jerusalem, who held women's suffrage to be immoral and anti-religious, they issued a call to boycott the election and secede from the Yishuv (Friedman, 1977:155–163).[3]

This was not an idle threat. The numerical power of the ultra-orthodox Jews could have easily been translated into political terms. According to the estimated data of M. Friedman, the Jewish community in Palestine numbered 56,000 people by the end of the First World War, and 26,000 of them lived in Jerusalem and were, for the most part, members of the Old Yishuv (Friedman, 1977:148, note 8). The meaning of the threat, the non-participation of a major part of the population in the election, was, therefore, a danger of delegitimization of the elected institution as representatives of the Jewish settlement before the British. A secession of this kind might have also undermined the authority of the elected body over the Yishuv itself.

The danger of an ultra-orthodox boycott was compounded by the fact that this sector had potential allies who might have joined it under certain political circumstances. The first of these was the Zionist orthodox party, the Mizrachi the "natural ally" of the Haredim (the ultra-orthodoxy), as it was apprehensive of finding itself weak and isolated against a "non-religious majority whose avatar were the militant, Left-wing, anti-religious parties", if the secession took place. It was also concerned about the possibility that the representation of the Orthodox Jewry would remain entirely in the hands of the Old Yishuv (Friedman, 1977:160).

Other allies were the Sephardi sector whose members, albeit politically marginalized to some extent, stood for a conservative line regarding Jewish tradition. And finally, there was the private farming sector (with some religious members) whose main concern was to prevent the economic and political takeover of the Labor Movement in the Yishuv. These groups formed, along with the Haredim, an important part of the right wing of the Yishuv (Friedman, 1977:149,170).

The magnitude of the threat and the bargaining power of the Right wing were fully realized both by the Zionist leadership and by the women activists. If the Balfour Declaration was the "constructive crisis" which triggered the formation of the women's movement, the threat of Orthodox-religious secession, the culminating point of the crisis, was the turning point in its organizational formation.

Jo Freeman notes that two additional conditions, apart from the "constructive crisis", are essential in the formation of a social movement. First, there should be a network of communication between groups and individuals. Second, the communications network should also be capable of assimilating the new ideas adopted by the movement in the process of formation (Freeman, 1983:9).

In our case, the communications network was formed by the Women's Associations, set up in the wake of the Balfour Declaration, and it was fully capable of assimilating the ideas of the movement. The Associations made it possible to establish the leading organization in the women's movement, the Association of Hebrew Women for Equal Rights in Eretz Israel.

The Association of Women for Equal Rights set up branches in towns and moshavot (rural settlements) as the Women's Associations ceased to exist as autonomous organizations, and its headquarters was set in Jerusalem. The Association prepared for elections by forming a list of independent women which ran for election, a step which was particularly daring and apparently with no precedent in women's movements abroad at the time (Azaryahu, 1947:18). The leaders of the organization thus tried to encourage women, who did not belong to any organization, to struggle for public positions and, at the same time, they hoped to move the political parties, by indirect influence, to secure prominent positions for women candidates on their own lists.

2. 1919–1920

In spite of the resolution of the third Constitutive Assembly in December 1918, calling for the right to vote for all adults regardless of sex, the elections were postponed six times until April 1920. The main reasons for the delays were the procrastinations of the Mizrachi, who aspired for "co-operation with the non-religious sector for reasons of national need and an affiliation to a liberal value system" (Friedman, 1977:151), but at the same time could not dissociate themselves entirely from the ultra-orthodoxy of the Old Yishuv. Only in February 1920, after over a year, the Mizrachi agreed to take part in elections which were to take place no later than May 1920. Two factors appear to be central in this change of attitude:

1. The name of the assembly to be elected was changed from the Founding Assembly to the Elected Assembly, thus removing the apprehensions of the Mizrachi lest the Assembly, defined as

"Founding" should, on the strength of its name, promulgate fundamental anti-religious laws, which would apply to the entire Yishuv in the future.

2. The Mizrachi, who viewed the issue of women's suffrage as a "cultural-social matter", supported the resolution of the extended Executive of the Zionist Organization to hold the election with no further delay and without sexual discrimination (Friedman, 1977:163).

But it was not only the Mizrachi which changed its mind. Some of the Haredi delegates also agreed to take part in the election for the Elected Assembly, women's suffrage notwithstanding. The "moderates" among the Haredim had apparently estimated that they would get the majority of the votes in the election, and their weight in the Assembly would enable them to revoke the resolution on women's suffrage.[4]

Throughout the negotiations on the election, the women continued to organize themselves, mainly through those members who were active in the Women's Association for Equal Rights. In addition to that, there was the refusal of the women leaders, from both left, center and right, to give in to pressures of "peace makers" who asked the women to "give in and wait for a more appropriate time" (Maimon, 1955:213). Thus, it happened that when the situation in the political arena changed, i.e., when the delegates of the opposing groups changed their minds, the women's movement was well prepared for it. At the critical moment, the women of Palestine could go to the ballot boxes.

The election for the national assembly of the Yishuv was held in Palestine on April 19, 1920. The ultra-orthodox Jewry and the inhabitants of Jerusalem did not vote at the same time. They voted only on May 3, 1920, after a compromise settlement was reached which allowed the religious sector to have "Kosher" ballot boxes. Ultra orthodox Haredi women did not vote, but every male vote in that sector was counted as two. The general public in Jerusalem used ordinary ballot boxes as in the rest of the country. Out of 28,765 potential voters, 22,000 took part in the election: 20,160 in general ballot boxes and 2,040 Haredi voters in special ballot boxes. This amounted to 77 percent of all eligible voters (for detailed outcome of elections, see Rubinstein, 1979:156).

Out of 314 delegates 14 women were elected, about 4.5 percent of the total number, although there were only four out of twenty parties who put women candidates on their lists. Five delegates were elected from the list of the Women's Association for Equal Rights, which ran for elections under the name of the "List of Women's Associations": Esther Yeivin, Nehamah Pukhatchewsky, A. Gissin-Shroit, Hemdah Rosenberg, and Hannah Shopin. Sara Azaryahu and Yehudit Katinka, both active in the Women's Association were elected as 2 of the 13 delegates of the Progressive Party. Among the workers' parties, Ahdut Ha'avoda had 5 women among its 70 delegates: Esther Becker, Sarah Glicklich, Ada Geller, Rachel Yanait Ben-Zvi, and Manya Shohat, while Hapoel Hatzair had 2 delegates out of 41: Hayuta Bussel and Hanna Meisel (Atias, 1963:13–14, Rubinstein, 1979:156–157, Azaryahu, 1947:18–19).

The election for the first Elected Assembly was, then, a victory for the women's movement. Their opponents in the ultra-orthodox sector were defeated. By taking part in the election, the ultra-orthodox leaders legitimized the Elected Assembly as the representative institution of the entire Yishuv, but their participation was founded on a scenario which failed to materialize: they did not emerge as the largest faction, and could not join forces with their allies to revoke the resolution on women's suffrage. Women were not only entitled to vote, they were also elected. Admittedly, the percentage of women delegates in the first Elected Assembly was still low, but in view of the difficulties they had to face, and in comparison with the status of women in other countries who were still mostly deprived of suffrage at that time, it was, indeed, an impressive victory for the women's movement in Palestine.

3. 1920–1926

But the women could not rest on their laurels for long. It soon became apparent that the achievement of the movement might be eradicated, and they might have to start all over again. The ultra orthodox sector simply refused to accept the results of the election. They left the first session of the Elected Assembly (October 7, 1920), after their demand to hold another election which would exclude the women within six months was denied. However, they did continue to take part in the sessions of the Va'ad Leumi (The National Council), the executive body of the Elected Assembly,[5] even after Rachel Yanait Ben-Zvi was elected to replace one of the delegates in this forum (Friedman, 1977:172–173). The crisis broke out again at the second session of the Elected Assembly (March 6, 1922), when the refusal of the ultra-orthodox sector to participate in the session was compounded by an announcement, made by the

Mizrachi, some of the delegates of the private farming sector and the Sephardi factions, that they would not take part in the session so long as women's suffrage was not abolished (Friedman, 1977: 176).

It was clear to the Zionist leadership that the demands of the Haredim would have to be reckoned with, as they might secede from the Assembly and take the entire Right wing along. That feeling accounted for the constant pressures that were exerted on the women to withdraw from the Assembly, and the fact that they were "implicitly told that their obstinacy might ruin the organization". But the women delegates held fast, "as though they were sitting on burning embers rather than leave the assembly hall, since they did not believe that they were ruining the organization" (Maimon, 1955:215).

In fact, the position of women in the Assembly was strong enough to withstand these pressures.

A. Since 1920 the political power relations in the Yishuv changed in favor of the women. The power of the ultra-orthodoxy turned out to be quite limited, while the Labor Movement, the women's ally, began to emerge as a leading force in the Yishuv. The women were reinforced by the arrival of 35,000 members of the Third Aliyah (one third of which were women) at that time (1919–1923). Women's suffrage was part and parcel of the ideological outlook of these newcomers who held "progressive views", socialist or liberal (Erez, 1964).

B. Women delegates were now part of the Elected Assembly. A surrender to the pressures exerted on them would have been interpreted as a consent on their part to a political system in which women will be second-class citizens, to which they certainly would not agree (Azaryahu, 1947:23).

C. Finally, the organizational growth and the pluralism of the women's movement also reinforced the position of the women delegates at the Assembly. The early 1920s saw the emergence of other women's organizations in the Yishuv, organizations which set the demand and the struggle for "full civil and personal rights to women" as one of their integral goals (Thon, 1926:10). These organizations included the Federation of Hebrew Women and the National Organization of WIZO in *Eretz-Israel* from among the civic sectors and the Women Workers' Council, the central organization of the Women Workers' Movement, under the auspices of the Histadrut, the General Federation of Labor.

The changes which took place in the Yishuv and in the

women's movement were significant enough to strengthen the women delegates in the Elected Assembly but they were not significant enough for women's suffrage to be definitely established in the election constitution. Thus the Mizrachi once again attempted a compromise and in the autumn of 1923 brought up the idea (initially suggested in 1919) of a referendum on the issue of women's suffrage with exclusive male participation (Friedman, 1977:159–177). From that point until the surprising end, the threat of the referendum loomed large.

In March of 1924, the Women's Association organized a campaign for women's rights in the country to counteract the idea of the referendum. Women from all parts of the Yishuv, Left and Right, took part in this event, as well as some men who spoke for civil equality to women. The spirit of the campaign was expressed by Henrietta Szold in a public meeting held in Jerusalem, when she called on the Yishuv to "guard and protect the principles of equality and justice which are at the core of our national enterprise" (Azaryahu, 1947:28).

But the threat of the referendum was not removed, and in an attempt to eradicate it, the Women's Association enlisted the help of Jewish and Zionist Women's organizations in Europe and in America. These organizations responded by flooding the National Council with letters of protest against any attempt to deprive women of their civil rights (Azaryahu, 1947:29).

Finally, the third session of the Elected Assembly was convened on June 15, 1925. It was hoped that after a long delay the issue of women's suffrage would finally be resolved, but the delegates were surprised when Dr. Y. Thon presented them with a draft agreement signed by the ultra-orthodox leadership and the executive of the National Council after an informal negotiation which took several months. The agreement defined women's suffrage as a religious issue which cannot be resolved through democratic procedures. In order to find a parliamentary way out, the ultra-orthodox leadership agreed to put the subject to a secret ballot. However, they announced that they would join the Assembly only if the results were satisfactory from their viewpoint, and would secede if they were not satisfied (Kahana, 1984:75–6). The agreement met with strong objections from the majority of the delegates who summarily rejected the abolition of women's suffrage, the idea of a secret ballot, and the a priori refusal to accept the majority decision (ibid.).

When the agreement was finally brought to the vote, it was

voted down by a majority of 103 to 53. At the end of the session the constitution for the election to the second Elected Assembly was ratified on the basis of equality of the sexes. However, even as the election constitution was being ratified, opposition continued making it impossible to hold the elections. In order to get out of the maze, the Mizrachi brought up the idea of the referendum again. In September 1925, with the abstention of the Left, the National Council—apprehensive of internal divisions and the loss of its authority—decided to accept the suggestion of the Mizrachi on two conditions: 1). Women should also take part in the referendum. 2). The Right wing would undertake to accept the results of the referendum. These conditions were accepted by the Right wing and the date for the referendum was set for November 8, 1925.

The women had no choice but to get organized in order to obtain a positive result in the referendum. It is hard to tell what would have happened if the referendum had been held, but after a short while a bulletin against the referendum was posted in Jerusalem on behalf of the Haredi Rabbinate. The immediate result of this development was a dismantling of the Haredi party and subsequently of the entire Right wing. It appears that the Rabbinate issued the bulletin without consulting the leaders of the Haredi party who were placed in a ridiculous position, where their political steps were unequivocally rejected by the religious authorities. As they could neither oppose the religious authority, nor withdraw their consent to the referendum, they chose to disappear from the political map of the Yishuv (Friedman, 1977:181).

The election was held, with the women and with the Mizrachi, on December 5, 1925. Once again the Women's Association for Equal Rights ran for elections with its own women's list called— The Association of Hebrew Women for Equal Rights in Eretz Israel. Twenty five women delegates were elected to the Assembly, raising the percentage of women from 4.5 percent in the first Elected Assembly to 12 percent in the second Assembly. The women's list was particularly successful in that 13 out of the 25 elected delegates were its members, among them Leah Cook, the representative of the religious stream within the organization. The increase in the representation of women in the second Elected Assembly made it possible to increase their representation in the National Council. As a result, there were 4 women delegates among the 38 members of Council: E. Yeivin and S. Azaryahu (Association), R. Yanait Ben-Zvi (Ahdut Ha'avoda) and A. Maimon (Hapoel Hatzair)—all veteran feminists.

At the end of the first session of the second Elected Assembly on January 15, 1926, an official declaration was issued confirming "equal rights to women in all aspects of life in the *Yishuv*—civil, political and economic" (Azaryahu, 1947:38, Maimon, 1955:217). The declaration was legally ratified by the Mandate government only in 1927, when, after a long delay, the constitution of "Knesset Israel" was laid as the foundation of the national autonomy of the Jews in Eretz Israel. The struggle of the women's movement for suffrage concluded in a victory. It was one of the cornerstones of Israeli democracy.

The Power of Women: The Politization of the Status of the Woman

In this part of the chapter, we will focus in depth on one major question: what was the source of the power the women's movement held in the Yishuv? The question emerges in view of two major facts: 1) At that time, even in the most democratic or revolutionary societies, women had not had suffrage, or had only recently obtained it (women got suffrage in Finland in 1907, in Norway in 1913, in Denmark in 1915, in Russia in 1917, in Sweden and England in 1918, in Germany in 1919, in America in 1920 and in France in 1944). 2) In all those countries, the struggle for suffrage was long and exhausting, and sometimes took dozens of years (Badinter, 1986:205–214; Flexner, 1975; Deckard, 1979:213–300).

However, in order to understand the source of women's power in Palestine, it seems equally important to understand why it was the Women's Association, from the center and right wing, rather than the Women Workers' Movement, from the left, which took the lead in the struggle for suffrage. A number of factors can explain women's power, as it related to the issue of women's suffrage.

A. The fundamental source of power of the women's movement in the Yishuv between 1917 and 1926 was the Zionist-Feminist consciousness of the women who initiated and led the movement. Feminism was, for these women, an inseparable part of the Zionist revolution, which aspired to create a new society, based on liberty and human equality, in the Liberal or Socialist sense of these terms.

It seems to us that the feminist consciousness of the leaders of the movement made it possible for them to translate the issue of the woman's status from the private, individual level, to the public, general sphere. In addition to that, their Zionist orientation enabled them to learn the rules of the political game, as established at that time in the Yishuv, which revolved on the accumulation of power through the formation of organizations and organizational mechanisms, and by means of constant political activity (Shapiro, 1975; Horowitz and Lissak, 1977).

It was for these reasons that when the threat to women's suffrage became real, the leaders of the movement understood that to gain influence they must act through political channels, and they did not hesitate to form an exclusively female political organization and to go as far as to form a women's list for the first and the second Elected Assembly, while acting vigorously within their own parties. One should remember, however, that the Zionist Feminist consciousness of these leaders would not have been sufficient, if there had not been other women who thought alike, and saw the struggle for suffrage as part of the struggle of women for human rights. These women formed the first core of the Women Workers' Movement in 1911 and the Women's Associations in the towns and moshavot after 1917. Without this consciousness of the leaders as well as the rank and file of the movement, and without the networks which bound them together, the women's movement would not have been able to get off the ground.

B. The Feminist-Zionist consciousness of the women can account for another source of power, unique in the history of women in the Yishuv—the co-operation between the women of the civic sectors and the workers' sector. This consciousness seems to be the only explanation of such co-operation between women who were so central and active in two rival sectors competing for the leadership of the Yishuv. This co-operation was expressed in several ways, such as overlapping membership of the General Federation of Labor (the Histadrut) and the Women's Association (Azaryahu, 1947:16, 26), participation of the women workers' leaders in the general meetings of the Association and in its first national conference held in Jerusalem in 1922 (Azaryahu, 1947:25–26), and a united front of the women delegates in the first Elected Assembly against the pressures exerted on them to renounce women's suffrage for the sake of the unity of the Yishuv. As we have mentioned, this co-operation was unique, and it lasted only until the ratification of women's suffrage by the third session of the first Elected Assembly (Azaryahu, 1947:26). From that point onwards, the women were divided.

C. A third source of power of the women's movement was the affiliation of its leading figures to the elite of the new Yishuv. This affiliation was based on:

1. Family relationships between leaders of the women's movement and leaders of the Yishuv (such as the fact that Rachel Yanait Ben-Zvi of the WWM and Yitzak Ben-Zvi, one of the leaders of the labor movement, were husband and wife).

2. The professional occupations of the leaders (teachers, writers, journalists, doctors, agronomists, social workers) which placed them at the top of the social hierarchy of the new Yishuv, not only because these professions required a higher level of education, but because they were part of the daily construction of the Zionist enterprise. Some of the leading figures contributed to the revival of the Hebrew language. Others, to the establishment of Jewish agriculture. Still others, to the development of medical and social services on a modern professional basis.

3. The leaders of the women's movement were also key figures in their own parties. S. Azaryahu and Y. Katinka, to name just two examples, were at the head of the Progressive Party and were elected to the first Elected Assembly as part of its list. Their affiliation to the elite of the new Yishuv offered the leaders formal and informal access to centers of political power, and increased their influence. It also imparted legitimacy and respectability to their demand for civil equality.

D. Another source of the power was derived from the fact that the women's movement was an organic part of the new Yishuv, and its closest allies were the workers, a fact which placed them on the winning side in the struggle between the Old and the New Yishuv. Even those who opposed women's suffrage, but saw themselves as Zionists, had to resign themselves to suffrage when they joined the institutions of the Yishuv.

E. Finally, it is impossible to understand the success of the women's movement without taking account of the male support it had among the leaders of the labor movement and the Progressive Party. Admittedly, these allies were more than once prepared to sacrifice women's rights, it is also true that the support of the men was obtained to a large extent through the political organization of the women and their refusal to compromise. However, it cannot be denied that the male leadership—Labor and Progressive—saw women's suffrage (as did the women and the Haredi leadership, from their respective viewpoints) as a touchstone to the character of the future national homeland, and the male leadership, like that of the women, wanted a democracy where civil rights would be respected regardless of sex.

Having described the sources of power of the women's movement in general, we should now try to account for the predominance of the women of the civic sectors in the struggle for suffrage.
We believe that the reasons for this are the following:

A. The women of the civic sectors were the first to respond as an
organization to the issue of suffrage after the Balfour Declaration,
when they set up the leading organization, the Women's Association. As heirs to the Liberal feminism of the late nineteenth century, they perceived an end to the legal discrimination of women
and the establishment of legal equality regardless of sex, as the
necessary and main condition for equality between the sexes, as
evidenced in their motto, "one constitution and one law to man and
woman" (Fogiel-Bijaoui, 1981:3–6).

B. The leading figures of the organization knew how to bring together women from all sectors in the Yishuv, by a clear definition
of the goals of the organization—the acquisition of civil and political rights—while making it possible for rank and file members and
for the delegates in the national institutions to act according to the
dictates of their conscience on the "general concerns of the Yishuv"
(Azaryahu, 1947:16–17).

C. There was no internal division between the women activists of
the Second and the Third Aliyah in the civic sectors. On the contrary, the main organization established by the women of the Second Aliyah, the Women's Association for Equal Rights, was reinforced by the women's organizations established by the Third
Aliyah, the Federation of Hebrew Women and WIZO—Eretz Israel. This is not to say that there was no competition among the
organizations of the women's movement for prestige as well as for
human and economic resources, but at the time we are concerned
with, there was full co-operation among these organizations: they
all worked for the women's list for the Elected Assembly, they
called upon women to support it, and placed their own candidates
(such as Dr. Helena Kagan of the Federation of Hebrew Women,
Jerusalem, who was nominated for the 1925 election) in the list of
the Women's Association (Azaryahu, 1947:17–38; the Annual report of the Federation of Hebrew Women, 1926).

D. The professional and organizational activity of the women of the
civic sectors were conducted in the towns and moshavot, where the
majority of the Jewish population lived. They extended various
services according to the needs of the general female population,
ranging from child care clinics to professional training, community
work or legal counseling to families. This relationship must have
carried weight when it came to convincing women to support the

ideas of the movement. It can explain how women "dared" to vote
for a women's list, which more than doubled its strength from five
delegates in 1920 to thirteen in 1925. It also explains the fact that
the elected delegates were not only from Tel Aviv or Rishon
le'Tzion, but also from the Old Yishuv, Jerusalem, Safad (1920),
Tiberias and Petah-Tikva (a moshava with traditional-religious
leanings).

E. Finally, the predominance of the center and right wing in the
women's movement can also be explained by their serious attitude
to the "organizational aspect". They set up, from the very beginning, a formal organization in order to make the most efficient use
of their resources. In order to set up the organization, they obtained the assistance of Dr. Welt-Strauss, who was elected as
chairperson of the Association. Dr. Welt-Strauss had been one of
the most active members of the suffragettes movement in the
United States, and she contributed much of her experience and
contacts abroad in outlining the work of the organization (Azaryahu, 1947: 85–95).

The women's organizations of the civic sectors made contacts
with organizations abroad, particularly, but not only with Zionist
women's organizations, in order to obtain advice, support and resources. The Women's Association for Equal Rights and the Federation of Hebrew Women made contacts mainly with Hadassah,
whereas the WIZO—Eretz Israel was reliant on and reinforced by
its mother organization—WIZO, notwithstanding the initial tension between them. This was further proof of the political acumen
of the leaders as, according to M. Friedman, "in the reality of that
time no political movement could survive or struggle for positions
of power and dominance in the Yishuv, without allies in the Zionist movement" (Friedman, 1977:152).

We should now try to account for the relative weakness of the
Workers' sector in the women's movement.

A. The women workers were the first organized feminist group in
the Yishuv (set up as early as 1911), but as far as women's suffrage
was concerned, they acted alongside the women of the civic sectors
rather than as an independent consolidated sector. The reason for
this had to do with the political philosophy of the women workers'
movement in the country and in the world, which saw women's
suffrage as a secondary goal (at best) in the liberation of women.
Their main goal was the "conquest of labor" through the egalitarian integration of women in the production process. As far as they
were concerned, women's suffrage was to be taken for granted in

the "new world of tomorrow", and it did not appear to be an issue requiring the specific organization of women. This was also the basic outlook of the women workers' movement in Palestine, which was ideologically and organizationally founded on the "conquest of labor" in the Zionist-Feminist sense. In the situation which prevailed in the Yishuv at the time, it seemed necessary to devote the meager resources of the movement for the "conquest of labor" by the woman, particularly in the rural sector (Fogiel-Bijaoui, 1981: 110–218; Bernstein, 1987:101–103; Izraeli:1981).

B. The differences in the political philosophies of these two sectors are not the only explanation of their different roles in the women's movement. The women workers had to struggle, at the same time, for the legitimation of their own organization, The Women Workers' Council, within the labor movement. The question behind this struggle was the legitimacy of a separate and autonomous women's organization within the General Federation of Labor (the Histadrut) which was supposed to represent and serve all workers. The WWC remained a step-daughter in the Histadrut until the mid-1920s, a fact which compelled the leaders of the Women Workers' Movement to invest redoubled personal and organizational energies in the attempt to obtain resources from the father-organization, and these energies could not be spared for the struggle for suffrage.

C. Finally, there were internal tensions and organizational problems within the Women Workers' Movement, which are beyond the scope of this chapter, which restricted its influence in the struggle for suffrage.

However, the contribution of the Women Workers' Movement to the struggle for suffrage was crucial and significant. As we have already mentioned, the awareness of a common cause on the subject of suffrage united the women workers and the women of the civic sectors and enabled the joint effort—co-ordinated or not—of these two sectors. In addition to that, the concrete political steps taken by the Women Workers' Movement in the struggle for suffrage (pressures put on the leadership of the workers' parties to reject compromises at the expense of the women; their placement in prominent places on the party list, etc.) were all cornerstones in the success of the joint struggle. These steps created precedents in the public arena of the Yishuv which made it difficult for the male leadership of the labor movement to sacrifice the civil rights of women, even if they were occasionally tempted to do so. Finally, the contribution of the Women Workers' Movement to the struggle for suffrage was not least in the figures it put forth for the struggle, (Manya Shohat, Hayuta Bussel, Rachel Katznelson-Shazar, Rachel Yanait Ben-Zvi, Ada Maimon and others)—all women of exceptional political courage and stature. Of all these outstanding figures, a place of honour should be reserved for Ada Maimon, whose total commitment to a socialist and feminist revolution prompted her to co-operate fully and unreservedly with the women of the civic sectors in an attempt to realize the ideal of human equality.

Summary and Conclusions: A Limited Victory

In this chapter, we have described the struggle of women between 1917 and 1926 for the right to vote for and to be elected to the national institutions of the Yishuv. The issue behind the struggle was the nature of the future Jewish society in Eretz Israel, i.e. democracy or theocracy.

The power of the women's movement was in the fact that it placed the issue of the woman's status on a political level and struggled for positions of power to obtain its goals. It was supported in this struggle not only by the Liberal Right wing but mainly by the sector which was becoming the dominant one in the Yishuv, namely the Labor Movement.

The second half of the 1920s, after the achievement of suffrage, marked the end of the co-operation between the Right and the Left wings of the women's movement. One of the immediate results of these developments was the gradual weakening of the women of the civic sectors. The Women Workers' Council, supported by the ruling party, now had an economic and organizational advantage over the women's organizations of the center and right wing in its services to the women of the Yishuv. The demise of feminism in the Women Workers' Movement during the 1920s, with the growing acceptance of women's traditional role, and the gradual disappearance of feminism in the civic sectors, marked the end of feminism in Palestine (Fogiel-Bijaoui, 1981:219–94).

The question which emerges in view of all this is, to what extent did the struggle for suffrage bring the women closer to equality with the men? At first it appears that the achievement of suffrage did not bring about any significant changes in the position of women in the Yishuv. Politically, they were still virtually absent in the centers of power of the national institutions, i.e. the National Council and the World Zionist Organization. They also had to go through additional struggles to gain suffrage on the local level in the towns and in the moshavot (in Petah-Tikva, for example, the women were allowed to vote for the local Council only in 1940).

From a legal viewpoint, the achievement of suffrage did not change the status of women with regard to divorce and marriage laws, which remained in the hands of the rabbinical courts in the Yishuv and in the State of Israel, after the failure of the attempt to set up a non-religious Hebrew judiciary system on the basis of sexual equality (Azaryahu, 1947:54–81; Maimon, 1955:215–217).

Women's suffrage did not change the inferior position of women in the economic and occupational hierarchy, and they remained a cheaply available labor force, with no control over the economic development of the Yishuv (Bernstein, 1987).

However, the triumph of the women on the issue of suffrage has set an extremely important example of how a weak social group can determine its own destiny if certain ingredients of success are present: the politization of the status of women, co-operation among women, organizational capability (which entails an understanding of the needs of the target population undergoing a process of social change), and above all, a refusal to compromise the rights of the woman as part of the struggle for human rights.

In addition, the victory contributed to the establishment of a norm of civil equality in the Yishuv, just as the struggle of the women of the Second Aliyah in the kvutzot contributed to the norms of equality in the kibbutzim (Shilo, 1981). This resulted in the development of a cluster of laws ensuring civil equality between the sexes (with the exception of matrimonial and divorce laws), which was later adopted by the State of Israel. The second article of The Declaration of Independence (1948) confirms the commitment of the state to ban sexual discrimination in the political and social sphere. This was one of the "earliest legal documents in any legal system, which included an expression of equal rights to women, not only with regard to a single civil right, such as suffrage, but as a principle applying to a large spectrum of civil rights and legal competences granted by the state to its citizens" (Raday, 1982:173).

The achievement of suffrage was, in these respects, in Israel as in other countries, a necessary but not a sufficient step on the way to equality.

Notes

1. With the exception of a few studies (Friedman, 1977; Fogiel-Bjaoui, 1981; Kahana, 1984). Of these, Friedman's study (1977), which discusses the issue of women's suffrage in detail, does so from the perspective of its impact on the ultra-orthodoxy, the Haredim. Fogiel-Bjaoui's study (1981) and Kahana's (1984) are an unpublished Ph.D. and Masters thesis respectively, and thus have not had similar circulation to the major studies of the Yishuv mentioned above.

2. For a more detailed discussion of the bias of the conventional historiography on this issue see Herzog, this volume.

3. Friedman makes a distinction between two factions within the ultra-orthodox sector: the "extremists" who were resolved not to join the institutions of the Yishuv, in view of the resolution on women's suffrage; and the "moderates" who preferred to take part in the leadership of the Yishuv rather than secede, but still objected strongly to women's suffrage (Friedman, 1977:149). At this stage, we are still dealing with the entire ultra-orthodox sector, "extremists" and "moderates" alike.

4. The "extremists" did not change their attitude. See note above.

5. The National Council (Va'ad Le'umi) was a semi-government of the Yishuv. It had 20–40 members and its plenary was often in session. This forum, which was constituted by the Elected Assembly, determined the policy of the Yishuv.

References

Atias, Moshe. 1963. *The Book of Records, 1918–1948*. Second and expanded edition. Jerusalem: R. H. Hacohen (Hebrew).

Azaryahu, Sara. 1926. "The Woman and the Elected Assembly." *Ha'Isha*, 1:26–30 (Hebrew).

Azaryahu, Sara. 1947. *The Association of Hebrew Women for Equal Rights*. Jerusalem: The publication of the Association of Women for Equal Rights in *Eretz Israel* (Hebrew).

Badinter, Elisabeth. 1986. *The One is the Other—Relations between Men and Women*. Paris: Editions Odile Jacob (French).

Bernstein, Deborah. 1987. *The Struggle for Equality, Urban Women Workers in Prestate Israeli Society*. New York: Praeger.

Deckard, Barbara S. 1979, *The Women's Movement*. Second Edition. New York: Harper and Row.

Eisenstadt, S. N. 1967. *Israeli Society*. London: Weidenfeld and Nicholson.

Erez, Yehuda. 1964. *The Third Aliyah Book*. Tel Aviv: Am Oved (Hebrew).

Flexner, Eleanor. 1975. *Century of Struggle: The Women's Rights Movement in The U.S.* (revised edition). Cambridge, Massachusetts: The Belknap Press of Harvard University Press.

Fogiel-Bijaoui, Sylvie. 1981. *The Rib of Eve—The Women of Palestine, 1881–1948*. Ph.D. Dissertation. University of Paris-X, Nanterre (French).

Freemen, Jo. 1983. "On the Origins of Social Movements," pp. 8–30 in *Social Movements of the Sixties and Seventies*, edited by Jo Freeman. New York and London: Longman.

Friedman, Menahem. 1977. *Society and Religion, The Non-Zionist Orthodox in Eretz Israel, 1918–1936*. Jerusalem: Yad Yitzhak Ben-Zvi (Hebrew).

Gamson, William A. 1975. *The Strategy of Social Protest*. Homewood, Ill.: Dorsey Press.

Goldberg, Giora. 1982. "The Performance of Women in Legislative Politics: The Israeli Example." *Crossroads*, 9:27–49.

Greenberg, Ofra and Hanna Herzog. 1978. *A Voluntary Women's Organization in a Society in the Making*. Tel Aviv: Department of Sociology and Anthropology of the Tel Aviv University (Hebrew).

Gurr, Ted. 1970. *Why Men Rebel*. Princeton, N. J.: Princeton University Press.

Horowitz, Dan and Moshe Lissak. 1977. *The Origins of the Israeli Polity*. Tel Aviv: Am Oved (Hebrew).

Izraeli, Dafna, N. 1981. "The Zionist Women's Movement in Palestine, 1911–1927: A Sociological Analysis." *Signs*, 7:87–114.

Kahana, Nurit. 1984. *Women's Participation in Politics: The Case of the Struggle for the Vote for Women in the Yishuv*. M. A. Thesis. University of Haifa (Hebrew).

McAdam, Douglas. 1983. "The Decline of the Civil Rights Movement," pp. 279–320 in *Social Movements of the Sixties and Seventies*, edited by Jo Freeman. New York and London: Longman.

Maimon, Ada. 1955. *Fifty Years of the Women Workers' Movement, 1904–1954*. Tel Aviv: Ayanot (Hebrew).

Raday, Frances. 1982. "Women in Israeli Law," pp. 172–210 in *The Double Bind, Women in Israel*, edited by Dafna Izraeli, A. Friedman and R. Schrift. Tel Aviv: Hakkibutz Hameuchad (Hebrew).

Report of the Annual Conference of the Hebrew Women's Association. 1926. *Ha'Isha*, 2:33–34 (Hebrew).

Rubinstein, A. 1979. "The Zionist Institutions in *Eretz Israel* and the Institutions of the *Yishuv*," pp. 29–202 in *The Yishuv during the Period of the National Home*, edited by Benyamin Eliav. Jerusalem: Keter (Hebrew).

Shapiro, Yonathan. 1975. *The Formative Years of the Israeli Labor Party*. London: Sage.

Shapiro, Yonathan. 1977. *Democracy in Israel*. Ramat Gan: Massada (Hebrew).

Shilo, Margalit. 1981. "The Women's Farm at Kinneret 1911–1917: A Solution of the Problem of the Working Woman in the Second *Aliyah*. *The Jerusalem Cathedra*, 2:246–283.

Shur, Shimon. 1976. "The Kibbutz and the Israeli Nation Building: The Problem of Periodization." *Hakkibutz*, 3/4:185–201 (Hebrew).

Smelser, Niel. J. 1983. *Theory of Collective Behavior*. New York: Free Press.

Thon, Hana. 1926. "The Woman in the *Eretz Israeli* Public." *Ha'Isha*, 1:4–10 (Hebrew).

Tilly, Charles. 1973. "Does Modernization Breed Revolutions?" *Comparative Politics*, 5:425–447.

Touraine, Alain. 1971. *The Post-Industrial Society: Tomorrow's social history: Classes, Conflicts and Culture in the Programmed Society*. New York: Random House.

Turner, Ralph. H., Killian, Lewis. 1972. *Collective Behavior* (2nd ed.). Englewood Cliffs, N. J.: Prentice-Hall.

Wilson, John. 1973. *Introduction to Social Movements*. New York: Basic Books.

Zald, Mayer. N., McCarthy, John. D. (editors). 1987. (ed.) *Social Movements in an Organizational Society*. New Bruswick and Oxford: Transaction Books.

12

The Fringes of the Margin: Women's Organizations in the Civic Sector of the Yishuv

—— Hanna Herzog ——

Marginality in Society and in Historiography

The social sciences and humanities have frequently been criticized with respect to their gender bias. The argument is that historians have not paid attention to crucial events in history concerning women (Beard, 1971; Rosen, 1971; Eichler and Nelson, 1977). "Sexism in historical writing" claims Rosen (1971:541), "is much like sexism in daily life. For the most part women are made invisible".

As Marx claimed, researchers are influenced by the current modes of thinking and the social situation in which they live. Thus traditional historiography has used the formal archives, and dealt with constitutional and administrative developments of nation-states and diplomatic relationships among them (Stone, 1981; Tilly, 1981). It was elite historiography and had a winner's bias. Israeli historiography travelled the same path.

A review of the literature dealing with the social historiography of the Yishuv, commonly referred to as the period of Israeli nation building, reveals that the changing research orientations reflect the social and political processes which have taken place in Israeli society.

The dominance of the labor movement in the political, economic and cultural spheres, is reflected in the historiography and is expressed mainly in the questions raised and in the focus of social research. It is only natural that history and the historians of every society favor the victors and deal mainly with them. The first to trace the Yishuv's history were members of the labor movement who wrote their own history (Braslavsky, 1955; Even-Shoshan, 1963). The history of the women's movement was written in

the same manner (Maimon, 1955). They were later joined by historians and historical sociologists, most of whom dealt with the labor
movement and its role in the formation of the new society (Gorni,
1973; Eisenstadt, 1967; Shapiro, 1976; Horowitz and Lissak, 1978).
Little research was devoted to the center and right wing of the
Yishuv's political spectrum (Giladi, 1973; Shavit, 1983).

The gradual weakening of the labor movement (Shapiro, 1977)
is expressed in the proliferation of new research orientations. On
the one hand, we find a growing volume of research engaged in
questioning accepted myths, such as the myth of equality in the
Histadrut (the General Federation of Jewish Labor) (Sussman,
1974), the myth of Jewish labor (A. Shapira, 1977), and the myth
of democracy (Shapiro, 1977). On the other hand, we witness a
growing interest in other groups and parties which, owing to the
dominance of the labor movement, had previously been rendered
marginal, both as far as their political power and their place in the
historiography of the Yishuv were concerned. Examples of such
sectors are the religious circles (Friedman, 1977), ethnic groups
(Druyan, 1982; Herzog, 1986), the First Aliyah (wave of immigration) (Kellner, 1979) and the middle-class circles, called in Hebrew *Hugim Ezrahi'im* or in English—the civic sector (Drori,
1981).

Research dealing with women in the period of the Yishuv falls
into both categories. It explodes the myth of equality, particularly
within the labor movement (Bernstein, 1987), but also poses questions and deepens our understanding of the status and role of
women, and analyzes the problems faced by them during that period.

This interest in non-dominant groups has no doubt been kin-
dled today by their increasing importance in contemporary politics
and by the growth of social protest expressed by groups which have
been forced onto the sidelines. Growing interest in women's liberation and equality between the sexes around the world, and in Israeli society in particular, has given an impetus to research on
women. The researchers naturally address the social circumstances
of the weaker groups and analyze the reasons for their lack of
power or for their failure to achieve their aims.

This chapter, as its title suggests, deals with the periphery of
this marginal group: the women's organizations of the civic sectors,
and their role in the Yishuv's activity of the period.

I contend that these organizations made a unique contribution
and that they may be defined as pioneering bodies according to the

image of the halutz (pioneer), which developed during the period of the Yishuv (Eisenstadt, 1967:17–19). Their double marginality—as part of the right wing and as women—left them on the fringes of society and historiography, despite their unique contribution.

It shall be argued that the fragmentation and lack of broad political consciousness, which characterized the women of the civic sectors and the sector to which they belonged, had the effect of keeping part of their activity outside of the mainstream, where it failed to gain recognition and support. Furthermore, even such innovative social activity as did receive recognition was assimilated and adopted by the dominant groups and was not attributed to its originators in the Yishuv's historiography. Moreover, the tendency to "forget" the contribution of the civilian women's organizations was strengthened by the fact that their spheres of operation were traditionally thought of as typically feminine ones. These spheres were not accorded prestige and social esteem and were not perceived as an important component of the public activity through which the new society was formed.

The Research Population, Research Method and Issues

There is no accepted uniform social categorization of the sectors that composed the Palestine Jewish community (for different demarcation lines, see Horowitz and Lissak, 1978; Giladi, 1973; Drori, 1981). In order to locate the women's organizations relevant to this study, a negative definition has been adopted: any body or any organization that did not define itself, or was not defined by others, as belonging to the right, the left, the religious or the ethnic sections, was part of the civic sector (Hugim Ezrahi'im).

A sociological-historical method has been adopted, with material drawn from the organizations and private archives, biographical details about the active women, newspapers, interviews with the veteran members and secondary analysis of existing research.

The central concern of this article is to account for the minimal reference to the women's organizations of the Hugim Ezrahi'im in the historiography of the Yishuv. The article folds together two lines of argumentation. The first claims that sexism in *historiography* has played down women's role in the Yishuv history. This line of argumentation leads to a brief presentation of "herstory" through the description of the following organizations: The Women's Equal Rights Association, The Federation of Hebrew

Women, the WIZO's Palestine Branch. Based on "herstory", the
second line of argumentation is that sexism in *history* limited
women's political achievements. Together these two lines of argumentation point to the double marginalization of women's organizations of the civic sector, Hugim Ezrahi'im.

The Association of Hebrew Women for Equal Rights in Eretz Israel

The Women's Association for Equal Rights lays claim to the
most impressive achievement in the history of the women's movement during the period of the Yishuv, namely granting women the
right to vote. Following this achievement, the organized Jewish
community, as early as 1920, was among the earliest western societies to grant equal political rights to women though the right to
vote was formally and conclusively confirmed only six years later,
in 1926 (Fogiel-Bijaoui, 1981). This event has been largely forgotten in the historiography of the Yishuv.

In the leading works of the social history of Israeli society,
women's activity is invisible. Discussing the infrastructure of the
society in the making during the period of the Yishuv, Eisenstadt
(1967) deals with various spheres, including the political, but fails
to mention the women's achievement. Horowitz and Lissak (1978:
42) state that the universality of suffrage, the "one man one vote"
issue and proportionality of representation, were the crucial issues
at the pre-state time. The authors note that the debate about
women's voting rights established the boundaries of the political
framework of the organized Jewish community, after the extreme
religious circles withdrew from its political organization. They discuss the position of the Haredim (ultra-orthodox) and of the Mizrachi (a mainstream, Zionist, orthodox, religious party), without
mentioning the women who constituted a major factor in determining this boundary. Amidst the long list of parties and organizations
discussed in the above book, which deals with the process of the
formation of the Yishuv, the place of women is ignored. The reader
gains the impression that the entire society favored women's suffrage, and that the achievement should be credited to "society".

Drori (1981), who deals with the civic sector, the Hugim Ezrahi'im, and its organizations, makes no mention at all of the
women's groups, ignoring even the Women's Association for Equal
Rights, which appeared as a political party. Discussing the Pro-

gressive Party (ibid: 35–38), he notes that it supported personal freedom and equal rights, irrespective of sex, but when listing the delegates chosen by this party to the first elected assembly, he does not mention the two women chosen by it, who were among the leaders of the Women's Association for Equal Rights.

In contrast to the rest of the scholars who deal with the formation of the Yishuv and ignore the women's struggle for equal rights, Friedman (1977) raises the issue of women's equality in his discussion of the old Ashkenazi Yishuv and of the struggle over the social and religious character of the new Jewish society. Two chapters (ibid: 146–184) are devoted to the struggle by the Haredim to prevent the granting of women's suffrage. The entire discussion naturally revolves around the attitudes of the Haredim, but it is nevertheless difficult to understand why the women and their organizations—which precipitated the dispute and constituted its focus—are almost not mentioned.

The struggle for the vote and for equal rights for women in the Yishuv was documented by one of the protagonists (Azaryahu, 1977), and is dealt with in another chapter in this anthology (Ch. 11, Fogiel-Bijaoui, "On the Way to Equality?"). The aim of this chapter is to try and understand why this illustrious chapter in the history of Israeli democracy has been consigned to the periphery.

"The Association of Hebrew Women for Equal Rights in Eretz Israel" was established in 1919 as a non-political national women's organization. After some hesitation it decided to attempt to implement its slogan, "one constitution and the same law for men and women", by organizing as a political list and participating in the elections to the assembly of the organized Yishuv. This strategy was without precedent among women's organizations in other countries. The decision was no doubt influenced by the legitimization given at the time to every organization, whatever its social and ideological base, as long as it participated in the organized Yishuv, i.e., was affiliated with the elected institutions of the Yishuv. Participation in the contest itself endowed the institutions of the Yishuv with legitimacy (Horowitz and Lissak, 1978). The women explained this decision in terms of their aim of "spurring unorganized women to concerted action in order to gain public stature", in the belief that "the very appearance of the women's list will enable us to exert indirect pressure on the parties to allocate secure positions to women on their lists" (Azaryahu, 1977:18).

The founders of The Women's Association for Equal Rights[1] were of Russian origin and had immigrated during the First and

Second Aliyah. By the time the Yishuv began preparing for the establishment of representative institutions, they were well established and involved in the life of the country. All its members had both a Jewish and a general education, while some had a university education and were engaged in the free professions (teaching, medicine, etc.). Their area of residence was mainly in the cities and the moshavot (private agriculture settlements).

At the time of the founding of the Association, a broad base was created and, as Azaryahu (1977:26) notes, a number of women laborers actively fought shoulder to shoulder with the members of the Association for the women's right to vote in the Yishuv. However, following the granting of women's suffrage by the third session of the first Elected Assembly, their ways parted. The differences between the middle-class founders of the Association and the women workers led to different paths. The social background and way of life in the cities and the moshavot, that typified the Association women, were very different from those of the working-women who were struggling for equality within the labor movement. The laborers were intent on furthering their rights and interests within the General Federation of Labor, the Histadrut, whereas the Women's Association for Equal Rights continued to include women from all movements and sectors.

This broad organizational base ensured the support of women from various sections at the outset of the Association's activity, but also prevented its continued existence. The Association's members also belonged to other organizations and thus found themselves at times the object of contradictory demands. Those seeking to further women's political integration tended to join political parties. For example, two women, prominent in the Association (Azaryahu and Katinka), were members of the Progressive Party which included them in its list of candidates for the first Elected Assembly. During the debate on the election constitution, some members of the Progressive Party, called on these women to desist "this time" and wait for a more auspicious opportunity, for the sake of "peace and unity" (Azaryahu, 1977:23). Women who were members of WIZO (Women's International Zionist Organization) found themselves under constant pressure from their headquarters, which sought to maintain political neutrality.

The Association co-operated at times with other organizations and also received moral support (Azaryahu, 1977:29,85–93), but had no permanent affiliation with any large Zionist organization either in Palestine or abroad. Most of the large parties in the country were affiliated with parallel parties operating within the Zionist Organization. The lack of such strong organizational backing impeded the Association's continued existence.

Once the right to vote in the election of the assembly had been ensured, the Association fought for the extension of voting rights to local authorities, and at the same time established legal bureaus, whose function was to render legal aid in matrimonial matters. In the course of these activities, the Association negotiated with the British mandatory authorities on one hand and with the rabbinical courts on the other. The issues taken up by the Association were considered marginal by those engaged in building and in settling the country. The bodies with which it came into contact were marginal, as far as foci of power and activity were concerned. Its struggles failed to gain general support, did not engender public debate and made little impression.

Owing to the inherent nature of the issues it raised, the Association dealt with exceptional matters which did not occupy the attention of the general public. Its attraction among women waned. After the establishment of the state, the organization merged with WIZO and its activities were assimilated with WIZO's other activities, which were considered to be feminine and marginal (see discussion below). The Association's major achievement—women's suffrage—became a taken-for-granted part of the political scene, the origins of which were soon forgotten. The historiography of the labor movement virtually ignored the issue. Although it had supported the cause of voting rights for women, it had not been in the vanguard of the struggle, and thus, had nothing to gain by publicizing the event as a milestone in the development of Israeli society.

The Federation of Hebrew Women
(*Histadrut Nashim Ivriot*)

The Federation of Hebrew Women (FHW) was established in 1920 with the aim of rendering public assistance. In this it was no different from the women's organizations that had preceded it. Its innovativeness expressed itself in a search for methods and spheres of activity (Herzog and Greenberg, 1981:33–38).

The founders of the Federation of Hebrew Women (FHW), arrived with the third wave of immigration known as Third Aliyah 1919–1923. From its inception they attempted to deal with two problems. The first of these concerned the poverty and the nutritional and hygienic deficiencies which they encountered in the Old Yishuv, which was composed largely of ultra-orthodox communities originating from Europe on the one hand, and communities from Moslem countries, on the other. The second problem they tackled was their own need, as immigrants, for assistance and guidance in the ways of the land, in general, and in raising children, in particular. Climatic and nutritional conditions in Palestine were different from those in their countries of origin and they were young, without family, in a new country. They encountered language problems and a lack of cultural and social frameworks. In answer to their problems, they organized social meetings in their homes, from which developed the nuclei of voluntary activity. They came to the aid of veteran women settlers in the country, who were in even greater distress than they, and assisted women immigrants seeking support and advice.

The first branches were organized independently of one another, in Jerusalem (1920) and in Tel Aviv (1923), joined soon after by Haifa and Tiberias. Each branch maintained a large measure of autonomy even after an umbrella organization was established and regulations drawn up. The decentralized and loose organization was due to the independence of the various committees and central branches. Each committee and branch was required to finance its activities almost independently, and therefore also viewed itself as responsible for its financial management. The Federation of Hebrew Women was active among the new immigrants and had strong ties with the working strata. In contrast with many voluntary organizations during the period of the Yishuv (Eisenstadt, 1966:255), FHW was not affiliated with any political organization or movement abroad. Partial financial support was given by Hadassah, the organization of American Jewish women Zionists. However, they stressed that the money should be for activity in the medical field, and were unenthusiastic about broadening the scope of activity to which the Federation aspired. Hadassah furthermore prevented the FHW from fundraising in the U.S.A., whereas in Europe it was met with opposition from the WIZO women. The latter argued that fundraising by various women's bodies tarnished the Yishuv's image and made it more difficult to raise funds. These organizational problems eventually led to the union between the Federation of Hebrew Women and the National WIZO Branch (1931). The united organization was named *"Histadrut Nashim Zioniot"*, i.e., the Federation of Zionist Women (FZW).

Figure 17. Waiting room of the Federation of Hebrew Women.

The Federation of Hebrew Women is credited with initiating two types of activity which, as in the case of women's suffrage, are so much part and parcel of everyday life in Israeli society that they seem always to have been there; namely, mother and child clinics and social work.

The Federation members were mediators between Hadassah, which offered medical care, and the population, persuading women in the later stages of pregnancy, to be examined by a doctor and to give birth in hospitals. They established advice bureaus for the treatment of infants. The women's response was initially poor, but this changed once it was decided to distribute milk at the advice bureaus in an attempt to rectify deficient nutrition which resulted from insufficient breast feeding. The milk distribution program was termed *"Tipat Halav"* (a drop of milk), a name which was later extended to encompass the weekly consultations with doctors or nurses which took place at the clinics.

Although the Federation of Hebrew Women initiated and operated the first Tipot Halav, it was forced to hand over the two clinics it had established in Jerusalem to Hadassah, owing to budgetary constraints (January 1st, 1922). FHW members did not stop working in the Tipot Halav after they had been taken over by Hadassah, and they continued to raise funds and to establish new independent clinics. In later years, WIZO's national organization, other branches of the Federation, the Histadrut sick fund and the *Amami* sick fund of the General Zionists party, also joined in this pioneering project. The Tipot Halav became centers for advice, provision of milk to needy mothers, as well as provision of clothes and food. The guiding principle was that these items should be sold, albeit at minimal prices, so as to obviate any feelings on the part of the women that they were receiving welfare.

The infants' clinic and distribution of milk gradually became an accepted feature of the Yishuv. Their importance was recognized by public authorities, which gradually took responsibility for them in co-operation with the women's organizations. With the establishment of the state, the Tipot Halav became the responsibility of the Ministry of Health, which opened clinics for the general public (1952).[2] Virtually every family in Israel uses this service today. How many of them know of the part played by the women's organizations and the Federation of Hebrew Women in particular, in creating this institution? The history of the Yishuv, dealing with contributions made in the economic and political spheres, simply ignores areas of activity identified as feminine.

A similar process occurred with regard to social work (Herzog and Greenberg, 1981:38–51). The rendering of assistance to the needy is by no means a novel feature of Jewish culture. The innovation in this case was in the methods of operation and in the concept of the essence of the activity. The needy were not viewed as recipients of charity, but as receiving their due as members of the community. The work was not of a philanthropic nature but rather intended as constructive aid. The aim was not to increase the extent of assistance rendered, but to reduce the number of those in need of it. The members of the Federation of Hebrew Women regarded public activity as a Zionist undertaking.

The idea, however, met with a markedly reserved reception from circles in the Old Yishuv, which viewed it as a duplication of the efforts of various societies engaged in the provision of assistance and charity. Even sections of the New Yishuv were not initially in favor of the idea. The term "aid" invoked opposition, as it symbolized for the pioneer the distribution institutions of the Old Yishuv and contradicted the image of the new Jew who created and built on his own accord.[3]

Reservations about social work were also expressed during the course of negotiations prior to the amalgamation of the FHW and the national WIZO organization in 1929. Those opposed to the union maintained that the inclusion of the Federation's activities in WIZO's program of action would lead to a change in WIZO's orientation and a shift of emphasis away from agricultural training towards unproductive and non-economic spheres. With hindsight, these fears proved justified, not only because the focus of activity was altered, but so was the public image of the organization as engaged in traditionally female areas of activity.

The focus of the FHW's activity was the neighborhood. It built up a statistical card index by means of which it kept track of those in need. This was the beginning of planned, systematic assistance. At the same time, it established centers for training in sewing, Hebrew lessons and a variety of cultural activities. The Federation initiated many pioneering enterprises, such as the establishment of the Jerusalem infants' home (which both took in abandoned infants and provided training in childcare for orphaned girls, who also worked in the institution but paid no tuition fees), and the first infants' day-care center in the country (in the Nordia neighborhood of Tel Aviv, 1927).[4]

The first salaried social worker, in those days referred to as a "public inspector", was employed by the Federation of Hebrew Women. The individual family, with its variety of problems, constituted the unit of treatment. Social work became more professional, shedding the amateurish nature of philanthropic activity which had been accepted until then.

Social work was initially undertaken among the people of the Old Yishuv. It was here that the FHW developed and opened its first branches (in Jerusalem, Haifa and Tiberias). As the waves of immigration in the 1920s swelled in dimension, and particularly with the onset of the economic depression in Palestine, the scope of activity expanded, focusing on the centers of the new immigration, mainly in Tel Aviv, which was hardest hit by the crisis of the late 1920s. The FHW was a small organization with meager resources and was thus not in a position to meet the pressing needs of the times single handedly. It was during this period that other women's organizations adopted modern methods and joined the effort of aiding the needy. The lack of resources and the unwillingness of World WIZO to support social work, provided the impetus for the establishment of a social services department by the elected executive body—the *Va'ad Leumi* (National Council).

In 1931, the Federation of Hebrew Women, a non-political body, decided to field candidates in association with the Women's Equal Rights Association, for the elections to the third Assembly of the organized Jewish community, with the express purpose of founding a social services department in the national council. The joint list, identified by the letter "vav", returned three delegates, headed by Henrietta Szold the initiator and leading figure in Hadassah. The three elected delegates to the Assembly were insufficient to win representation for the list on the national council. *Mapai*, the labor party only recently formed (1930) by the union between Ahdut Ha'avoda and Hapoel Hatzair, relinquished one of its places on the national council executive in favor of Henrietta Szold, so as to enable her to organize the social services department. Henrietta Szold later wrote:

> . . . Until I arrived here, I was not aware that I owed my position on the national council's executive to the Labor party, which had previously strenuously opposed me. They gave up one of their places for me . . . (Quoted in Herzog and Greenberg, 1981:46).

Mapai clearly adopted a tactic of co-optation. Its support of social work, which was already being undertaken by voluntary women's associations with the funding of Hadassah and the backing of U.S. Jewry, was another step towards the acquisition of power. The labor movement's ideological opposition was dropped, once considerations of power predominated. Mapai was ideologically inconsistent with regard to a number of bodies and issues (Shapiro, 1977:56–57,140; Herzog, 1986:46–59,115,139).

The guidelines for social work, laid down by Henrietta Szold, were those which had served the FHW, with local authorities providing the organizational base. The regulations stipulated that the chairman of the social services committee had to be a member of the local authority, whereas the committee's other members could be drawn from people in public positions and from well-known activists who were prepared to devote time to developing the local social services. In most cases, no member of the local authority agreed to head the committee and the positions were mostly filled during the 1930s by the Federation members and after the 1933 union with national WIZO, by the united organization—Federation of Zionist Women (FZW).

During the initial years, Henrietta Szold did not set up social service bureaus in locations without an FZW branch, which she regarded as the basis for their operation. With the passage of time, the labor movement's women's organization also became active in this sphere. As the labor movement increased its activities among the urban population (Shapiro, 1977:90–95), its attitude towards social work changed. At the same time, the feminist aspirations of working-women were "suppressed". The Women Workers' Council moved away from its struggle for acceptance of women in male occupations (as a means of furthering equal rights for women) towards rendering assistance to women engaged in the traditionally female roles of mother and housewife. The Organization of Working Mothers was formed in 1930 for this purpose, and soon became active in the sphere of social work (Izraeli, 1981; Bernstein, 1987). Thus, the area of activity initiated by women belonging to the civic sectors came to be identified with women in general.

The politicization of social work induced the Federation of Zionist Women (FZW), which sought to maintain its influential status within the social service bureaus, to run for elections to the local authorities, in association with the Women's Association for Equal Rights. As a result of its political achievements, it not only gained membership of social service committees, which were generally non-paid positions, but also received funding for its activities. In 1946, representatives of the women's list constituted 20.3 percent of the membership of social service committees, compared with 39 percent held by representatives of the Organization of Working Mothers, the labor women's organization, and Mapai. It should be noted that Mapai was then already the largest and dominant party in the Yishuv.

An additional factor in maintaining FZW's influence in the realm of social work was the agreement governing the division of activities between the social services department of the National Council and the FZW. According to this agreement, the social service bureaus dealt primarily with community social work, whereas Federation of Zionist Women specialized in work within institutions such as baby homes, day-care centers, clubs, mother and child clinics, vocational and agricultural schools.

The FZW's independent activity continued as long as its members succeeded in raising funds abroad. During the Second World War, when virtually no money reached Palestine from Europe and only Hadassah was active in the U.S.A., national resources came to play an increasingly important part in this sphere as well. With the establishment of the state, it was only natural that welfare roles were taken over by state bodies.

WIZO's Palestine Branch

At World WIZO's inaugural convention held in London in 1920, a decision to establish a central office in Israel was made.[5] WIZO's initial activity in Palestine was undertaken by individual women. Only in 1927 did they officially organize to form WIZO's Palestine Organization. The purpose of this national organization was to foster awareness among women of the importance of national needs and to develop and promote educational programs for women, in order to enable them to participate actively in the rebuilding of the country (Herzog and Greenberg, 1981:51–95).

The emergence of the national association as a WIZO federation met with opposition from two other women's organizations. The Federation of Hebrew Women viewed it as a competitor for financial resources and for volunteer workers in Palestine. Hadassah, while it undoubtedly regarded World WIZO as a serious rival, justified its opposition by maintaining the undesirability of linking an organization based in Palestine with one operating abroad. While the Federation of Hebrew Women which got support from Hadassah, maintained its organizational autonomy, the WIZO Palestine branch was closely linked to the London head office, which formulated policy and allocated resources according to its priorities.

Many of the spheres of activity undertaken by the various women's organizations overlapped, resulting not only in co-operation among them, but also in friction and rivalry. Some of the conflicts were resolved in 1933, following the union between the Federation of Hebrew Women and the WIZO's Palestine branch.

Whereas the majority of WIZO's Palestine members were recruited from the upper middle-class and did not define themselves as belonging to the labor movement, they nevertheless perceived their main task to be agricultural training for women. This they viewed as part of the Zionist endeavor in general, rather than a monopoly of the labor movement.

> The core of our aspiration in Eretz Israel [Palestine] is to create a free, Hebrew, working Yishuv, primarily a Yishuv of agricultural workers, which will strike vigorous roots in the soil and serve as a strong basis, economically, physically, spiritually and politically for the whole nation (Quoted in Herzog and Greenberg, 1981:41).

Agriculture was perceived as a means of transforming women into a productive force. "Our dream of dreams was a Jewish farmer, his wife at his side, both trained for agricultural work in Eretz Israel", (ibid), a direct derivative of the image of the pioneer (halutz) which took shape during that period.

In contrast to its present day urban-bourgeoise image, WIZO was a major initiator and supporter of agricultural schools and agricultural education. In this enterprise they worked together with the Women Workers' Movement. The agricultural schools initially accepted only girls and absorbed young immigrant women, constituting a means of obtaining entry certificates at the time of the restriction on immigration by the British. In the forties the schools began to take boys as well.

Agricultural education began to expand beyond the confines of formal educational institutions, and included training in the cultivation of vegetables in nurseries. This took place during the economic crisis of 1926–27, which began shortly after the cessation of a big wave of immigration from Poland, which reduced many families to poverty. The training in growing vegetables in nurseries was directed at assisting families in reducing their expenses, and at the same time at creating a bond between the immigrant women and the land. These activities accorded with WIZO's endeavor to transform women into a productive and not merely a consumer force, and with its objective of enriching the family's diet with essential items for rational nutrition, another of WIZO's ideas.

The vegetable garden idea was first tried out in Tel Aviv. Once the experiment proved a success, training was expanded to other areas of the country. WIZO's training department consisted of mobile instructors, who passed through urban settlements and moshavot, training women in all aspects of vegetable cultivation (from sowing seeds to fertilizing and irrigation) and in raising poultry. Instruction in preserving surplus yields and in introducing greater variety in the family's menu was also given.

In a parallel avenue of activity, vegetable gardens were developed in schools and in kindergartens with the aim of creating a bond between the children and cultivation of the land, and of teaching them to love the garden "as future pioneers, who would conquer the wilderness" (Quoted in Herzog and Greenberg, 1981: 67).

The agricultural orientation of this educational initiative was in accord with the spirit of the Zionist Movement, under the impact of the labor movement. It was also compatible with the widely accepted image of the pioneer and thus gained recognition. In 1931, the Va'ad Leumi (elected National Council) entrusted the overall supervision of the school and kindergarten nurseries to WIZO's training department. After the establishment of the state, the Ministry of Education took control of agricultural training in elementary schools.

WIZO was the first to initiate many areas of training which constituted an important source of information for immigrants in a land of migrants such as Israel. The majority of subjects in which training was offered were, however, those traditionally defined as female areas of activity: training for motherhood, cooking courses, operating public kitchens (in kibbutzim, moshavim, workers' kitchens and later army kitchens), preparation of budgets, compositon of menus, cleaning, decoration of dining halls, etc. Training in these spheres, unlike training in agriculture, was not recognized as important and was not adopted by state organizations. Agricultural training, which was recognized and adopted, came to be identified with the dominant group in society—the labor movement—while the women of the Hugim Ezrahi'im, the civic sectors, who had initiated these activities, were forgotten in the historiography of the Yishuv.

Conclusions: Why in the Margins?

The women's organizations that operated within the Hugim Ezrahi'im (the civic sector), belonged to the liberal feminist trend. The liberal endeavor focused on the exertion of pressure to eliminate discrimination against women in the British mandatory and religious judicial systems. At the same time it was active within the Yishuv in promoting equality, mainly through voluntary organizations in the areas of health, education and mutual aid.

The variety of associations described thus far demonstrates that the women of the civic sector were involved in extensive public activity, but were divided and failed to achieve a measure of political cohesion.

Among this sector, there were militant political organizations such as "The Women's Association for Equal Rights", alongside welfare organizations that dealt with everyday needs of women, children and the household (Federation of Hebrew Women and Federation of Zionist Women); an exclusive social association (University Women) and a professional association (The League of Women Physicians).[6]

A study of the biographies of the women who were active in

these organizations reveals that many were members of more than one of them. Notwithstanding this overlapping membership, the women's associations did not form a unified framework for joint action that would have enabled them to accumulate power. In 1925, the Federation of Hebrew Women floated a suggestion to form a council on which all the Jewish women's organizations in Palestine and abroad would be represented. In August 1927, it convened a "preparatory committee", with representatives of nine organizations, for the establishment of the "Council of Palestine Women's Associations".

Apart from the FHW and the Women's Association for Equal Rights, all the other participants were small, local organizations. The council failed to get off the ground. The FHW expended much energy in an attempt to support the abortive "Palestine Women's Council". In May 1929, World WIZO initiated the establishment of its own council, which was joined by WIZO's Palestine branch, the Women Workers' Council and the Palestine Women's Council. The organization's objective was to represent the women of Palestine vis-à-vis the women of the Diaspora, thereby influencing the decisions of women's organizations abroad with regard to their activity in Palestine. The potential strength of these women's organizations was never realized, since the proposed bodies did not begin to operate. Disagreement and competition between the organizations precluded co-operation among them.

The women's organizations of the civic sectors also neglected to align themselves with a political party, as the women of the labor movement had done. The Yishuv society was organized along political lines, with the various groups and organizations maintaining reciprocal relations within the organized community. Its central institutions were invested with a good deal of authority, which stemmed, in part, from their ability to mobilize resources abroad—both finances and personnel—and from the right to determine their allocation (Horowitz and Lissak, 1978).

The accumulation and allocation of resources took place via political channels. Women could have established contact with parties competing in the political arena, but did not make use of that possibility.[7] An alternative strategy entailed an independent organizational effort. The Women's Equal Rights Association, Federation of Hebrew Women, and later the Federation of Zionist Women chose the political avenue as a means of exerting influence in an attempt to achieve their specific objectives. The major achievements of the women of the Hugim Ezrahi'im, the civic sectors—women's suffrage and social work—were gained through political organization. However, the status of women and the enterprises initiated by women played no part in the political debate of the time, which was determined by the ideological struggles between right and left.

The majority of organizations, amongst them World WIZO, had reservations about political activity. Two factors were doubtless at play here; the external dilemma faced by minority groups as to whether attributive factors (sex, origin) constitute a sufficient basis for organization, even at the price of ignoring political differences on other issues. Of no less importance was the matter of the image of women. Since politics is seen as a masculine preoccupation, many women's organizations throughout the world have reservations about their involvement in political activity. World WIZO's resolute refusal to adopt political stands weakened its Palestine branch. WIZO controlled economic resources which could have been utilized for political gain, as Hadassah had done in supporting the idea of social work.

A different "political mistake" made by the civilian women's organizations was their "incorrect" choice of fields and foci of activity, which were perceived as lacking a pioneering and nation building nature. The Federation of Hebrew Women began its work amongst the Old Yishuv, whose orientations and organization were shunned by the New Yishuv (Herzog, 1984). This "mistake" was somewhat mitigated once FHW also began to work among the new population and in particular with the immigrants of the 1920s. Here, however, it found itself in competition with the labor movement's organizations, which also sought to establish themselves among this wave of immigration. For the latter, humanitarian motives were mingled with political considerations.

As a result of the failure by the women of the civic sectors to accumulate political power or to find themselves allies with such power, their activity and contribution, important as they were, remained unrecognized in the historiography of the Yishuv for many years. Failing to gain power put the women of the center and right wing Hugim Ezrahi'im in the same situation as the right wing in general at that period (Giladi, 1973), except that the women suffered from double marginalization.

The few activities that did gain recognition, such as social work and agricultural training, were adopted by the labor movement and became part of the policy of the elected institutions headed by the labor party—Mapai. This usurpation was so complete that for many years the recorders of history forgot that these had been enterprises of the women's organizations.

Lastly, the fact that much of their activity was directed to traditionally feminine areas worked against the women's organizations, as these were never endowed with much prestige or recognition. The choice of "feminine" pursuits resulted from the image of women held by members of these organizations. The Federation of Hebrew Women viewed the family as constituting society's natural nucleus, and related favorably to women's primary role, care of the home and children. Their traditional perception of the woman's role defined the sphere of activity in which they chose to work: care of women, children and the weak, which they regarded as a contribution to the pioneering endeavor. According to their image, while the men were involved in the economic-instrumental aspects of building the country, the women participated in building its social institutions, and as such were entitled to equal rights.

WIZO's Palestine branch regarded women's economic and professional integration into the economy as of prime importance, but nonetheless did not adopt the image of the pioneering woman as equal to the pioneering man. Women were equal to men as far as rights were concerned, but should be active in areas appropriate to them. WIZO viewed the rural woman as the farmer's wife, lending support to her husband—a woman who cooks and raises vegetables and poultry. But in her capacity as farmer's wife she should undergo training and take an active role.

This image of the woman's role focused the work of the women's organizations on education, on running baby homes and day-care centers, on medical and mutual aid institutions, with most of the work performed on a voluntary basis. The combination of voluntary work in feminine areas of activity detracted from the woman's image as a pioneer contributing to the society in the making.

Such a phenomenon is not unique to Israeli society. The dominant social consciousness values economic and political spheres of action, which are generally predominantly masculine spheres. It is these that are regarded as central and important to society, whereas areas of activity such as education and welfare, undertaken primarily by women and by voluntary organizations, are regarded as secondary spheres. Research in the U.S.A. has revealed that the economic worth of voluntary organizations in 1965 was put at 14.2 billion dollars, in other words, a significant contribution to the economy (Sapiro and Farah, 1980). Devaluation of these organizations' activities takes the form, among others, of relating them to women and to voluntary work.

Women's organizations in the Yishuv formulated policies, made decisions, allocated resources and implemented their policies, just as the men did. They were the first to undertake work in many spheres, but this was all done in traditionally "feminine" areas, and was not regarded, in the historiography of the Yishuv, as a pioneering endeavor worthy of mention, nor as a contribution to the society in the making. The few endeavors that were recognized, were usurped by the dominant groups, thus excluding the women of the civic sector from the Yishuv's history.

Notes

1. Rosa Welt-Strauss, Miriam Nofech, Fania Matman-Cohen, Esther Yeivin, Hassia Pinsol-Sokenik, Sara Azaryahu, Nehamah Pukhachewsky.

2. Since the health services in Israel are not state operated, various bodies are involved in running the "Tipot Halav" including the Histadrut sick fund, Tel Aviv municipality, Hadassah and the Ministry of Health.

3. Thus, for example, the "Agricultural Center" declared a boycott of clothes sent from America for distribution among the needy, considering that it smacked of philanthropy and was in direct contradiction to the ethos of the working-public. Together with Hadassah, which had organized the collection of clothes abroad, it was decided to sell the clothes at low prices. This was the beginning of "Beged Zol" (cheap clothes), a project undertaken by FHW and adopted by the Working Mothers Organization of the labor movement.

4. These activities actually anticipated the women's liberation movement which to this day maintains that the existence of day-care centers is a necessary condition for the achievement of its aims.

5. World WIZO was founded by women who had been active in the suffragette movement in England and who sought to establish the status of women within the Zionist movement, which had made Britain its main base of activity following the First World War (for an analysis of the growth of World WIZO, see Herzog and Greenberg, 1981:7–10).

6. The last two organizations mentioned were not dealt with in this chapter.

7. A faction within FHW co-operated with the General Zionists, but I have no details of the nature of their links apart from a table drawn up by Drori in his study (Drori, 1981:218).

References

Azaryahu, Sara. 1977. *The Women's Equal Rights Association*. Haifa: The Fund for Support of Women (Hebrew).

Beard, R. Mary. 1971. *Women as Force in History*. New York: Collier Books.

Bernstein, Deborah. 1987. *The Struggle for Equality. Urban Women Workers in Prestate Israeli Society*. New York: Praeger.

Bráslavsky, Moshe. 1959–1963. *The Jewish Workers' Movement in Palestine*. Tel Aviv: Hakibbutz Hameuchad, Vols. 1–4 (Hebrew).

Drori, Yigal. 1981. *"Hahugim Ha'ezrahiyim" in the Jewish "Yishuv" in Eretz Israel 1920–1929*. Ph.D. dissertation, Tel Aviv University (Hebrew).

Druyan, Nitza. 1982. *Pioneers of the Yemenite Immigration*. Jerusalem: The Zalman Shazar Centre for the Furtherance of the Study of Jewish History and The Historical Society of Israel (Hebrew).

Eichler, M. and Nelson, C. A. 1977. "History and Historiography: The Treatment in American Histories of Significant Events Concerning the Status of Women." *The Historian*, 40:1–15.

Eisenstadt, S. N. 1966. "The Social Conditions of the Development of Voluntary Association," pp. 251–276 in *The Social Structure of Israel*, edited by Eisenstadt S. N. et al., Jerusalem: Akademon (Hebrew).

Eisenstadt, S. N. 1967. *Israeli Society*. London: Weidenfeld and Nicolson.

Even-Shoshan, Zvi. 1963. *The History of the Workers' Movement in Eretz Israel*. Tel Aviv: Am Oved (Hebrew).

Fogiel-Bijaoui, Sylvie. 1981. *The Rib of Eve—The Women of Palestine 1881–1948*. Ph.D. Dissertation. University of Paris, X, Nanterre (French).

Friedman, Menahem. 1977. *Society and Religion—The Non-Zionist Orthodox in Eretz Israel, 1919–1936*. Jerusalem: Yad Yitzhak Ben-Zvi Publications (Hebrew).

Giladi, Dan. 1973. *Jewish Palestine During the Fourth Aliya Period (1924–1929)*. Tel Aviv: Am Oved—Tarbut Vehinuch (Hebrew).

Gorni, Joseph. 1973. *Ahdut Ha'avoda 1919–1930—The Ideological Principles and the Political System*. Tel Aviv: Hakibbutz Hameuchad (Hebrew).

Herzog, Hanna and Ofra Greenberg, 1981. *A Voluntary Women's Organization in a Society in the Making—WIZO's Contribution to Israeli*

Society. Tel Aviv: WIZO and The Institute of Social Research, Department of Sociology and Anthropology, Tel Aviv University.

Herzog, Hanna. 1984. "The Terms 'Old *Yishuv*' and 'New *Yishuv*'—A Sociological Approach." *Cathedra*, 32:99–108 (Hebrew).

———. 1986. *Political Ethnicity—The Image and the Reality*. Tel Aviv: Yad Tabenkin, Hakibbutz Hameuchad (Hebrew).

Horowitz, Dan and Moshe, Lissak. 1978. *Origins of the Israeli Polity—Palestine under the Mandate*. Chicago: University of Chicago Press.

Izraeli, Dafna, 1981. "The Zionist Women's Movement in Palestine, 1911–1927: A Sociological Analysis". *Signs*, 7:87–114.

Kellner, Yaacov. 1979. "The Anti-Philanthropic Approach During the Days of the First Aliyah." *Cathedra*, 10:3–33 (Hebrew).

Maimon, Ada. 1955. *Fifty Years of the Women's Labor Movement 1904–1954*. Tel Aviv: Ayanot (Hebrew).

Rosen, Ruth. 1971. "Sexism in History, or Writing Women's History is a Tricky Business." *Journal of Marriage and the Family*, 33:541–544.

Sapiro, Virginia and Barbara G. Farah. 1980. "New Pride and Old Prejudice." *Women and Politics*, 1:13–36.

Shapira, Anita. 1977. *Futile Struggle—The Jewish Labor Controversy 1929–1939*. Tel Aviv: Hakibbutz Hameuchad (Hebrew).

Shapiro, Yonathan. 1976. *The Formative Years of the Israeli Labor Party*. London: Sage.

———. 1977. *Democracy in Israel*. Tel Aviv: Massada (Hebrew).

Shavit, Yaacov. 1983. *Revisionism in Zionism, the Revisionist Movement: the Plan for Colonizatory Regime and Social Ideas 1925–1935*. Tel Aviv: Hadar (Hebrew).

Stone, Lawrence. 1981. *The Past and the Present*. Boston: Routledge and Kegan Paul.

Sussman, Zvi. 1974. *Wage Differentials and Equality Within the Histadrut*. Ramat-Gan: Massada (Hebrew).

Tilly, Charles. 1981. *As Sociology Meets History*. New York: Academic Press.

Contributors

Ran Aaronsohn is a lecturer in the Department of Geography at the Hebrew University, Jerusalem. Areas of research include the historical geography of settlement, mainly the first Jewish colonies in nineteenth-century Palestine, and rural geography. Aaronsohn's book titled *The Colonies and the Baron, the beginning of the Jewish resettlement in Palestine and Edmund de Rothschild*, was published by Yad Izhak Ben-Zvi, Jerusalem (1990), (Hebrew).

Yaffa Berlovitz is a lecturer in the Department of Am-Israel (Hebrew and Jewish literatures) at Bar-Ilan University, Ramat Gan, and is affiliated with the Kurzweil Institute for Hebrew Literary Research, Bar-Ilan University. Main fields of research are the study of the literature of first settlers (Eretz Israel literature, American Colonial literature), Jewish-American literature (1880–1920) and women's literature in Eretz Israel. Author and editor of *Women's Stories of the First Aliyah*, Tel Aviv, 1985 (Hebrew) and *Short Stories of Aaron Meged*, Tel Aviv (1989), (Hebrew).

Deborah Bernstein is a senior lecturer in the Department of Sociology and Anthropology at the University of Haifa. Spheres of interest include ethnic and class relations in Israel, women and work, and women in the Yishuv. Author of *The Struggle for Equality: Urban Women Workers in Prestate Israeli Society*, published by Praeger, N.Y. (1987).

Nitza Druyan is Director of Long Island Center for Jewish Studies and Associate Professor of Jewish Studies at Hofstra University, New York. Professional experience includes teaching at the Hebrew University in Jerusalem and Yeshiva University in New York City. Areas of research include: Jews and Arabs; Yemenite Jewry; Immigration of Jews from Moslem countries; Sephardi Jews and Zionism; social and cultural development in Israeli society. Druyan's book *Without a Magic Carpet* (Yemenite Settlement in Eretz-Yisrael, 1881–1914), was published by Yad Ben-Zvi, Jerusalem (1981), (Hebrew).

Sylvie Fogiel-Bijaoui is a lecturer of Sociology at Beit Berl College and in the Department of Sociology at the Hebrew University, Jerusalem. Also affiliated with the Yad Tabenkin research center of the Kibbutz Hameuchad. Main spheres of interest include political sociology, sociology of the kibbutz, and women studies. Fogiel-Bijaoui is author of *Cooperation, Integration or Alienation? The Relationships between the Kibbutz and the Development Towns*, published by Yad Tabenkin (1988, Hebrew), and *Motherhood and Revolution: The Case of the Kibbutz Women, 1910–1986*, published by Everyman's University, Tel Aviv (1990), (Hebrew).

Nurit Govrin is an associate professor in the Department of Hebrew Literature at Tel Aviv University. Her research has dealt mostly with the beginnings of modern Hebrew literature in Palestine, with early literary journals and with such contemporary writers as Berdyczewski, Brenner, Baron and Shoffman. The two most recent of the numerous books she has published are: *The First Half—the Life and Work of Dvora Baron* (1882–1923), published by Bialik Institute, Jerusalem (1988), (Hebrew) and *Honey from the Rock, Studies on the Literature of Eretz Israel*. Ministry of Defense Publishing House, Tel Aviv (1989), (Hebrew).

Hanna Herzog is senior lecturer in the Department of Sociology and Anthropology at Tel Aviv University. Areas of study include political aspects of ethnicity; political communication; women and politics; identity and politics. Ongoing research includes, among others, a study on elected women in local government in Israel. Has published *Political Ethnicity—The Image and the Reality*. Tel Aviv, Hakibbutz Hameuchad, (1986), (Hebrew) and *Contest of Symbols—The Sociology of Election Campaigns Through Israeli Ephemera*. Cambridge: Harvard University Library, (1987).

Dafna N. Izraeli is an associate professor of Sociology in the Department of Sociology and Anthropology at Bar-Ilan University. Co-author of *The Double Bind: Women in Israel.* Tel Aviv, Hakkibutz Hameuchad (1982), (Hebrew), and co-editor of *Women's World: The new scholarship* (1985) and *Women in Management Worldwide* (1988). Her current research is on the interface of family-work and public policy and dual career families.

Musia Lipman was chief archivist of the Labor Archive, at the Lavon Institute for the Study of the Labor Movement, Tel Aviv. Has specialized in personal archives and the period of the Second Aliyah. Has written extensively on the Second and Third Aliyah, on the beginnings of kibbutzim and on Jewish journalism.

Shulamit Reinharz has taught psychology and women's studies at the University of Michigan, and is currently an associate professor of Sociology at Brandeis University. Reinharz has written, among other books, *On Becoming a Social Scientist* (transaction, 1984) and *Methods of Feminist Research* (Pergamon, 1990). Reinharz has done extensive research in Israel, including participant observation on a kibbutz focussing on the aging experience, to be published in *Aging on a Kibbutz* (Chicago).

Margalit Shilo is a lecturer in the Department of Israel Studies at Bar-Ilan University, Ramat-Gan. Her main field of study is the Jewish settlement in Palestine at the end of the Ottoman period, with emphasis on forms of settlement and organization. Author of *Experiments at Settlement, 1908–1914*, published by Yad Ben-Zvi, (1988), (Hebrew) which was awarded the Haifa Municipality prize. Has also written a short biography of Arthur Ruppin, to be included in the *Second Aliyah Book*, forthcoming by Yad Ben-Zvi (Hebrew).

Index

A

Aaronsohn, Sara, 32
Agriculture, 45, 82, 90, 113, 122–124, 130, 138, 140, 185, 213–216, 220–221, 224, 298
Agricultural colonies. *See* Moshavot
Agricultural training, 90, 126, 136–137, 191, 271, 293, 294, 296
Anya, 145–148, 155–157, 163n
Arabs, 13, 19, 34, 37, 40, 51, 80, 99, 100–101, 104–106, 110–111, 114, 185, 231n
Association of Hebrew Women for Equal Rights (in Eretz Israel), 197, 258, 261, 266–268, 270–271, 273, 275–276, 289, 293, 295, 298
Azaryahu, Sara, 268, 271, 274, 288

B

Baratz, Miriam, 122, 216
Bassin, Shoshanna, 80, 82
Bassevitz, Lilia, 163n
Bat Rachel, Yokheved, 220
Becker, Ester, 268
Ben Gurion, David, 108, 113, 197–198, 201
Ben Shemen, 81–82, 123, 145, 155, 156, 163n
Ben-Yehuda, Eliezer, 56, 70n
Ben-Yehuda, Hemdah, 27, 43, 53–60, 66, 70n, 71n, 166
Ben Zvi, Rachel. *See* Yanait Rachel
Ben-Zvi, Yitzhak, 107, 166, 274
Bialik, Haim Nahman, 91, 165
Bluwstein, Shoshanna, 133
Bussel, Hayuta, 134, 141n, 268, 278
Bussel, Joseph, 216–217

C

Charity. *See* social work
Child care, 14, 219, 242, 251
Chizick, Hanna, 141n
Civic Sectors, 257–259, 261, 264, 273, 275–278, 283–286, 298–300
Collectives, 89–91, 99, 103, 111, 113, 115–116, 157, 185, 218
Communes, 89, 191, 193, 228, 242
Constitutive Assembly, 263, 266
Construction, 218
Construction Workers' Union, 192

D

Degania, 115–116, 122–123, 131, 138, 164n, 216, 229n
Division of Labor, 92–94, 194, 204, 220, 223, 243

E

Education, 3–4, 9, 27, 31, 44–45, 50–52, 57, 76, 83–85, 96, 120, 126, 129, 219, 222, 226, 236, 297, 301
Ein Harod, 220, 228
Elected Assembly, 266, 268–273, 280n
Employment, 6, 53, 79, 95, 105–106, 110, 120, 126, 185, 189, 191–192, 195, 218, 247. *See also* Labor
Ettinger, Akiva, 136–137, 140, 142n

F

Family, 6, 10, 12, 16–18, 26, 31, 43, 49–51, 76, 78–80, 92–93, 98, 101, 140, 207n, 219, 221, 225–226, 235–